2-5-24

Hi CAROL & DALE,

Enjoy our Adventure!

FYI, since my heart issue,
(triple) I've (with Mari)
cycled Bergen, Norway
to Leysin Switzerland,
crossed the USA southern
bike by bike, & New
Zealand top to bottom by
Bike.

TransCanada this summer,
but with an E-bike this time.

Happy Retirement CAROL!

Terry

Pedal Pushers

Coast-to-Coast

A Cross-country Bike Tour Fueled by Kindness

MARIANNE WORTH RUDD

authorHOUSE®

AuthorHouse™
1663 Liberty Drive
Bloomington, IN 47403
www.authorhouse.com
Phone: 1 (800) 839-8640

Published by AuthorHouse 06/07/2019

ISBN: 978-1-5462-7822-1 (sc)
ISBN: 978-1-5462-7823-8 (hc)
ISBN: 978-1-5462-7824-5 (e)

Library of Congress Control Number: 2019901483

Print information available on the last page.

This book is printed on acid-free paper.

To Terry, my partner in grime

CONTENTS

PROLOGUE

"I have bad news," the physician's assistant told us at the urgent care in Minnesota. "Terry has a hairline fracture near the elbow."

My gut twisted.

The PA looked at us and paused. "This is the end of your bike trip."

Silence. A broken arm for Terry. A broken dream for me.

I'd been dreaming for thirty-two years about this coast-to-coast bike trip, and now, after seven weeks and over 2600 miles of bicycling, a car collided with Terry on a Minnesota highway.

Our cross-country bike trip was abruptly over.

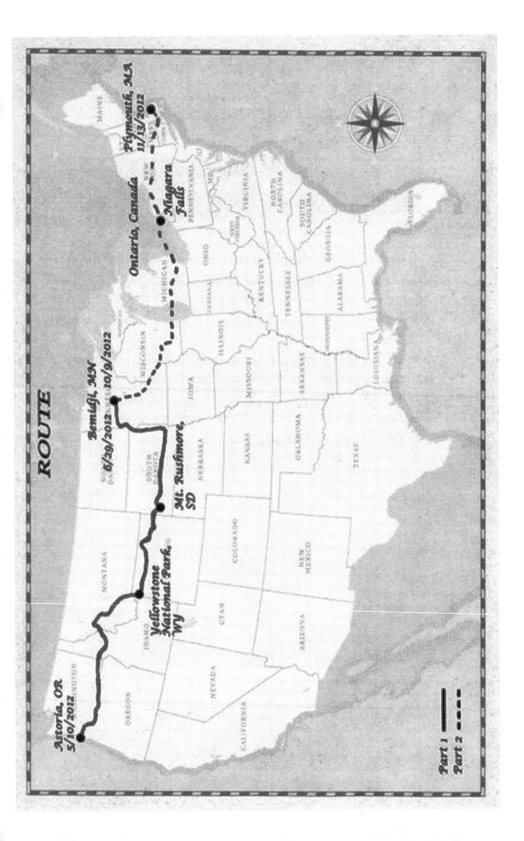

Part 1

CHAPTER 1

Anticipation

I belong on a bike.

A bicycle trip across the continent holds many unknowns, but that wasn't one of them. I do belong on a bike, heavily loaded with panniers, a sleeping bag, tent, and all the paraphernalia required for a bicycle tour across the North American continent, from the Pacific to the Atlantic Ocean.

This trip was my obsession—not my husband Terry's. He liked bike touring, but unlike me, he wasn't permanently dialed in on thoughts of a cross-country bike adventure. I, on the other hand, had dreamed of this trip for over thirty years. What was the source of this obsession? I didn't grow up bike touring. Time spent on my bike was typical of kids growing up in the 60's and 70's—bikes simply took you where you wanted to go. Go to school? Ride a bike. Go to a friend's house? Ride a bike.

My biking world significantly expanded with my 1976 high school graduation present from Aunt Ruthe, my mom's sister. Her friend annually led students on a summer bike trip to Washington state's beautiful Olympic Peninsula and San Juan Islands, and I was invited to join the two-week adventure. We biked and camped near mountains, sea, and farms, hopping ferries to explore peninsulas and islands north of Seattle.

Four years later, I repeated that route with a friend, expanding it to the nearby Canadian Gulf Islands. A seed planted. Why limit the bicycle trip to three weeks? Why limit it to the Pacific Northwest? Why not bike from one coast to the other? And so, my dream began.

Terry and I kept the dream alive with many shorter bike trips, which further whetted my appetite for a cross-country adventure, but real life always managed to collide with coast-to-coast bike plans. But at last, we had the time and resources, and Terry was onboard. We began planning in earnest.

First question: What bike to ride? I had one bike, a thirty-one-year old touring Trek I bought new after college. "Ancient", a friend snorted derisively. People told me I should get a new bike; it would be lighter and faster. I didn't need to be faster. I was already faster than Terry, and if I went any faster, I would just spend more time waiting for him than I already did.

My Trek was ancient, but thanks to a make-over during its middle years, it boasted twenty-one speeds instead of ten. That Trek took me twice along Oregon's 360-mile coast, and along big chunks of coastline in Washington and northern California. It carried me in the Canadian Rockies and to distant corners of Oregon. I loved my ancient Trek, and I found no need to forsake it.

Terry's Trek 520 was practically a twin of my bike, but two decades newer. Heavy and sturdy, each bike would carry substantial loads in their four panniers—two in the front, and two in the back.

Cycling through the Rockies in late May/early June practically begs for a snowstorm, and our panniers bulged with raingear and warm layers to stave off hypothermia. Our cold weather gear only needed to accompany us over the Rockies. Afterwards, we planned to shed the weight and bulk of mountain clothing before sweating in the hot mid-west plains.

Our panniers filled--with clothing, toiletries, electrical and emergency gear, and junk. We deleted items, and then added more. Ultralight touring cyclists thrive on speed and minimal gear; Terry and I were far from that. We just wanted to be comfortable for the next three months. Excluding food and water, my bike would begin its journey hauling forty-five pounds of panniers, tent, and sleeping bag. The weight didn't reflect what a good touring cyclist I was; rather, it reflected that I was a wimp regarding adverse weather, and that I liked to be warm and dry. The weight was mine to haul, however, and if I wanted to lug it around, that was my prerogative.

There was no indecision about one piece of equipment: the credit card. It was coming.

How does one budget for a three-month bike trip? We planned to frequently camp, saving motels for inclement weather. According to a cyclist friend, motels still count as camping—"credit card camping".

What to eat between one ocean and the other? Groceries are usually accessible at least every other day on a transcontinental bike trip. With stores providing the majority of our food, Terry planned regular visits to cafés, as well. Unbeknownst to us at the Pacific, the issue of food would headline a major dispute, driving a surprising wedge into our relationship.

What about that relationship? How do differing styles weave together, or not? How might a journey of this magnitude test a relationship?

Opposites attract, yin and yang, Terry and Mari. We met through mutual interests, but our comfort levels are often miles apart. I like speed, while Terry takes life with the brakes on. I welcome a little intermittent chaos, while Terry likes routine. I'm a social animal; Terry likes solitude. Terry is methodical, slow, and careful; meanwhile, I get antsy.

"Choose your battles" is sage advice, and with almost three decades of marriage behind us, we had plenty of battles from which to choose. We knew each other's quirks (or so I thought), and were veterans in negotiating the minefields of our relationship.

�⚲⚲

I thought I had Terry figured out. I thought our bike trip was about getting somewhere.

Was I ever mistaken.

I spent years imaging this trip, but I failed to imagine it wouldn't actually be about getting somewhere. It never occurred to me that I didn't have Terry figured out.

I was naïve about much that lay ahead. I didn't realize the trip would actually be about people, not sights nor our ending point. I never considered that Terry's and my quirks would become even quirkier, and that our relationship was destined for major challenges. I didn't realize our trip would become largely defined by one element we repeatedly encountered across the continent: the kindness of strangers.

There was so much I didn't know.

�⚲⚲

A six-day shakedown trip along Oregon's coast put our bodies and bikes to the test a month before our big adventure. Were the bikes working well? Did we have the necessary equipment for the conditions we encountered? With a few thirty-mile day trips behind us in Portland, the shakedown gave us almost a week to haul and test our gear, and to continue beefing up our legs.

After years of anticipation and a successful six-day shakedown, it was finally time to get this dream rolling.

CHAPTER 2

Farewell to the Pacific–Oregon

May 2012. Fort Stevens State Park, Pacific Ocean, near the mouth of the Columbia River and Astoria, Oregon.

成

They say that a journey of a thousand miles begins with a single step. Well, a multi-thousand, transcontinental bicycle ride begins with a tire dip in the ocean.

Our friends Erik and Karl drove us two hours west from our home in Portland, Oregon, to Fort Stevens State Park, on the edge of the Pacific Ocean. Close-knit brothers, Erik and Karl developed a track record over the years of driving Terry and me to various places, dumping us and our bikes off, and then driving back sometime later to pick us up in neighboring states. This time Erik and Karl were off the hook for our pick up, well over 3000 miles and who-knew-how-many weeks away.

At the parking lot, we overlooked a sandy beach, the Pacific, and the wreck of the *Peter Iredale*. In 1906, the ship sailed too close to shore, became grounded, and has been stuck in the sand ever since. There's less of that ship now than a hundred years ago, and less than I remember as a child. Now, only its skeleton juts up from the sand – an eerie and imposing ghost of a ship that was.

Lucky weather timing for us. The May afternoon was gray but dry, and Terry and I eagerly prepared to dip our rear tires in the Pacific Ocean near the *Peter Iredale*.

Bikes and sand are always a poor combination, so we carried our naked bikes down to the ship's ghost. A chill wind blew while we rolled up our pants and walked barefoot into the frigid water.

Low, pounding waves powered against us as Terry and I gripped our bikes and firmly planted ourselves in the sinking sand, bracing against the rush of water that tried to suck us into the ocean. While we stood shin high in the pressing water, Erik and Karl snapped photos while the crashing waters of the Pacific Ocean baptized our rear wheels.

Terry and I dipping our rear tires in the Pacific
Ocean near Astoria, Oregon, May 9, 2012

From that point, there was nowhere to go but east. Nothing stood in our way to the Atlantic, except a vast expanse of land.

Terry and I pedaled to a cabin, our night's luxury. No stranger to the infamous Oregon rain, I reserved indoor lodging at the campground for the four of us – I didn't want to break camp with a soggy tent on the first morning of our bike trip. There would be time enough later for that.

Seeing youth and adults gathered around a roaring campfire after dinner, we four sidled up to the group.

"You want some s'mores?" A middle-aged man handed us sticks, inviting us to join them.

We did, and learned they were from a charter school a few hours' drive away.

This summer would be the first time in fifteen years that I would not be working at a camp. I love camp, and the only thing strong enough to pull me away from it was this cross-country bike trip. Here was a mini-camp around the campfire, with welcoming folks from the charter school, jokes, antics from the students, conversations about creative teaching, and s'mores.

"What brings you to the coast mid-week?" a parent asked.

"We're starting a cross-country bike trip tomorrow. We dipped our rear tires in the Pacific this afternoon, and we'll head to Portland, Maine, where we'll dip our front tires in the Atlantic. We figure it will take us about three months. We plan to visit friends and family along the way, do some sight-seeing, and take our time. I've been wanting to do this trip for 32 years, and tomorrow is the day it starts." I grinned with glee.

"Wow. Fantastic. How many miles do you plan to do each day? Will you be camping, or staying in motels?"

"We figure we'll be cycling about 50-75 miles a day, and Terry wants to take a rest day once a week. We plan to camp when the weather is good, and snag motels when it rains."

Others listened in and joined the conversation. My excitement about the trip grew as Terry and I shared our plans and answered questions. Enthusiasm and warm wishes enveloped us when we retired for the night.

"Bon voyage!"

"Good luck!"

"Be safe!"

Inspired and energized, I went to bed one happy camper.

May 10, 2012

A light rain began to fall as Terry and I loaded our bikes in the morning. Western Oregon has a reputation for rain, and Oregon was giving us a proper send-off. We were ready for it: my #1 rule for bike touring is *Line your panniers with plastic bags.* Jumbo garbage bags were already in place, and more were ready to protect my sleeping bag, tent, and Thermarest sleeping mattress.

In addition to my forty-five pounds of gear, I added water and food. Food weighed in with a ridiculous five pounds of perishable produce and cheese; I was simply unwilling to throw out good food from home. At least it gave me an incentive to eat.

We were ready. A foot shorter than Terry, I tilted into his tall, lean frame and smiled. Two silver-haired cyclists, off to see the world. *Click.*

On went our helmets and our bright-green fluorescent safety vests. Into my vest's front pocket went my three essentials: camera, dog zapper, and voice recorder. The dog zapper emits a high-frequency sound, audible and uncomfortable to dogs, but not to humans. Terry and I became believers over the years; we would frantically point and zap at dogs that ran barking towards us, and the dogs would eventually stop before reaching us. We never knew whether it was because of the zapper or because the dogs lost interest, but it seemed to work.

My third pocket essential was my voice recorder. Since I was planning to send family and friends weekly e-mails about our trip, I could first capture my thoughts while I pedaled, and then transcribe them into detailed e-mails on my Blackberry.

Terry and I wobbled on our way to Erik and Karl's yurt, unaccustomed to the heavy bikes.

"See you soon!" we all called to each other.

Exhilaration swept me down the road. After all those years of imagining, now it was finally happening. But reality knocked, too. The unknown lay ahead, without a guarantee as to when, where, or how our trip would actually end.

Only a year earlier, a three-week bike trip unexpectedly ended when Terry crashed, lacerated his liver, and landed in a hospital's intensive care unit in South Dakota. That hadn't been part of our plan. Fortunately, Terry had a resilient liver, and a year later, we were back on the bikes.

As we left the Pacific, my euphoria wrestled with fear. Something bad could happen at any time—any minute—and I knew I would feel devastated if our bike trip ended before we saw the Atlantic.

Stopping to buy postcards of the *Peter Iredale* to commemorate the start of our adventure, I felt like shouting inside the store *We're just starting our cross-country bike trip to the Atlantic Ocean!* But with much restraint, I limited myself to *Thank you* as I took the postcards and left.

Crossing Young's Bay Bridge, I parked my bike and dashed on foot between speeding cars to take a photo of the mouth of the Columbia River. Talk about a big mouth – the Columbia's is over ten miles wide. From Canada, the river flows south through Washington state until it veers west and becomes the border between Washington and Oregon. During our first week, Terry and I would parallel much of that 300-mile border, as had the early American explorers Meriwether Lewis and William Clark in their Corps of Discovery Expedition, more than 200 years before.

Photos taken, I made another mad dash between the rushing cars back to my bike. It was a little dicey, and I thought what a shame it would be if I tripped, fell, and was killed so soon into our journey – and not even while on my bike.

Terry and I rolled along downtown Astoria's parade route, reliving parades from years before. Our son, Erik, grew up dancing in a Norwegian folkdance group, and those young *Leikarringen* (LAY-kuh-ring-en) dancers marched along this route as part of Astoria's annual Midsummer Scandinavian Festival.

With town, memories, and rain behind, the sun shone on gleaming blue water while an empty barge floated downstream. Beyond the broad river, the evergreens of Washington blanketed its hills. Giant fir trees lined our road on the Oregon side. I felt small and unassuming, quietly pedaling under the canopy of the dense, century-old trees.

🚲

Many people bicycle across North America in two months – Terry and I knew we were not those people. We weren't fast or strong or very bike-savvy, and we knew we'd make slow progress compared with hot-shot cyclists. Terry liked frequent, long breaks, and our daily mileage would be tempered by that. But the goal wasn't to do the trip quickly – the goal was just to do it.

🚲

Erik and Karl soon caught up and pulled over.

"You're doing great! You've come a long way."

Well, that was a lie. We hadn't come a long way, but that didn't matter. After several minutes of chit chat, hugs, and thanks, Terry and I were off again.

A stunning view of Washington's Mt. Rainer and the much shorter Mt. St. Helens greeted us from a hilltop in late afternoon. The Cascade Mountain range runs through central Washington and Oregon, sticking its numerous volcanic peaks up thousands of feet. Most of the volcanoes are dormant, but Mt. St. Helens awoke in 1980, spectacularly decapitating itself.

This time, Mt. St. Helens and Mt. Rainier looked peaceful and snow-laden against the big blue sky. Terry and I have an affinity for mountains. We met through a local climbing club, the Mazamas, just a few months after Mt. St. Helens blew up. Both of us registered to climb a mountain, and the climb leader mailed out a roster with everyone's address and phone number. Unbeknownst to me, Terry's *modus operandi* was to phone the nearest female to ask if she wanted to carpool for the climb. One time, that happened to be me. Ironically, the climb was for Mt. Bachelor, another dormant Cascade volcano, and within three years of Terry asking me if I wanted to carpool with him, he was no longer a bachelor. Terry and I spent many a grimy weekend hiking, backpacking, and climbing in the mountains.

Dinnertime found us in the town of Rainier, Oregon. We wheeled our bikes to the restaurant's patio, packed with diners enjoying the warm, sunny evening. We peeled off helmets and safety vests, and sat down.

Our young waitress handed us menus. "Where'd ya come from?" she asked.

"The Pacific Ocean, Astoria," I replied.

"Wow, that's such a long way!" she exclaimed. We were only sixty miles from the coast.

"We're on our way to the Atlantic Ocean," I announced with a big smile.

"Is that down by California?" she queried.

Oh brother. We told her where the Atlantic was. "Wow, that's so exciting!" She took our order and disappeared.

People inspected our bikes, and us. Getting up to leave, a man asked about our plans, while other diners intently listened. "Wow, that's great!" someone said. Others asked questions, and we happily answered.

"I told them back in the kitchen about you!" our waitress exclaimed as she returned with our food.

Dinner finished, we donned helmets, fluorescent-green bike vests, and biking gloves. As we wheeled our bikes from the patio, a waiter grinned and gave us the thumbs-up sign. I felt like we were celebrities—and we'd only biked sixty miles.

While pitching our tent at a nearby marina and RV park, the owner, Larry, introduced us to Pecker the Rooster. Pecker strutted about, bobbing his head as he wandered amid a gaggle of geese as the sky changed from blue to pink and yellow. A boat drew near in the twilight, and emerald forests claimed the land beyond the river. Peace and beauty defined our world.

Good weather, well-functioning bikes and bikers, and a beautiful technicolor sky were gifts to our first day. The temperature sank with the evening sun as we watched the day fade. Bundled in layers at 42 degree F., my hat and gloves stayed on as we burrowed into our sleeping bags for the night.

Emerging from our tent, shortly before discovering a rooster
pecked my tire during the night. Good morning, flat tire…

I went to bed with two intact bike tires and woke up to a flat- -my first flat tire in years. Rather than getting an early start on the road, we spent time fixing my flat.

While we pulled tools from Terry's panniers, I glanced at my bike. Pecker the Rooster was pecking at my other tire. Hmm. Prime suspect. Larry put him in the Pecker Pen so he couldn't keep pecking on our stuff.

Terry began working on the flat and then Larry joined in, suspicious of my claim that Pecker may have been the culprit. The tire bore marks that could have been beak slashes, but Larry found aluminum shards inside my wheel rim, and felt Pecker was innocent. Along came Ron the Shower Construction Guy, who whipped out a magnifying glass, examining my tire for sharps. He wanted to sand the inside of my wheel rim and clean it with his air compressor – sure, we let him.

Meanwhile, Pecker strutted in his Pecker Pen ten feet away, and the Columbia River rolled by.

While they worked, I charged my Blackberry inside the park's store. My source for writing long e-mails to friends and family about the trip, I knew my Blackberry would present a challenge to keep charged while camping.

With thanks and even a good bye to Pecker, Terry and I headed out for Portland, and more importantly for Terry, a chocolate milkshake. Milkshakes are Terry's rewards for fixing flats, and I'm happy to pay up. Inherited from my grandmother, my arthritic hands are too weak to remove or replace the industrial strength bike tires we use. While I was confident in my ability to ride across the continent, I knew I could not physically repair a flat tire. Independent in many things, I am not independent in that, and it ticks me off. I'm resigned to the fact that I'm physically unable to do it, and must rely on others. I have tools and knowledge, but I just need some willing brute force to assist. Fortunately, I had willing brute force accompanying me, who only asked for milkshakes as compensation.

Good thing our brains were still high on milkshake endorphins as we entered northwest Portland. The ugly, industrial view from Highway 30 conspired to attack my high spirits from the last eighty-miles of inspiring scenery.

But high spirits prevailed as we crossed the Willamette River and soon arrived home. Home so quickly, and we'd only begun this long adventure the day before.

Slacker Day.

Throughout my years as a Home Infusion nurse, I've worked with a stellar group of nurses, pharmacists, and support crew, and one was retiring. Because the nurses do their intravenous work autonomously in people's homes, a party is a rare occasion to socialize together. Camaraderie, stories, and laughter filled my day. Although the retirement party was in someone else's honor, I also felt celebrated. Love and warm wishes for our bike journey followed me out the door.

Meanwhile, Terry bought two new industrial strength tires for my bike. I wanted Peckerless tires, sans beak slashes, when we set out from Portland.

That evening, I spent time petting Tango, our fat orange cat. A purring machine, she didn't know we were leaving for three months. Would she still be around on our return? Once when we were gone for several weeks, she moved in with neighbors. Although being fed daily at our house, she moved across the street after discovering the neighbor's cat door. For the next many months, Tango was a joint custody cat, eating her way between the two homes. I was happy when someone with a cat allergy moved into the neighbor's house. Once our neighbors stopped feeding Tango, she was content to stay with us again.

A long-stemmed rose for Mother's Day greeted me Sunday morning. Terry's generosity with flowers has marked special occasions for years. One year during a cross-country ski expedition near the North Pole, he even strategically arranged for a floral delivery for our anniversary.

I tucked the rose under my bungee cord behind my bike seat. It was the crown jewel, atop the tent, sleeping bag, and my Thermarest. It was even on top of my violin, my latest piece of gear. My bike looked especially ridiculous with a violin case on top of everything else. Fortunately, the violin was going only as far as our church.

I'd been suckered into playing a duet with Frank, my violin teacher and our church choir director. I was the prodigal violin student – I kept leaving and returning, taking lessons for a few months and then stopping for months-to-years. Having done that multiple times, I was still a beginning violin student, with the cat fight sounds to prove it.

With a farewell to Tango, Terry and I pedaled off to our church, where I'd been a member for 32 years. After moving to Portland from college, I tried a church two blocks from my apartment and discovered friendly people-- and a group planning a day-long bike ride. I've been hooked on that church ever since.

Terry and I left our loaded bikes in the church's narthex and entered the sanctuary.

Throughout the service, I reflected on the people around me. So many were dear to me. Just like the previous day's work gathering, I felt loved by this community, and was excited to have them participate in the "sending forth" our pastor, Tom, had planned.

During the last song, Terry and I left our pew to join our bikes. While Tom began talking about Terry's and my trip, I walked my bike towards the front of the sanctuary. Terry paused, and then rode his bike up the aisle. People clapped.

"Mari and Terry are embarking on a great adventure of riding their bicycles across the entire United States. It will no doubt be a journey that will hold surprises; there will be rough roads along with the smooth," Tom read as Terry and I stood with our bikes before the congregation.

"Terry and Mari," he continued, "as you pedal your way across America, you will, along with changing weather, encounter different people. On your journey and in your encounters, we pray for your witness to your faith. We pray that through your words and actions, the love, patience, and hospitality of Jesus Christ will shine forth. We also pray for your safety: may your tires always remain on the road and your heads above water."

"Mari and Terry," the congregation responded, "we recognize you as ambassadors of this congregation in ministry with people that you will meet on your journey across the country. We dedicate you to this opportunity of sharing the gospel wherever and however you feel led by the Spirit of Christ. Through our prayers, and Mari's texting and e-mails, we will be united with you in your work. May God richly bless you in your adventure."

Terry and I read in unison, "With gratitude and excitement we begin our journey today. We go with the knowledge of your love and the never-ending grace of God at our backs as well as guiding us each day."

"Go with our blessing and the blessing of the Holy Spirit," the congregation responded.

It was poignant to stand before our church and feel the power of love and energy in that room. The service ended with hugs and good wishes from our church friends.

My anxiety mounted as I sat through the second service, waiting to play my violin. It was so dumb. Here I was ready to ride my bike across North America, but I had more angst about playing a minute-and-a-half on the violin than I did about riding my bike on highways for three months. When it was time to play, Frank gave me a reassuring look. The *Per Smed* waltz duet had the potential to sound beautiful.

It didn't. My violin playing was just as lovely as fingernails slowly clawing down a blackboard--I couldn't stay on pitch. Fortunately, the church was full of forgiving people. Nobody threw tomatoes or hymnals, but I bet they were tempted. I should have worn Terry's button that read "I played it better at home." I kept thinking that once we got to Yellowstone, I could forgo the bear spray and simply play my violin. That would chase off the grizzlies.

I happily chucked the violin after the service.

My panniers were already full, but I crammed in one more thing: love from our friends and family. They were also anticipating this adventure. Some were excited, others anxious--their feelings mirrored mine. While many questions remained about much of our trip, there was no question about my feeling of belonging, being accepted, and loved. Terry and I expected a journey of three months, and those months would connect us in person with friends and family across the continent, while staying connected via words and pictures with others. The positive energy and hugs from our church family made it feel like our trip was really starting--the first two days were only the warm-up.

Time to start our trip in earnest.

Terry and I pedaled out in the early afternoon heat--91 degrees of it; hotter than ideal to start a long day of mileage.

Soon we were on the I-205 freeway's bike path headed north towards the Columbia River. Mt. Hood and Mt. St. Helens were out in full splendor, draped in white snow against a blue sky. At the bridge, Terry and I dug out our earplugs for the noisy, 3.5 mile-long bridge, where the bike path lay sandwiched between opposing lanes of traffic. Cars whizzed by and planes from the nearby Portland airport roared overhead. Our ears took a pounding, but our eyes feasted on the Columbia River sparkling below us, reflecting the blue sky and bright sunshine. Midway across the bridge, we crossed our first state border. Good bye to Oregon.

Hello, Washington.

CHAPTER 3

River Travels— Washington

Across the river, the bike path descended like a tail between the legs of freeway. Soon we skirted pot holes and cracks of the Old Evergreen Highway, hugging the shore of the Columbia River. Massive evergreen trees lined the quiet, narrow road, so tall and thick that sunlight barely hit the pavement. To the side, weary old houses and imposing estates equally shared million-dollar views of the river.

This was familiar territory, having repeatedly biked this route for training rides. From our house, it was only seventeen miles to Camas Park, our normal turn-around point. Today there would be no turning around.

Near the park, a transit bus drove by. I couldn't see the driver, but I knew our friend, Paul, drove the Sunday Camas route. Paul wrote the next day that he recognized us on our bikes. Too bad he hadn't stopped the bus so the three of us could shoot the bull and say our good byes.

Temptation stopped us in the form of a business's water jet, and Terry knew exactly what to do. Off came his helmet, vest, gloves, and shirt. He soaked his shirt in the waterfall, and then slowly eased himself into it, making tortuous sounds as the cold, wet fabric agonized his skin. Cheap entertainment for me.

"You could do it too," Terry teased.

I wasn't so sure about taking off my shirt along the busy highway, but I did consider just standing underneath the cold water. Terry's wails and grimaces gave minimal encouragement, though. I passed.

Beyond Camas, we pedaled east, up and down the hills of the rural highway, appreciating good shoulders and the light Sunday afternoon traffic. A teenage boy pedaled up beside us, eyeballing our loaded bikes.

"Where are you going?" he asked.

"The Atlantic Ocean!" I replied.

He stared at us. "Well, just think of it this way – you're almost halfway there." With a wave of his hand, he was gone.

I liked his optimism, if not his understanding of geography.

Getting started is often the hardest part of a big dream. "I could never do that" many people said when hearing our plans. Well, yes, they could. You could. You don't have to start with a cross-country trip. Start small, and let the momentum and experience build. Don't allow yourself to become frozen by the immensity of the project—just start. You move, discover, and soon find yourself doing. Then you find yourself doing more, and the momentum keeps the process in action.

A marvelous aspect of bike touring is that there are so many ways to do it. Do you want to bike twenty-five miles a day, or a hundred? Do you want to camp, stay in a motel/hotel, or couch surf? Do you want to eat from grocery stores or restaurants? Do you want to be self-supported, or have a sag wagon? Do you want to do all of the above?

Anything is possible—just begin and let the momentum grow. Terry and I had begun.

My phone rang miles later. "Happy Mother's Day!" our son, Erik, exclaimed.

A detour to northern Minnesota would bring Terry and me to Erik and Concordia Language Villages, where he worked at their German and Norwegian language camps. But meanwhile, a lively five-minute phone call substituted nicely. "*Tschüss! Jeg elsker deg!*" Erik ended our call blending a German farewell and Norwegian words of love. My spirits soared.

I feasted on Erik's words and the beauty before us as we entered the Columbia River Gorge, which cradled us in its crook. The next day would bring us to beloved trailheads and waterfalls plummeting through forests on both sides of the river—we stood at the gates of splendor.

Tired from the heat and hills, Terry hit the wall before North Bonneville. Forty-one miles into our day and fifteen miles short of our planned goal, we pulled into the Lewis and Clark RV Park – what an oxymoron. What would those explorers have thought of an RV park, let alone having one named after them?

Pitching our tent in a secluded area next to Hamilton Creek, I wondered if Lewis and Clark ever bathed in its cold, fast flow. I sought comparative luxury instead: the shower house. For my four quarters, I bought time in a rusty smelling shower stall, but the refreshing water did purge my skin of its sweat and grime.

Terry and I slipped into the tent for the night, listening to the soothing sounds of the creek. The power of love had energized me throughout the day, and it enfolded me for the night.

Noisy trains shattered our peaceful night, running surprisingly close to our tent until hours past midnight. Either they finally stopped running or I just conked out.

"Trains? Really?" Terry asked as I queried him in the morning. Mr. Sleep-Through-The-Trains was oblivious to the noise and enjoyed a good night's sleep.

It took over an hour to break camp, load the bikes, get ready for the day, and get started. That was typical for us, and another reason we wouldn't be doing a quick, two-month cross-country trip. While Terry took his time getting ready, I stood immersed in words, with my Blackberry plugged into the bathroom wall.

Eastbound on Highway 14, we paralleled the river and the train track. Busy at night, the track didn't get rest during the day, either, with freight trains rushing past in either direction. Sometimes trains were hidden by woods as they rattled by, and sometimes we were all in the open, with train tracks and bikes in close proximity. In the open spaces, I waved to the engineers as the front engines passed. Many times, the engineers waved back.

Cycling next to train tracks and the Columbia
River, looking south into Oregon

For engineering of a different kind, we cycled past Bonneville Dam, the first of several dams we would encounter spanning the Columbia. My mother's father worked on Bonneville as part of President Franklin Roosevelt's New Deal in the mid-1930s, earning 50-cents an hour during the Great Depression. Eighty years later, I cycled by his work.

Headwinds delivered news of roadkill ahead--we could smell it before we saw it. Eviscerated raccoons and possums dotted the pavement for the next few miles, their guts glistening in the sunshine. The odor briefly faded as we pedaled beyond, only to reappear in advance of the next dead body.

The headwind was no surprise as we neared Hood River, Oregon, which proclaims itself the Windsurfing Capital of the World. A few colorful windsurfers and kite-surfers zipped along the Columbia's wide surface in the bright sunshine.

Wind is an inevitable part of a long journey. Sometimes it's a headwind that slows progress, sometimes it's a crosswind that blows the traveler off course, and sometimes it's a beautiful tailwind that makes travel effortless. Moderate wind is a welcome breeze that cools and refreshes on a hot day.

Strong headwinds began our three-week bike trip from Missoula, Montana, the previous year. At one point my pedaling was no match for the headwind at the crest of a hill; I pushed and pushed, but came to a complete standstill. And then I fell over. I just thought I was a wimp. The next day we heard that trees had blown down near Missoula, and I didn't feel so wimpy anymore.

Today's headwind wasn't that extreme, and I welcomed its cooling effect on my sweaty face.

To our right, the train tracks began to hum. A train shot through at full sound and speed with a deafening blast of its horn. A measly ten feet and a guard rail separated us from the train. Simultaneously to our left and less than ten feet away, trucks roared past, but without guard rails to protect us. For two long, tense minutes, I tightly gripped my handlebars as speeding, noisy monsters hurled by us on either side.

"Let's stop for a minute," I exhaled when the train disappeared and Terry could again hear me.

I was spooked. We gave our clenched hands and rattled brains a well-deserved break. How quickly our cycling rhythm could change. One minute we felt relaxed and comfortable in our stride, while the next minute was filled with tension and fright. We never knew what the next minute would bring.

🚲

A series of five short tunnels pierce through basalt flows on Highway 14, and a sign stands sentry on the road's shoulder outside each tunnel's entrance. Cyclists pedal up, press a button, and a flashing light outside the tunnel warns motorists of cyclists ahead.

"I'll just hit the button with my foot as I ride on by," Terry said as we approached. Yeah, right.

We stopped at the first tunnel. Terry dug through his panniers, pulled out two lights, and clipped them to the back of his bike. Blink, blink, blink went his red lights. On went our front lights.

I tapped the button and a yellow light flashed above the tunnel entrance. Terry entered first, his blinking lights easily visible as the rest of him disappeared into the shadow.

I pedaled like fury into the tunnel and was surprised how dark it was—until I realized I still had on my sunglasses. What a dork. Turns out Terry did the same thing. Two dorks.

The cool, dark, interiors of the tunnels were a welcome relief from the sweltering heat outside, but they were no place to linger on a bike. It was a relief to get beyond those five tunnels--they were simply dangerous. Motorists might ignore the flashing light outside, and the dark, narrow tunnels had skinny shoulders. If push came to shove inside the tunnel, I knew who would get the shove.

🚲

The Columbia River and Oregon's Mt. Hood

Like pedaling, the day had its own rhythm. Miles, breaks, and food. Our scenery transformed. To the south, Mt. Hood became bigger. The lush greenery of western Washington gradually gave way to large volcanic rocks of central Washington. Fewer trees meant less shade, and big rocks meant rattlesnakes. Everything was hot and dry, except us. We were hot and sweaty. The afternoon gave no place to hide from the sun. It was time to pull out our helmet brims –flat doughnut-like contraptions that fit over the top of our helmets, giving us a wide visor in front and back.

Terry and I wilted to a stop. After a cursory inspection for rattlesnakes, we plopped down on large rocks. My black leather cycling gloves were soaked with sweat, as was the rest of me. The headwinds had ceased, and there was no wind of any kind. In the withering heat, I may have even welcomed some headwinds.

I propped my pink umbrella over my head for shade. I love umbrellas, rain or shine, and might be the only person in the Pacific Northwest that admits to that. For some reason, people see it as a badge of honor to walk in the rain without one. I wondered how it looked to motorists to see someone underneath a pink parasol sitting on the desolate rocks.

Welcome respite from the sun

We drank up. Terry drank Gatorade and I drank Crystal Light peach tea. I'd divide a package of Crystal Light into two compartments of a contact lens case, half in the left and half in the right. I'd prepackage two contact lens cases in the morning, and periodically open an eyeball and dump it into a bottle of water. One eyeball per liter made for a good drink.

Terry was a Gatorade guy due to its electrolytes. He tried to convince me of its superiority, but Terry always wilted in the heat before I did. Meanwhile, I drank my Crystal Light, ate bananas and salted nuts, and remained unconverted.

Leaving rocks and slumbering rattlesnakes, we continued sweating our way east until reaching Horsethief Butte. Rock climbers sat on the ground talking and laughing after their day on the crags. I reveled in good memories from my own rock-climbing days: the feeling of accomplishment and a tired body. Hey, I still had that now, especially the tired body.

I dug out melted gummy bears, a going-away treat from my sister-in-law, Lynn. They were especially gummy in the 100-degree heat, but were a satisfying blend of sugary ooze and love from family. Eyeing the melted mess of my yogurt-covered raisins, I knew I'd be eating them with my spoon.

By 4:30, it was still bloody hot. Fortunately the wind returned, sending a warm breeze over hot skin. Waiting for Terry at the top of a hill, my pink umbrella open and leaning against my head, I used both thumbs to write on my Blackberry. But the wind also blew letters around on my Blackberry screen. I had this problem on previous bike trips and assumed it was a normal wind/Blackberry thing. I mentioned it once to someone, who looked at me like I was crazy.

"What do you mean, the wind blows your letters around?" he asked.

"When I write when it's windy, letters don't get written on the screen in the order that I type them. They jump around, and land in words that are up a few lines above what is already written. The letters end up all over the place. Whatever I type sometimes just ends up being gibberish and turns what I've already written into gibberish, too."

"That's weird."

I agreed.

I talked to the Blackberry people about it, and they thought it was me that was weird. They said they had never heard of that happening before, and had no solution other than for me to stay out of the wind.

But I was back in the wind, and the letters were once again blowing around, attacking words I already wrote. If I typed s-l-o-w-l-y and paid close attention, I could catch it when letters took off into previously written sentences, but I hated to type that slowly. I had lots to write about and wanted to get it into the Blackberry while I waited for Terry.

At least my voice recorder still worked in the wind.

Terry arrived, and after a break for him, we reaped the rewards of coming up that long hill by zooming down the other side. At least *I* zoomed down. Terry wasn't much of a zoomer and frequently used his brakes. Cycling east with the afternoon sun at our backs and not in our eyes was a sweet feeling. Going downhill was even sweeter.

Lush vineyards and orchards grew down by the river, a stark contrast to the big, dry rocks to the north of Highway 14. Bare, parched hills thirsted across the Columbia in eastern Oregon, without a tree in sight beyond the river's border.

Maryhill State Park was our day's reward, a steep, sweet mile-and-a-half ride down to the Columbia. That reward would become a chore the next day, since we'd need to climb back up.

Maryhill State Park is an oasis in central Washington – green grass, trees, and shrubs next to a river. We pedaled into our oasis, plopped on the shady grass, and didn't move.

Eventually, we began setting up camp. Terry laid out the tent's ground cloth on the grass.

"Hey, Terry, the sign says no tents on lawn," I called out, pointing to a sign close to our campsite.

"Piss on it," Terry replied. "Can't put stakes in the gravel," referring to the only surface by our site that wasn't grass. I had to agree. Besides, who wants a hard bed of gravel when you can have a soft bed of grass?

Apparently, the camp ranger felt the same way, because when he came by a short time later, he didn't make us move. Or maybe he just felt sorry for two worn out, beaten looking cyclists. At any rate, the tent stayed on the lawn, right next to the sign that read "No tents on lawn."

We weren't done biking for the day. Leaving pounds of junk behind, we biked across the bridge to Biggs, Oregon, for dinner.

We ate at a café, and it was worth every dime just to sit inside that air-conditioned building.

As we biked back across the bridge into Washington, I spied six quarters lying on the side of the bridge. Quarters! That was six minutes of hot water at the state park, just lying on the ground. I would have stopped, but there was no shoulder, and a lot of traffic. I couldn't justify an accident just to get six minutes of a hot shower. Earlier in the day, a hot shower would have sounded ghastly, but as the evening temperature dropped, it was downright appealing.

I obsessed about a hot shower all the way back to the state park, determined to have one. My personal stash of quarters gave me four glorious minutes, and the bathroom gave electricity to charge my Blackberry. I crawled into our tent feeling deliciously clean at the end of our hot, sweaty, 71-mile day.

If you want a peaceful night's sleep next to the Columbia River, don't expect to get it at Maryhill State Park. The beautiful, grassy campground belies the fact that it is surrounded by a busy highway, two train tracks, and a freeway. Throughout the night, trucks barreled down steep Highway 197, trains ran on both sides of the river, and from the Oregon side, the traffic from Interstate 84 hustled continuously. River trains tortured me until after 4 a.m., when I finally fell into a sleep-deprived coma.

Upon awakening at 7, my brain zapped me with an immediate sense of excitement about our trip and an eagerness to resume. First, however, Terry and I enjoyed a leisurely breakfast in bed. It's handy to reach over to a food bag and eat a meal without even leaving the sleeping bag. Our tent was cozy, warm, and dimly lit from the sunshine penetrating through the two layers of tent.

Once outside, the daily routine began. We pumped tires before burdening our bikes with heavy panniers and gear, and filled our many water bottles with fresh, cool water. We again crammed our world into colorful stuff sacks and panniers. Orange and yellow safety triangles dangled off the back of our bikes, and we wore bright fluorescent-green safety jackets. All that color was a stark contrast to the monotonous brown and yellow land of the day before.

The steep one-and-a half-mile climb back up to Highway 14 looked intimidating, but like much of life, the anticipation turned out to be worse than the reality.

Stonehenge greeted us two miles later. Sam Hill, a wealthy Quaker, commissioned a full-size Stonehenge replica as a World War I memorial. Completed in 1929, it sits in isolation on a bluff overlooking the Columbia River. Locals are familiar with it, but I imagine it must be a shock to unexpectedly encounter Stonehenge when traveling in the Columbia River Gorge.

A crop of wind turbines reached for the sky. The gorge turbines fuel not only wind energy but also controversy. Many people feel turbines ruin the beauty of the landscape, but I think they look elegant. With the 200-foot towers and each towers' three 100-foot blades, it's easy to become mesmerized by the rotating blades.

My five pounds of perishable food that I'd rescued from our home refrigerator gave me woe, just as Terry predicted. Inside my pannier, the cheese cooked in its plastic bag. I finally wised up and threw it out—something I should have done at home. I steadily gnawed my way through a pound of carrots that Terry abandoned.

Soon I began to curse my helmet brim. Fine at lower speeds, it provided great eye shade in the morning as we cycled towards the eastern sun. When I barreled down a hill, however, the air lifted the broad, firm brim, flopping it wildly. It either obstructed my vision or choked me by pulling up on my helmet strap. Terry liked his helmet brim and wasn't cursing his – perhaps he liked being blinded and choked. I didn't.

I was zooming downhill at 30 miles an hour near the John Day Dam when my brim flew off my helmet. I had to brake suddenly, park my bike, and walk back up that dam(n) hill just to retrieve my visor. After losing it multiple times, I resolved to remove it before I headed down the next big hill.

Another grueling hot day pushed the temperature to 100 degrees. We found shady refuge under a gigantic mailbox at the end of someone's driveway, until a man exited his house, eyeing us suspiciously. That break ended awkwardly.

We cycled into increasing isolation with fewer houses and less traffic. The wide blue ribbon of the Columbia cut through the monotony of the dull, treeless hills.

The dusty village of West Roosevelt provided welcome shade, as well as expensive food from a mini-mart. The produce looked old and neglected, but we bought it anyway—no food options remained until the next day. Revived by the mini-mart's cold chocolate milk and ice cream, we set out for the next 20-mile push through the desolation and heat.

Crow Butte Park was our reward, an oasis on a bridged island in the Columbia, where grassy, wooded campsites overlooked the river.

"What's the charge to camp here?" we asked the camp host.

"There's no charge since you are cyclists."

"Really? Is that true of Washington's state parks?"

"No, it's just true here. At Crow Butte, cyclists stay free."

Not only were Terry and I at an oasis, but a free oasis at that.

It's a good way to get the adrenaline going…

The sign next to our campsite read *Beware of Rattlesnakes.* Yikes. Terry and I carefully walked a path through the woods to a nearby cove. I wore my Keen sandals, which left plenty of flesh exposed in case a snake wanted to sink its fangs into me. Our plan was to swim, but we only made it as far as our feet—cold! I retreated to the shower, paid my two quarters and then received a dribble of cold water that felt like it came straight from the river.

Conditions, however, were perfect for laundry. I wriggled my clean body into my semi-clean night clothes, and washed grimy bike clothes in the bathroom sink while I charged my Blackberry. Our two bikes provided plenty of hanging space. I strategically draped wet clothes between the bike frame and brake cables, hung underwear by its leg holes from my handlebars, and let my bike seat serve as a head for my shirt. Perfect. The wind whipped my clothes.

I wandered the campground, talking with campers. One couple sat outside their RV next door, drinking cocktails. I hoped someone would invite Terry and me to join them for dinner or cocktails, but not surprisingly, that didn't happen. Terry and I were forced to scrounge from our panniers again. Crow Butte would have been the perfect setting for us to have cooked food, but we had deliberately left our stove and pot at home. We ate the same old pannier food we'd been eating for days: nuts, dried fruit, energy bars, candy, and an endless supply of carrots.

The wind picked up, a train rumbled by, and it appeared we were in for another noisy night as our tent rattled in the wind. After a long, hot day, I collapsed in my bag.

The beauty of being dehydrated is that you don't need to pee during the night.

I slept – even through trains – and woke up refreshed. The morning was cool, easing our exit from the verdant campground and the entrance back into the brown and yellow world of central Washington.

I think sunscreen is marvelous stuff. I could have been charbroiled by that point of our trip, but I slathered on sunscreen repeatedly and remained unburnt. Unlike Terry, I'm rarely diligent with sunscreen, and have had many sunburns to prove it. I was motivated on our trip, however--it was either use sunscreen or fry.

Twelve miles down the road, I ate a spicy taco salad for breakfast at Paterson, resulting with lips on fire when I resumed cycling. I discovered that sunscreen is useless for salsa lip burns.

Crossing the Columbia River, we briefly left Washington for a foray into Oregon again. Three hundred miles upstream from our start, the river's breadth significantly diminished, and it took only a few minutes to cross into Umatilla.

A big grocery store filled us with joy: food and shade. I sat in the shade with our bikes while Terry shopped. I excitedly spied a quarter on the ground—a minute's worth of hot shower somewhere.

"Where are you going?" a man asked as he walked by, eying the bikes and me.

"The Atlantic Ocean," I replied. I loved saying that.

We were still talking when Terry returned with his sack of food. While Terry continued the conversation, I went inside, and had a beautiful time choosing my next twenty-four hours' worth of food.

I bought chocolate milk, skim milk, three yogurts, string cheese, a green pepper, a couple of bananas, cans of juice, and nuts. The macaroni and cheese at the deli looked gooey and tempting. I bought that, too. It was a lot of food.

Outside, I concocted my favorite milk mixture: 50/50 chocolate milk and skim milk. I drank some, polished off a yogurt, and dug into my hot macaroni and cheese. Although it tasted great, I only wanted a couple of bites. It settled heavily in my stomach.

Terry was smarter. He sensibly bought smaller amounts, and didn't overdue it with the perishables.

"You have a ton of food!" he exclaimed incredulously as I struggled to cram the rest of it into a pannier.

I couldn't deny it. It was too much, and I knew I would be hard pressed to eat it before it spoiled. It just looked so wonderful inside the grocery store and I was carried away by the freshness and abundance of it all.

With full bellies and panniers, we rode east from Umatilla on Highway 730. At Hat Rock State Park, the bright colors of swimsuits and sails gave a reprieve from the arid brown rocks and hills, where anything green worked hard to survive.

Blue and beautiful, our final stretch of the Columbia River ended our first geographical chapter of our trip. The river bent north, but Terry and I veered east on Highway 12, once again in Washington.

Goodbye, Columbia. You were a marvelous companion for the start of our trip.

We paralleled the Walla Walla River, a slip of a thing compared to the broad Columbia. Along the river, the world transformed to green, but elsewhere was parched. Pierce's Green Valley RV Park was aptly named, with grass, trees, and even a breeze. I had no need for the quarter I found in Umatilla; there weren't any showers. Outhouses did the trick for restrooms, and a long green hose did the trick for water. An electrical outlet at our campsite put me in heaven with the Blackberry.

Terry and I plopped down on grass in the shadow of a leafy tree, happy to be done for the day. The temperature hadn't climbed above 90, and we were grateful for the ten-degree difference.

We even had internet coverage, something that came and went during our 350 miles so far.

Terry accessed Warmshowers, a couch-surfing organization for cyclists. We hoped to augment our camping with hospitality from bike friendly folks across the nation. The tricky part was that we couldn't give people much lead time in our requests to spend a night. Terry wrote to a household in Dayton, asking if we could spend the next night with them. Before pressing *Send*, I added a line to his e-mail: "Are you Norwegian by any chance?"

We spread our buffet on the picnic table. My soupy yogurt practically exploded from the heat when I peeled back the foil. Inspired by the cocktails that we weren't invited to the evening before, I pretended my pineapple/coconut juice was a pinã colada.

The RV park owner wandered over.

"Just want to let you know about the critters in this area," she said. "We have raccoons, possums, cougars, rattlesnakes, and bull snakes around here. Keep your tent door zipped to keep out the snakes."

Roger that.

Goodnight rattlesnakes and cougars. Please stay away.

May 17 – Syttende Mai (17th of May), Norway's Constitution Day and its national holiday.

The rattlesnakes and cougars did stay away, and far from the Columbia River's train tracks, I finally had a good night's sleep.

Syttende Mai deserved a rousing rendition of Norway's national anthem, but I wasn't ready to bust out singing in the RV park. On our three-week bike trip from Missoula to Spearfish the previous year, I stood next to a frozen lake in Montana on Syttende Mai, where I belted out *Ja Vi Elsker*, confidently knowing that no one except Terry could hear me. Not even the fish could hear me, since they still lived under a thick sheet of ice. Safely isolated, it was the perfect place for me to sing. But there were other people around at the RV park, so I wisely kept my mouth shut.

Good news on my Blackberry. Our Warmshowers contact responded that Terry and I were welcome to stay at her and her husband's home in Dayton that night. No better way to celebrate that news and Norway's big day than by drinking my remaining pseudo-piña colada for breakfast. *Skoal!*

Soon were in Walla Walla, home of the Walla Walla sweet onion, which is legendary in the Pacific Northwest. We biked into downtown and there it was – a giant sweet onion painted on a brick wall. I stood with my bike in front of Onion World's advertisement, happily posing with an onion.

We dinked around Walla Walla while Terry had adjustments done on his bike and I looked for sweet onion postcards. Sadly, although there were postcards of the beautiful area around Walla Walla, there were none of onions.

Terry found the perfect power nap conditions on the Whitman College lawn: soft, green grass in the shade of a big tree, and a temperature of 75 degrees. He sprawled on his side and covered his face with his helmet visor, still wearing his fluorescent-green safety vest and biking gloves. A woman came out from a building and did a double take.

"He's okay, he's just sleeping," I called to her from the shade of my tree.

"Well, he shouldn't be sleeping on this lawn," she admonished me. She looked at him critically and walked off.

I shrugged and let him sleep.

The afternoon sun played moving games with the shade, and soon Terry's shade went elsewhere. Exposed in the bright sunlight, he awoke from his power nap, oblivious to the scorn he'd created. I told him he was in trouble.

"Piss on it," he responded.

A few minutes later there was no trace of either of us on Whitman College's exclusive lawn. On a mission, we landed at a big grocery store where I asked a young clerk if there were postcards.

"What's a postcard?" he asked.

Oh brother.

I educated him about postcards, but the store had none. Unable to spend my entire afternoon looking for onion postcards, Terry and I were forced to finally leave town without them.

A group of cyclists congregated outside the store. They looked like real cyclists, dressed in tight, brightly colored shirts, with tight biking shorts that displayed their muscular legs. I was dressed in capris pants and a loose short sleeve shirt, and did not have muscular legs. Terry wore his loose, long sleeve shirt and long beige pants. We looked like country bumpkins compared to this sleek crowd.

"I've always wanted to do a tour like that," a cyclist remarked after asking about our trip.

As Terry and I struggled with headwinds later on Highway 12, a voice called from behind.

"On your left!"

The string of cyclists easily overtook us.

"Good luck!"

"Have a great trip!" some exclaimed as they flew by.

We watched them quickly disappear up the road. They were cycling animals, the type of cyclists that could crunch out a 200-mile bike day. Terry and I were the type of cyclists who had time, and we were planning to use it. We didn't care about how fast or slow we were; we just wanted good adventures along the way.

And good scenery didn't hurt, either. Today's scenery earned top marks, with the snow-capped Blue Mountains backdropping emerald, wheat-covered Palouse hills. Back in fertile farm country, the arid, rocky land of central Washington languished behind us.

Like instructions from a spy movie, our Warmshowers hosts directed us to arrive at Dayton, and phone at 8 p.m. At the appointed time, Terry and I stood outside the little town's grocery store just as I reached for my phone.

"Are you the traveling Norwegians?" a woman asked Terry as she walked to the store's entrance. Ja, I guess we were--or close enough. Two miles later, Terry and I pushed our bikes up a steep gravel driveway.

Not cyclists themselves, Genie and Fred host cyclists traveling the Lewis and Clark Bicycle Trail that runs near their house. The 3000-mile bike route, highlighted in cycling maps by Adventure Cycling Association, rolls between Hartford,

Illinois and Seaside, Oregon, staying fairly faithful to Lewis and Clark's westward expedition route of 1804-1805. ACA's detailed maps were essential trip ingredients for Terry and me, listing campgrounds, stores, bike shops, lodging, miles, and elevation along ACA's recommended route. Terry and I were following the Lewis and Clark Bicycle Trail from our starting point in Astoria to Missoula, Montana. Lewis and Clark's route would lead to Illinois, but at Missoula, Terry and I would strike out on our own towards Yellowstone National Park.

Relaxing in Genie and Fred's engaging company, we all feasted on pie plant. That's an old name for rhubarb, but it was a new one to me. Both agriculturalists, Genie retired from the USDA, and Fred's work as a plant pathologist and international garlic expert took him around the world. Recent gigs as a garlic consultant found him in Georgia (of the former Soviet Union) and in Egypt.

Pie plant, friendly people, good conversation, and then—the warm shower. Warmshowers lived up to its name, and Terry and I had our first one in three days. Not only were we clean, but entertained as well. Colorful postcards from past cycling guests adorned the bathroom walls.

We melted into a soft, cozy bed, humbled to be the recipients of such welcoming hospitality. Terry and I merely showed up, and Genie and Fred took us in.

Sweet dreams to us.

Genie and Fred pulled out all the stops for breakfast. Hearty bread, a hot dish, huckleberries, and even fresh tarragon. Fresh tarragon was a new treat for me; tastes like licorice. Farewell, and many thanks to our generous hosts.

The bright sun bore down I saw my reflection in a window as we set forth. My helmet brim tilted at a rakish angle. I looked stylish, like perhaps I should have been at the Kentucky Derby or on the cover of Vogue magazine.

Terry and I returned to Dayton and began climbing Highway 12. The day before, we climbed a thousand feet, but most of it was gradual. From Dayton, the road became more serious about its incline, until we summited a few miles later, and then reaped the rewards with a long, downhill zoom.

Three powerful forces intervened simultaneously: zipping downhill, a gust of wind, and the draft of a large truck. Whoosh! Off flew my helmet brim. I squeezed hard on my brakes to stop, leaned my heavy bike against the guard rail, and plodded back up the hill. Guessing where my brim flew off, I climbed over the guard rail, gingerly descended the steep slope, and searched through the tall green grass. Ten minutes later, and fully irritated, I finally found it.

Though providing great sun protection when it stayed in place, I was tired of the helmet brim choking me or flying off. To avoid the problem, I had options. I could brake frequently like Terry, and give up zooming down the hills. But I liked zooming. Or I could just remove the brim and, as Terry would say, piss on it. But I liked the shade it provided. So I did nothing different, and it kept intermittently flying off or choking me. I became well-versed at swearing at it.

The Palouse is a cyclist's delight with its gentle hills of wheat and vineyards. As much as I enjoyed the gradual hills, what I really liked was zooming down the steeper ones—when my helmet brim didn't cause me grief. My speedometer hit thirty-six miles per hour before I braked. That's not a big deal to bike racers, but it felt pretty darn fast to me. Thirty-six is easy to hit when you're flying down a three-mile stretch of six percent grade.

Terry didn't fly. He frequently braked and took his time—a lot of time on steep hills. Meanwhile, I waited at the bottom and wrote.

More wind turbines dotted the land, and as I traversed the hilly terrain, I pondered. Those turbines were moving, and I was, too. I know this about myself: I like to be in motion. Bike, feet, car, or train-- I like them all. I steadily rolled along on my bike, savoring my world. Nearby beauty came and went in rhythmic intervals, and the beauty in the distance was mine for hours.

My feet were disciplined, but my mind was not. My mind had no itinerary, no agenda, no mission. Miles and hours of pedaling left me ample opportunity to think. I could put whatever I wanted into my head and let it rattle around. A world of thoughts roamed my head and left my mind content.

Terry and I left the rolling hills behind and tackled bigger ones. After a thousand-foot elevation gain, a sign for the upcoming Tumbleweed Festival greeted us at the small town of Pomeroy. Too bad we were three weeks too early.

A long, steady ascent and occasional breaks finally ushered us to the summit and its sign: *Alpowa Summit Elevation 2785.* We ate, drank, and were merry on the rest area's grass, where I finally finished the pound of carrots that I had salvaged from our refrigerator at home. Was I ever tired of carrots.

Lounging on the grass, Terry and I basked in the accolades of the motorists who noticed our bikes.

"Wow, you came all the way up here on your bikes?" one man asked. "You're crazy!"

Well, maybe all the comments weren't accolades.

Done with the toughest part of our day, we knew that whatever goes up must come down. The descent from Alpowa Summit didn't play around – it was significantly steeper than our ascent, and its multi-mile downhill canyon came with a ramp for runaway trucks. I didn't play around either. I braked often – a crash from an unchecked flight down that hill was guaranteed not to end well. Predictably, Terry played it even safer, and I spent time between those steep canyon walls waiting for him to catch up.

The road finally leveled, and in one lovely, magical moment, it suddenly opened to the Snake River. We rolled into Chief Timothy Park, swarming with people splashing in the wide, placid river. The Snake River has a reputation as a wild river, but it is broad and tame at the bottom of the Alpowa Summit Road. A sign at the entrance booth announced a day-use fee.

"We just want to lie in the shade and take a short break. Then we'll move on," I explained to the woman at the booth. I thought she would welcome us and our bikes with open arms.

"You need to pay," she said.

"Could we just sit in the shade for 15 minutes and then we'll leave?" I countered politely.

She looked at us suspiciously.

"Okay, you can stay for fifteen minutes. But stay over there where I can see you." She pointed to an area where she could monitor us. At least it had shade. The stopwatch began.

We rode over to the shade, parked, and plopped down on the grass. We wanted to use the restroom, but I hadn't asked permission for that, and now the woman was watching us. The restroom wasn't in the shade, and it didn't appear to be part of the deal.

"Piss on it," Terry exclaimed. He walked off to the restroom.

He seemed to get away with it, so when he returned, I went too.

We were in the park beyond our fifteen free minutes. When I returned to Terry and our bikes, I avoided looking in the direction of the woman. We mounted our bikes and rode slowly past the entrance booth.

"Thank you," I called. The woman glared at us as we left the park.

Almost to our goal for the day, we struggled with headwinds riding eight miles upstream along the Snake towards Clarkston, Washington. We were hot, tired, and hungry. That last stretch along the river seemed to stretch forever.

So did the dead snakes—we'd seen a score of them since leaving Portland. Because snakes are generally long, parts of them were often bloody and smashed into the road, while other parts were in great shape. My world as a city slicker didn't generally include snakes, and I was fascinated with them, taking photos from a distance. Afterwards and safely away, I zoomed in on my photos to look for rattles or fangs.

A day earlier, I posted a smashed and bloody snake photo on Facebook. A friend responded "That's yucky." Just for him, I kept my eye out for a snake that wasn't yucky. Shortly after leaving Chief Timothy Park, I passed a snake on the road that looked in great shape. I turned around to get a photo, but the snake was gone. I guess it was alive, which explains why it was still in such great shape.

Terry and I finally entered Clarkston, where a Lewis and Clark heritage marker stood adjacent to a golf course.

"Here's where Lewis and Clark played eighteen holes of golf on May 5, 1806," Terry said. I looked at the heritage marker. It read that Lewis and Clark arrived to what is now present-day Washington on that date and location.

I usually gain weight when I'm on bike trips. It's not fair. The month before starting our coast-to- coast tour, Terry and I did a six-day shake down along the Oregon coast. I did my usual trick, gaining four pounds in six days. If that trend continued, I figured I was slated to gain seventy pounds over the next three months of our cross-country trip – a troubling thought. But I was famished at Clarkston and an Italian restaurant drew us in. I had a personal pizza, and then ate half of Terry's spaghetti. I wasn't hungry when we left.

Minutes later, we stood at the entrance to a narrow, busy bridge that spans the Snake River, connecting Clarkston, Washington, to Lewiston, Idaho. Lewiston/Clarkston—Lewis and Clark. Get it? Squinting into the evening sun and nearly five hundred miles from our beginning at the Pacific Ocean, Terry and I sat at the stone pillar and grinned. The pillar's engraved message read:

Entrance to State of Idaho.

CHAPTER 4

Water— Idaho

Immediately off the bridge into Lewiston, Terry and I turned south onto a bike path paralleling the Snake River. The twilit sky dazzled us with a kaleidoscope of pinks, yellows, and oranges, a gift at the end of the day as we leisurely cycled to Hellsgate State Park. Terry bought a bundle of wood, and soon our campfire crackled cheerfully. Coziness on a warm evening, and all was right with the world.

Slacker Day. Our cross-country plans included a weekly rest day, and Terry wanted his in Lewiston. Not realizing it was our day to rest, birds warbled reveille at 4:30 a.m. Eventually, I emerged from the tent and set out to clean myself and my clothes in the state park's restroom.

There's an art to taking showers at campgrounds and RV parks. First, the shower areas are often wet and cold, so there's an initial reluctance to even remove your clothes. Once naked, there are frequently no hooks, so you must carefully drape your clothes and towel over something to keep them dry while you shower. If you drape stuff over the door/wall of the shower stall, you hope that someone doesn't grab your stuff and take off with it – forcing you to run naked back to the tent. Sometimes, there is an inside bench, and if you're lucky, there might even be a curtain that separates the shower from the bench so that the bench and your items stay dry.

If it's a shower that eats quarters, you must either be quick, have enough quarters to keep the shower fed, or deal with shampoo/ soap on your body when you run out of quarters. Drains are often poor, with water flooding the floor near the shower. Finally, there's the problem of how to put on long pants without dragging them through the water on the floor. It can be logistically complex, but it feels good at the end to be clean. Warm, too, if you are lucky with the water temperature.

My most memorable campground shower involved meeting a naked man in the women's bathroom when I also happened to be naked. But that's another story.

My shower at Hellsgate wasn't as interesting as that, but I did get some clean clothes out of the deal--no quarters needed and I had an ample supply of hot water. After I cleansed my body, I turned my attention to my dirty clothes, scrubbing them with shampoo and soap as I stood under the shower's stream. Back at our tent site, my dripping clothes watered the grass from rope I tied between two trees.

Terry examined our brake pads, fenders, and bike racks. I had a front fender go cattywhompus the year before while biking through Wyoming – it was raining, late at night, and I was thrown to the ground from a loose fender that suddenly speared my spokes. No good. Terry and I hoped to keep bicycle parts and bicyclists intact on this trip. So far, so good, and Terry's exam indicated that our equipment still looked solid.

Our bikes, gear, and my colorful laundry attracted attention from neighboring campers. Not only were Terry and I the only cyclists, but we also had the only solo tent in that campground loop. If it had a tent, every other campsite also had an RV, trailer, or a camper.

"I saw your stuff and had to come over and ask what you're doing," said a woman.

Unlike our first cycling day when we had only sixty miles under our belts, we had a more substantial story to tell at this point. We'd biked nearly five hundred miles from the Pacific Ocean, and had made it to Idaho.

"We're curious about your trip." A couple came over from another camp site, and stayed for ten minutes.

"Looks like you're on an adventure!" A man on a walk stopped to get the scoop.

We happily answered questions, absorbing the energy from curious folks.

Eventually we had to pack up, though. Terry wanted a motel for our second night so he could wash clothes in a more conventional manner; plus, he wanted to lock his belongings while we explored Lewiston. It was perfect camping weather and I would rather not have wasted it for a motel, but *c'est la vie*. I didn't want Terry to object if I ever asked for a motel, so I knew better than to object when he wanted one.

We rode our loaded bikes to the Lewis and Clark Discovery Center. At restaurants, we would park the bikes so they were visible from our table. At grocery stores, we often took turns going in so that one of us could stay with the bikes. At the Discovery Center, we locked the bikes--and crossed our fingers about leaving our easily detachable panniers and gear unattended.

I felt especially wimpy after watching a movie about the expedition. Seeing the hardships of Lewis and Clark's two-year expedition reinforced how soft my life is, bicycle trip and all. Those folks were tough cookies.

While we unlocked our undisturbed bikes afterwards, people stopped to talk. A few miles later at a grocery store in Lewiston, a man questioned us for several minutes. Our bikes ignited conversations.

Still feeling humbled by Lewis and Clark's Discovery Corps and their accomplishments, Terry and I arrived at a Lewiston motel for the night. Instead of shooting, gutting, skinning, butchering, and cooking a deer over a fire made with wood we had chopped or gathered, Terry and I had panniers loaded with food that we selected from shelves in the grocery store. We could even keep food cold inside the motel room's little refrigerator. Nothing like Lewis and Clark's expedition.

We rolled our bikes into our room to unload, and in ten minutes the place looked completely trashed. Sleeping bags, Thermarests, and tent were dumped on the bed. My damp laundry was the frosting on top, and took over chairs, a table, and a lamp as well. Panniers littered the floor. Terry threw his dirty clothes into the motel's public washing machine and off we went, back into the sunny day. Our bikes were naked, except for one pannier each for errands.

I forgot to pack a belt, and my gray cotton capris, which were my normal cycling pants, were falling down. I loved those pants; they were loaded with pockets. I could stash my Blackberry in one thigh pocket, my camera in another, and my sunglasses in yet another. With six pockets in those pants, I could really load up with stuff, but with a loose waist, my pants were apt to fall down just from the weight. I kept hoisting them up and rolling down the waistband. We biked to a fabric store and bought some thin webbing and a plastic buckle to make a belt. With my travel sewing kit, I'd be keeping my pants up very soon.

A post office received our maps of Oregon and Washington, and since we were mailing home maps, Terry also ditched clothing and gear he decided not to lug across the continent.

We emerged from dinner just before sunset. Lewiston and Clarkston lay below us, as did the Snake River to the west and the Clearwater River to the north. We could see the towns and the clefts where the rivers lay, but we couldn't see the rivers themselves. It was another lovely view of the twilight – all those pinks, yellows, and oranges in the vast sky to the west. As much as the sunset tempted us, our red rear safety lights were back at the motel, and we didn't want to be biking through town without them. Besides, it was cold. Dressed in clothing for a warm afternoon when we left the motel, it was now a chilly evening.

Our motel's hot tub warmed us right up. Lewis and Clark used animal skins to keep warm, but we found the tub worked just fine as we languidly stretched out in its bubbling hot water.

Our Slacker Day was lovely. Tomorrow, we would return to work.

It was a Sunday, and not our day of rest. Our trip's toughest uphill climb so far beckoned us to Winchester State Park, promising a 3000-foot elevation gain from Lewiston. We did that same stretch four years earlier on a beastly hot day and it nearly did us in. On that same bike trip, we climbed over Lolo Pass, the Rockies, and the Bighorns, but our trip to Winchester State Park was the toughest climb of them all.

Fortunately, the temperature this particular Sunday was more humane.

My #1 rule of bicycle touring: Line your panniers with garbage bags before you start.

My #1 rule of general bicycling: Cross railroad tracks on the perpendicular.

Every cyclist who has learned about railroad tracks the hard way ensures that subsequent railroad crossings are done with care and focus. Train tracks abound on a long trip like this, and sometimes they cross the roads at funky angles. My last bad encounter with a train track had been a couple of years earlier. The nearly parallel track ate my bike tire, and my bike suddenly stopped. I kept moving, though, right onto my helmeted head. Thank goodness for the helmet.

Terry and I crossed funky angled rail tracks on our way out of Lewiston. I carefully negotiated them and stayed upright on my bike.

The next thing Terry and I knew, we were seated at a rodeo, watching the warm-ups.

"All contestants must wear long-sleeved shirts, tucked in, and a cowboy hat. Contestants must be in full western attire for each event," instructed a voice over the loudspeaker.

A rodeo hadn't been on our agenda, but when we cycled by the Lewiston Rodeo Grounds, the crowded parking lot and booming loudspeaker drew us in. With our bikes locked below the grandstand, Terry and I sat with the crowd on the bleachers, eating our snacks and absorbing the sights and sounds of the local amateur rodeo.

The young cowboys and cowgirls, outfitted in their requisite boots, jeans, long-sleeved shirts, and cowboy hats, were straight out of a Norman Rockwell painting. With their sharp clothing and long hair hanging down from the girls' hats, they looked imported from earlier and more innocent days. They buzzed with purpose and excitement.

Terry and I watched the warm-up, where dozens of horses and riders circulated in the arena, as if on an ice rink.

"If anyone would like to sing the national anthem, please come to the announcement area." The loudspeaker put out an invitation.

The previous week I butchered playing my violin for people at our church. I still hadn't recovered from that experience and it didn't strike me as a good idea to volunteer to sing the national anthem, even for a crowd of people that I would never see again. I stayed put.

The announcer's voice continued. "If there are any visiting royalty, please let the announcer know." Visiting royalty?

Terry and I waited twenty minutes, but the first event still hadn't started. Neither had the national anthem nor the presentation of royalty, and as Robert Frost reminded us, we still had miles to go before we could sleep. Reluctantly, we left the bleachers. It looked like we were going to miss a whole lotta fun.

Cycling conditions were excellent, however, with an overcast sky and cool temperatures. Highway 505 is a sleepy back road on a Sunday morning. Western meadowlarks serenaded, and Terry and I could even cycle next to each other and converse sometimes. What a contrast to last week's heat, noise, and congestion, sandwiched between roaring trucks and trains next to the Columbia River.

A loaded recumbent cyclist headed our direction. Someone like us! After more than a week on our bikes, he was the first touring cyclist we'd seen. We crossed the highway and met Papa Mike on a Trike.

Papa Mike had an impressive rig. His trike was a three-wheeled recumbent-- two wheels in front and one in the back. The seat looked like a low-slung camp chair, with a wide cloth support for his rump and back. Reclining slightly, his rump was only inches off the ground. When outstretched, Mike's legs were almost parallel to the road, pushing the pedals that propelled him forward, and he steered and braked with levers on either side of his hips.

Two poles extended above his head, flying three flags which were easily visible by motorists. His panniers hung over the rear tire, and mounds of gear were piled above the tire rack. Terry and I were intrigued. Neither of us had ever ridden a recumbent, but we'd heard great things about them.

"This recumbent is so comfortable, and I've never had a sore butt at the end of the day. It's like sitting in a chaise lounge and putting on the miles," Mike told us. My own butt wasn't yet sore because the day was still young, but I knew that a sore butt was likely just hours away.

A big, tanned guy, Mike was enroute to meet his 14-year old grandson, and the two of them were planning to cycle to Alaska. Mike already had 3600 miles of recumbent adventures under his legs.

"Be careful of thorns in this area. I hadn't had any flat tires for weeks, and then I had five of them yesterday," Mike warned.

Five flat tires in one day!? I'd just throw away my bike.

"Yeah, I spent a lot of yesterday fixing flats and I hope I'm done with that for a while. Don't take your bikes off the road and don't wheel them through the grass," Mike cautioned.

Now I was scared. Terry and I had been warned about thorns at Hellsgate State Park. We'd survived that area, but I wasn't so sure we'd survive what was coming up. Five flats in one day – that made me nervous.

Terry and I took turns sitting on Mike's recumbent, and I was ready to just trike off with it. It looked like a blast. But Mike settled in to his sweet trike again and headed off towards Alaska. His muscled legs looked like they could move a train.

My legs might be able to move a train, too. Well, maybe a short train. My legs are like tree trunks. It's not pretty having tree trunks for legs, but at least they do the job. One of my mountain climbing friends once said of my short legs, "They're long enough to reach the ground, and that's what counts." Yep, and on our bike trip, they were long enough to reach the pedals, and that's what counted there. Terry is a long guy, with long legs, long arms, and a long torso. Apparently on a bike, it doesn't matter whether you have long legs or short legs, as long as you can reach the pedals.

What's the difference between a friendly honk and an unfriendly one from passing motorists?

I collected data. Two short honks from a distance – that seemed friendly. A long, deafening blast right as a car went by – that scared the crap out of me and definitely was not friendly. The Language of Honks. I'd never thought about the Language of Honks before this trip, but I was beginning to understand it. I liked it when oncoming drivers would honk and wave at us, or pump their outstretched arm at us and whoop.

Terry and I continued our gradual climb up Highway 95, stopping at the bottom of Winchester Grade Road. We took a "before photo", and I already looked worn out, just anticipating what lay ahead.

Winchester Grade Road is a steep son-of-a-gun that switchbacks up for about eight miles from the little town of Culdesac. Once it gets the switchbacks out of its system, it continues climbing for another five miles to Winchester. Winchester Grade is the old road, replaced by the more efficient Highway 95. Highway

95 isn't as steep, but it is dangerous for bikes due to fast traffic and poor shoulders. Our bike map showed Highway 95 as being gently curved, while Winchester Grade Road looked like someone had taken a red marker and angrily drawn squiggles. Terry and I experienced those angry squiggles four years earlier on a day when the temperature was in the 90s--a brutal day.

Today it was at least 20 degrees cooler. Hallelujah and a big Amen. It was a gift to have the temperature in the low 70s as we started up that hill.

I stopped for my first break, fascinated by a hawk circling above us at close range. It would briefly land in a tree and then take off again, flying and soaring. After five minutes, Terry was hawked-out, but I was absorbed--there's tranquility in watching a bird glide above. Of course, the hawk probably wasn't feeling very tranquil. It was most likely hungry, and intent on swooping down to kill something for lunch. I was glad I wasn't a field mouse making my way up the road.

An hour later, we returned to the house where we had been served lemonade on an earlier bike trip. Four years before, when we were being tortured by Winchester Grade's steep hill and the heat, Terry and I rode our bikes up the driveway to ask if we could use the outside hose to refill our water bottles. We were given more than that. Sharon served us ice-cold lemonade, which we relished with her under the shade of her patio umbrella. Her kindness and hospitality still resonated with us four years later.

Our church in Portland talks about radical hospitality, and Sharon's simple gift of lemonade always comes to mind. Could some cold lemonade become one of the highlights of a bike trip? It sure could. Sharon probably had no idea the impact her lemonade had on us, but there we were years later, still remembering the significance of her kindness.

Once again, Terry and I pulled into her driveway. We sat near the road, tired from a steep section, wondering if we should go up to her house and say hello. As we pondered, a car came down the long driveway from the house, a woman got out, and unloaded a garbage bag close to where we rested. It was Sharon.

"Hi," I said. "You may not remember us, but we biked by your house four years ago on a hot day and asked if we could have some water. You invited us up for lemonade. We have thought about you and remembered your kindness more than you would know. We're on a cross-country bike trip now and we just stopped for a rest, wondering if we should come up and say hello to you."

Sharon didn't remember us, but she invited us back to her house so she could give us her card. That led to more lemonade, which led to roast beef sandwiches, which led to a 45-minute conversation at her kitchen table. Terry and I told her that her house was on the Lewis and Clark Bicycle Trail.

"I often see bicyclists go by our house," she said. "I've never heard of the Lewis and Clark Bicycle Trail, but maybe some of the cyclists are biking that route. I'm often lonely here, as my husband is frequently out of town. It would be fun to have some nice cyclists to talk with."

"There's an organization called Warmshowers, which is like couch surfing for cyclists," I told her. "If you're interested, you can sign up to host, and I bet that lots of cyclists would love to spend a night here. You would make a wonderful host for them, plus you could hear about their cycling adventures."

"Yes, I'd like to meet more people. I might just do that." Sharon paused. "You never know the impact you have on people, do you?" Whether she referred to the lemonade she gave us four years earlier, or to our current conversation, I don't know. "You two have just made my day."

She certainly made ours.

"You are the Winchester Angel," I told her. She smiled.

Terry and I gratefully said goodbye to our Winchester Angel. Well rested with food, drink, and thought-provoking conversation, we rolled out and resumed inching our way up the road.

Had I been more astute, I would have realized something important was emerging. When planning our trip before we left home, I primarily focused on getting from Point A to Point B, both across the continent and on a daily basis. In our planning, I gave less thought to what might happen between the daily points than to actually getting to them. Naïve me.

It's the in-between that matters, and it's kindness that stands out.

Kindness is common among healthcare staff, and I've been privileged to work with many such people. Being patient and supportive typifies my co-workers. Our bike trip taught me the value of a different type of kindness, though: an offer of drink, food, a gesture, or words hollered out open car windows.

Conversations originating in curiosity often ended in the kindness of encouragement, giving Terry and I an emotional boost. Short and friendly beeps, or thumbs up extended from passing cars offered kindness in a less conventional manner.

We benefited from it all. Throughout our cross-country trip, we would learn more about the impact of kindness, not only during the moments of the words or gifts, but in their lasting impressions.

Our Winchester Angel was just the beginning.

Shortly after leaving Sharon's, a parrot driving a pickup passed us. Oh, wait, it was a man driving the pickup, and the parrot was perched on his left shoulder. The pickup stopped, and I rolled alongside the open window.

"What's your story?" the man asked with a smile, while his parrot quizzically surveyed me.

"We started at the Pacific Ocean by the Columbia River, and we're headed to the Atlantic," I answered, never tired of saying that.

He was interested in our story, and I was interested in the story of someone driving with a big green parrot on his shoulder.

"Bogie's fifteen years old, and is especially happy when I drive at high speeds with my window down. He always manages to stay balanced on my shoulder, and has never disappeared out the window yet."

Terry pulled up, and while we three conversed, Bogie attempted a conversation, too. I couldn't attend to Terry and Ron and understand Bogie all at the same time. Too bad, because maybe Bogie's discourse was worth hearing, too.

I loved it that a man with a parrot on his shoulder stopped to hear our story.

Our ride up Winchester Grade was easier this second time around. The hills hadn't changed, and it was doubtful that either Terry or I had changed for the better in the last four years, but the inclined road was easily manageable with our many breaks. Having the temperature in the 70s instead of the 90s helped turn Winchester Grade from the worst ascent of our trip four years ago into merely another long, steep hill for this trip.

Done with the switchbacks, we settled in for the last five miles of gradual ascent to Winchester. Once in town, we stopped beneath a gigantic replica of an iron rifle suspended over the street.

"Is it just a coincidence that the sign reads *Winchester, population 308?*" Terry asked.

Having been fond of guns in his youth, Terry was quick to make the connection between the .308 Winchester rifle and the town's population. It was true – the town's population was 308 in the 2000 census. Another census had come and gone, and the population was no longer 308, but it appeared that Winchester ignored the 2010 update.

I awoke with my usual feeling of excitement about our trip. I would wake up and – boom! –an immediate sense of excitement for the day and anticipation for the miles we planned would grip me. It occurred every morning since we'd started the trip, and was a fine way to wake up.

It was a good thing our tent was cozy and we had warm sleeping bags, for the temperature had dropped to 48 degrees, making a chilly start to our day. I wanted my fleece headband but couldn't find it, and then I discovered that my fleece hat and

Gortex overmitts were also missing. I had used the fleece headband two days earlier, but that was back in Lewiston. My hands were cold, and I used the electric hand dryer in the restroom to warm them before putting in my contact lenses. Contact lenses and frozen fingers are a bad combo.

The dark sky threatened, and I wrapped my sleeping bag, Thermarest, and tent in garbage bags, ready for a swim. We left the forest and cycled through wheat fields towards rain clouds and lightning--yikes. I was fine with rain, and since we'd been cycling for ten days and hadn't had any, we felt overdue. Ten days without rain to a Portlander seems like a drought. But lightning made me nervous, especially since we were biking in open ranch country. Where do cyclists go for cover when stalks of wheat are the tallest things around?

As we watched with anxious eyes, the lightning ceased. In its place, the wind kicked up, the rains tumbled, and we scrambled to find rain gear buried deep inside our panniers. Racing against the plunging rain, we donned rain pants, jacket, helmet cover, and shoe covers. Terry had overmitts for his hands, and I once again wondered where mine were. At least I had some rain gloves. It was a five-minute process to find and hurriedly stuff ourselves into rain gear, and by the time we finally had it all on, the rain stopped.

Within ten minutes, we were sweating under those extra layers of clothes as we cycled. The layers came off. A half hour later, the rain returned, and so did the layers. On, off, on, off. It's annoying to repeatedly be taking clothes off and on. This happens all the time with mountain climbing, too. You layer up while you are standing around, strip once you've started moving, layer up again for any breaks, and often strip again after a few minutes of climbing. Standard operating procedure. It's a pain in the neck... but it's better than hypothermia.

That inconvenient off/on ritual plagued us for hours, until we stood at the threshold of a steep, eleven mile descent. Our layers stayed on.

Eleven miles of downhill – "Whee!" you say. Not so. Normally that would be great, but our eleven miles were on steep, bumpy, wet pavement, and the braking exhausted our hands. I don't trust wet pavement, especially on the downhill. We braked long and hard, and we even needed breaks from our braking. We passed the Fort Misery Road intersection, but I felt we were already on Misery Road. Fortunately, Kamiah, a charming mountain town alongside the Clearwater River, greeted us at the bottom.

A bakery revived us. We gratefully sank into a cozy, padded booth and warmed our hands around hot drinks. I peeled off my damp shirt in the restroom, replacing it with one that was warm and dry. Heavenly.

After lunch, Terry was a man on a mission. I waited outside with our bikes while Terry went into a mercantile to search for a foam sit pad, as his had mysteriously disappeared. He walked out with his new sit pad and gave me welcome news.

"They have a fleece headband," he announced.

The store did have a fleece headband. One. And it was thin. If there had been two thin ones, I would have bought both and made a thicker headband out of them. As it was, I was happy to at least get one, even if it was on the skimpy side. Terry's pad was for sitting on the ground when we took cycling breaks. I wasn't interested in a pad. I typically spend my breaks standing up, as I want a break from sitting. Yin and yang.

We had forty-five miles under our pedals by lunchtime and still had another thirty to go. We were done with downhills for the day.

Soon, we were leaving Kamiah on Highway 12 – the same highway we'd traveled in Washington that brought us to Lewiston. Terry and I hadn't actually been following the Lewis and Clark trail since arriving at Idaho; it goes along the Clearwater River, and Highway 12 paralleling it isn't recommended for bicycles. Dense traffic and stretches without shoulders prompted the Adventure Cycling Association to recommend detours to Winchester. From Kamiah, our route forward was still described as "narrow, curvy, and shoulderless in stretches," so we wound up with the same conditions that we worked hard to dodge in the last two days. This time, there was no avoiding them.

The road lived up to its threatening description, but the scenery along the Clearwater was terrific. River and road cut through towering forests, and we zipped alongside the flat, fast flowing water. Seven miles upstream at Kooskia, we entered another world—wet. The Middle Fork of the Clearwater sloshed and roiled its way downstream on our right, pouring rain again attacked us from above, and passing vehicles threw their tire splash from the left. Below, our tires hissed on the wet road. There was no escape from the water.

Water, water all around. The Clearwater River to our side, wet pavement beneath us, and rain and mist surrounding all

Finally, the rain stopped. A mist rolled in above the river, bathing its surface with a soft, silvery veil that looked magical. Ahead in the distance, lightning and thunder replaced the rain. Spooked by the morning's lightning when we were the tallest things around, I felt relieved to be small fry compared with our neighboring trees by the river. Still, lightning gave us something to think about. Should we get off the road and take cover? But all we did was talk and ponder. Much to my relief, I saw only one more bolt of lightning after that. Rain took its place, instead.

Eventually we came to the small community of Syringa. In the pouring rain, we pulled up under a pub's eave and gave a show for the inside dinner crowd as we peeled off our soggy layers. Off came the bulky rain gloves. Off came the dripping, bright yellow helmet covers and helmets. Off came the drenched jackets. Rain pants and the shoe covers stayed on. We draped wet gear over our bikes, pulled warm, dry clothes from the panniers, and went in.

"Welcome inside!" a voice called.

"What are you doing out there?" someone asked.

"Wow, you're really wet," someone else astutely observed.

Terry and I dripped our way to the bar, which offered the only available seats in the room. I felt conspicuous, as almost all eyes were upon us.

"Do you have a pay phone here?" Terry asked our server.

"Yes, over there."

We were seven miles from Lowell, which offered indoor lodging. With the cold rain, we had no desire to pitch the tent and sleep outside at Lowell's campground. Terry and I had three cell phones, but none of them had reception. Our chances of reserving a room decreased with the approaching evening. I was glum.

Terry disappeared for ten minutes. That wasn't a good sign. Meanwhile, the guy next to me at the bar chatted politely, distracting me from thoughts of sleeping outside in the cold rain. I considered asking him if he would like to put us up for the night, but I refrained. Barely.

Hearing about our cross-country bike trip, my neighbor gave me a gigantic tube of lip balm, telling me it was the best stuff. I use lip balm frequently and already had a couple tubes packed, but I accepted his giant container of the aptly named Chubby Chap. The tube was about three times the size of a normal lip balm tube. A lip balm vender, the guy extolled the virtues of his strawberry banana lip balm, and had tons of the stuff in his pocket. And now I had a ton of it too, just in one large container.

Terry finally returned. I couldn't read the expression on his face.

"It took a long time to get through." The noise in the pub drowned out the rest.

"Did you get it?" I anxiously asked.

"Yes, we have a room." Terry smiled.

Now we could relax. No camping for us that night, and we could get completely soaked cycling the next seven miles because we'd have a warm, dry motel room for the night. My mood perked up.

Mr. Lip Balm Guy offered a big tube to Terry, which he sensibly declined. I was so happy about the motel room that I would have gladly taken all of the guy's lip balm. Once I knew we had a room for the night, nothing bothered me.

Nothing, that is, until it was time to leave.

Our outer clothes were still soggy. There's nothing fun about putting on cold, wet outer gear. Last to go on were my bulky rain gloves. They were the worst-- soaking wet and cold. My hands were warm while we were cycling during the afternoon, but the gloves cooled during our break. A pair of fleece mittens waited in my pannier, but I sadly lacked overmitts to keep them dry in the rain. I donned my cycling gloves instead, pulling down the sleeves of my rain jacket to make a little tent for my hands.

"I have just the right amount of overkill," Terry proclaimed.

Terry has long been recognized by friends and family for his equipment overkill. Terry's the only one who believes he has the right amount; everybody else thinks it's excessive. But as he put on clothing outside the restaurant and said he was warm and dry, I had to concede that maybe this time he was right.

With blinking lights, Terry and I rode off into the gray, rainy evening.

We arrived at the Lowell motel in a downpour. Once again, Terry and I were the center of attention. The motel connected with a café, and customers stared at us as we entered looking like drowned rats. But there were never happier drowned rats than us as we took the key to our room.

We trashed that place in no time flat, draping wet clothes over bikes and every spare inch of the room. Clothes hung from the curtain rods, the bathroom door, the shower faucet, curtain rod, lamp, table, and chairs. Everywhere but the bed. Terry cranked the heater to its highest setting— but it turned out to be a heater in name only, unfortunately, and not in function.

We did have hot water, though. We luxuriated in a hot bath and disappeared under the covers inside our dry room. Sweet dreams to us while it continued to pour outside.

The rain pounded roof and window throughout the night, and it was still pouring buckets when we awoke. Our ride to Powell Junction looked to be cold and rainy, so we cried uncle about camping and made indoor reservations up the road. Lodging options are few between Lowell and Powell Junction, and we would have gambled to show up at the day's end hoping there was a vacancy. That was a gamble we weren't willing to take.

Our lackluster heat dried thin garments like rain jackets and rain pants but barely made a dent on my thick, water repellent rain gloves. I'd have to keep my fingers moving for any hope of warm hands.

Fifty is nifty, except when it's the temperature in the pouring rain--even worse when you're about to bike 2000 feet higher to a still colder elevation up in the Bitterroot mountain range, the foothills of the Rocky Mountains.

After two hours of cycling, it warmed up a whole degree. The rain came, left, and returned. Rain clothes on, rain clothes off. Rinse, repeat.

The river changed names. Back at Lowell, two rivers merged to form the Middle Fork of the Clearwater, which we followed since Kooskia the day before. Had we camped at Lowell, Terry and I would have been on the banks of the Selway River. At the motel, however, we were on the Lochsa.

I asked someone how to pronounce it.

"Lochsa, like Lockjaw," he said. Lockjaw River had a nice ring to it.

The day before, the agitated Middle Fork of the Clearwater looked enticing for rafts and kayaks, but I'd seen nothing yet. Further upstream, the Lochsa was a wild thing, with churning whitewater and Class III and IV rapids. The swift water played out in chutes and upheavals as it surged downstream. Those rapids looked like they'd be a blast to ride.

A guy stood off the road, intently watching the rapids on the Lochsa. I stopped, waiting for Terry to catch up, and talked with Chris (aka Crash) Peterson. He told me he surfs this water.

"Yeah, with a surfboard. I grew up in Hawaii and California; I've been surfing my whole life. I've been surfing the Lochsa for years."

Chris showed me a video of him surfing the Lochsa rapids. Yep, there he was on a surfboard out in the rapids of the river. Amazing.

"You can check out my video on Vimeo: *Crash Surfs the River*," he told me.

I did check out his video a couple of days later. Pretty impressive.

Terry rolled up while Chris and I talked. While we all snacked during a lull in the rain, Terry and I told Chris about our bike tour. He thought it sounded great.

"Good luck with your trip!" He gestured us with the surfer's "Hang Ten" sign as Terry and I cycled away.

A few miles later, four colorful kayaks darted through the rapids. To my surprise, one shot up in the air and made a 360-degree flip. My heart hammered. The kayak landed, the kayaker raised his arms, whooped, and blasted down the river.

As we cycled upstream, more river traffic descended. A raft with seven helmeted people bumped their way through the river, and a sleek kayak caught up and passed them. A double-barreled kayak came through, with a lone kayaker who appeared to sit on a chair between and above the hulls. That looked risky. More rafts and kayaks bounced their way in and around the churning whitewater swells. The river quickly whisked them away.

The temperature made it up to a high of 52 for the day, just two degrees higher than the starting temperature of the morning. By the time we biked our 65 miles and climbed the 2000-foot elevation gain to Powell Junction, the temperature dropped to 46 and it was again raining. I was cold, wet, and tired.

Lochsa Lodge is a log structure with cute little log cabins. One of those cabins was ours for the night. It even had a covered porch, so we could lock our bikes outside and not have to clamber over them inside the room. Our cabin had a narrow entrance hall, a spacious room with a bed, a huge bathroom, and an instant glowing gas fire ignited with the mere flick of a switch. The entrance hall turned into a little lake, with dripping panniers and garbage bags. As usual, the entire cabin took on a familiar look as we spread our wet clothes and cycling shoes on any accepting surface, save the bed. We cranked up the gas stove to hot, hot, hot.

The shower was heavenly, as was my stash of dry, warm clothes. Thank goodness for plastic garbage bags lining my panniers. I slipped my grateful feet inside clean wool socks and dry boots.

Warm and dry, Terry and I relaxed in the lodge's restaurant. The lights were low, the chairs were broad, and the food and drink plentiful. Such a joy to be eating by candlelight and to be warm, dry, and inside for the night.

We scored some newspapers from the gift store. Back at our cozy cabin, we repeatedly stuffed newspapers into our cycling shoes to soak up the water.

My legs were sore, which was a first for the trip. I had been tired at the end of each cycling day, but I hadn't been sore, except for my butt once in a while. I guess we really had been going uphill all day. At least that's what my legs were telling me.

We turned out the lights, and from our bed enjoyed the heat and the flickering orange light from the gas stove. Our Lochsa Lodge cabin was divine.

We awoke to 41 degrees, more rain, and no hurry to get on the bikes. We lollygagged. Inside the lodge, we talked with a young couple.

"How do you pack for a cross-country bike trip?" the woman asked me.

"Three pair of underwear, three short sleeve shirts..." I started in on my standard response.

Before the trip, some teenage girls at my church were stunned that I was only taking three pair of underwear for a three-month bike trip. That was horrifying to them, but this woman took that disclosure in stride.

A lull in the rain, and it was time to go.

The interior of my cycling shoes were still wet, so into my panniers they went and I kept on my warm, dry boots. My water-repellent gloves were almost dry – only slightly damp inside. That was a step up. Gloves don't keep fingers as warm as mittens do, and what I really wanted to wear were my fleece mittens. I had no way to keep my fleece mittens dry, though, and I cursed the loss of my Gortex overmitts again, wherever they were.

We pedaled for a whole fifteen minutes before the rain returned. On with the layers.

Pretty pink rock studded the road, and we cycled slowly enough to appreciate it. In a fast car, the pink would have been lost, but in our slow-motion world, it was ours to enjoy.

The thirteen-mile slog up to Lolo Pass gained 1800 feet in elevation. The last six miles were the steepest and the sloggiest. We clocked in at a whopping four miles per hour at times, pushing slowly and gradually through the rain. It was a wet world, and the rain gradually morphed into a mix of snow and rain. As we neared the summit, small mounds of snow lay off the road's shoulders, evidence to a previous snowfall.

Eventually, there was no more up to go. We summited Lolo Pass at 5233 feet, just a few hundred feet from the border of Montana and Idaho, which lay on the opposite side of the pass. The snow and rain continued, with some wind thrown in as a special welcome. We knew what to do: we locked our bikes outside the Lolo Pass Visitors Center, removed our helmets, and dripped our way inside.

The Visitors Center is small and homey, built with logs and

charm. Soaked and weathered, with snow on our clothes, Terry and I contrasted with folks who entered from their warm cars.

"Welcome, and come on in," a woman greeted us.

"Wow, this feels great. We've been biking," I said, dripping while I looked around.

"You are welcome to stay and warm up. We have coffee over there." Jane, the volunteer, motioned to a refreshment table near some big, comfy looking chairs. "It just started snowing more."

Outside, snow continued to fall in earnest as we dripped, drank, and ate our way through our break at Lolo Pass. We considered getting back on the bikes so we could descend and get out of the snow, but there was no appeal going back outside in that kind of weather. Instead, we took our time looking at the exhibits, books, and talking with Jane.

The Nez Perce Indians used the Lolo Trail before the 1700s, and the Lewis and Clark Discovery Corps traveled it in 1805 on its way west. Due to its historical significance, Lolo Pass is now a National Historic Landmark. Fifty years ago, Lolo Pass turned into Highway 12. Few vehicles climb its steep grade anymore; most traffic bypasses it, speeding along Interstate 84 at a lower elevation to the north.

Sadly, Terry and I couldn't just keep drinking hot chocolate and talking with Jane. We thanked her for her warm hospitality (literally) and left the cozy building. Snow was falling, and under the eaves we piled on our rain gear, aka snow gear, adding balaclavas and face masks. We would happily have added ski goggles if we had them. Silly us, not to have packed ski goggles for our summer bike trip.

With his face covered by a balaclava and face mask, Terry looked more like a thug than a cyclist. I looked like a hazmat worker, according to someone who saw a Facebook photo later that day.

Terry looking like a thug

As we transformed ourselves with snow gear, the snow began to lessen. A few minutes later, we biked through the parking lot, stopping to read informational signs. It was barely snowing as we took photos at our new state sign. By the time we stored the camera, the snow had actually stopped.

"Welcome to Montana" the sign read. It was neither snowing nor raining at the Montana border.

I was in love with Montana already.

CHAPTER 5

Snow and Pain— Montana

I don't know how Montana pulled that off, but we liked it. We liked entering Mountain Time Zone, too.

Strong winds gusted at the summit, but nary a flake nor drop fell from the sky. I donned dark glasses to protect my eyes from the blasts of wind.

Terry looked alarming, but I didn't realize how weird I looked, too. After posting a photo that evening, I understood why someone asked if hazmat suits were a requirement for entering Montana. I looked like a hazmat rescue service on a bike. My blue balaclava, blue face mask, and dark glasses hid my face, and my rain/snow gear and gloves concealed the rest of me.

Between the two of us, we looked downright suspicious.

The road was wet but free from snow accumulation. Unlike our descent into Kamiah two days earlier, this descent wasn't as steep or threatening. We weren't killing our hands with fierce braking, and we weren't dodging bumps in the road at high speeds.

Instead, Montana gave us another gift: a carefree downhill spin. We gradually shed clothes as we dropped over 2000 feet to Lolo, at the bottom of Lolo Pass.

Goodbye to the light traffic, and hello to fast and scarily close traffic on Highway 93. Our thirteen miles north into Missoula were our thirteen most harrowing miles yet. Give me the physical challenge of a steep uphill any day over the mental challenge of riding on a dangerous highway. Shoulders on the highway came and went, but the heavy and nerve-jarring traffic was always there. Gigantic trucks sometimes left little space between us as they barreled by.

It was ironic that this last piece of road to Missoula was so harrowing for cyclists. The Adventure Cycling Association, headquartered in Missoula, enthusiastically promotes bicycle touring. The terrific bicycle maps we used for our 750 miles from the Pacific Ocean to Missoula came from Adventure Cycling, giving us elevation information as well as mileages along the various routes. The maps also gave information and safety recommendations relating to traffic, road, and shoulder conditions. The map from Lewiston to Missoula failed to mention that the thirteen-mile stretch of Highway 93 coming north into Missoula was our most likely place to be struck by a vehicle.

We made it to the "Welcome to Missoula" sign and stopped for photos. Just as we finished taking pictures of each other, a car stopped along a rare shoulder and out stepped Jane, the volunteer from the Lolo Pass Visitors Center.

"Hi you two! I recognized your bikes." Terry and I looked significantly different from when we stepped into the Visitors Center hours earlier. Gone were the rain/snow clothes and our jackets. Instead, fluorescent-green safety vests covered our long sleeve shirts, and we wore single layer fleece pants.

Perfect timing. It was fun to see her again, and especially nice to have a photo that featured the sign plus the two of us. No doubt about it – some of the best parts of our bike trip were the people. From brief encounters with curious people to substantial conversations and relationships with others, the people part of this trip was fun and energizing. Cycling the miles towards our destination was satisfying, but people crowned even that.

Jane wished us well, slipped into the late afternoon traffic, and Terry and I escaped the highway for errands.

First up, buying an extra Blackberry battery. Keeping my Blackberry charged was problematic, especially when we were camping. The last couple of nights I had easy access to electricity in motels, so I was able to start my days with a fully-charged Blackberry. But even with a full charge in the morning, I would often run out of juice before the day ended. Cold temperatures, roaming for internet service, and occasional photos sucked the energy right out of it.

We attempted to find overmitts and a fleece hat for me at a nearby outdoor store. No go. It was May, and the overmitts and warm hats were either sold or packed away for the season. The clerk phoned other outdoor stores, but they all said no go, as well.

At least I had the thin fleece headband that Terry found in Kamiah. That gave me some ear cover. I also had my thin balaclava. My helmet and helmet cover provided some head warmth while cycling, but once we were camping again, I didn't want to wear a helmet and helmet cover to bed just to keep my head warm. I left the outdoor store disappointed and irritated, mostly with myself. It wasn't the stores' fault that I lost some of my gear.

Back in rattlesnake country, we cycled up Rattlesnake Drive to get to Audrey and Mark's home. Audrey is my dad's wife's son's wife's sister's daughter, making us shirt-tail relatives.

We saw Audrey and her family a year earlier when Terry and I drove to Missoula and parked our van at their house. From there, we started a three-week reconnaissance bike trip through Yellowstone and over the Rockies, the Bighorns, and through Wyoming. That was the bike trip with an unexpected ending, with Terry crashing and being admitted to an intensive care unit with a lacerated liver. Terry and I last saw Audrey and family a day after Terry was released from the hospital. Now, we were back for a night.

What a tranquil evening. We sat at the kitchen counter eating ice cream while third-grade Zoe and first-grade Roman worked on their homework nearby. How relaxing just to sit and watch a family do its school evening thing.

I was pretty excited about access to bleach. Crud grew inside my water bottles from two weeks' worth of juice, chocolate milk, Crystal Light, tea, and water. An overnight soak in bleach would take care of that.

Our evening ended with Zoe giving us the grand tour of her bedroom where Terry and I would be guests for the night. Hotel Zoe was awesome, with zebra striped sheets and a karaoke machine.

"I'll show you how to use the karaoke machine in case you want to do it," she offered.

I liked the idea that Zoe thought Terry and I might want to do a little karaoke before going to bed. That's the way a third-grader thinks, and it was far more interesting than the way an old person thinks. It was an intriguing concept, but I didn't have the energy for a night of karaoke before going to `sleep. Maybe next time.

Because of the previous day's wind and an afternoon of rising temperatures, our rain gear had already dried before reaching Missoula. Zoe would have been appalled if we had done our normal room-trashing. As it was, we awoke feeling clean and refreshed in a room that also looked clean and refreshed.

The morning abounded with simple pleasures. I mooched sunscreen from Audrey and squirted it into the pill bottle that functioned as my sunscreen container. Those hot, shadeless days along the Columbia during our first week had taken a big toll on my sunscreen inventory.

With clean water bottles and plenty of sunscreen, I was in fat city again.

One of our friends' sons used to charge visiting guests a dollar a night to sleep in his room. Ever since that surprising bit of entrepreneurship, Terry and I have made a habit of leaving a dollar anytime we caused children to be evicted from their rooms due to our visits. Zoe gave up her bedroom for us, and Roman shared his room with Zoe, so we wrote thank you notes to both and left them each a dollar.

Goodbye to my dad's wife's son's wife's sister's daughter and her family. It's good having kin.

We stopped at a grocery store to load up on food for the next couple of days. I waited outside while Terry shopped, and as usual, several people stopped to ask questions and strike up conversations.

I pondered the lure of riches as we pedaled by a casino. It held no appeal. What would I do differently if I won a million bucks? Nothing. I was doing exactly what I wanted – taking our bicycle trip. How would our bike adventure be different if we had deep pockets? Unsure. We liked to camp, so even if we were rich, we'd still camp in good conditions. Expensive grocery food doesn't travel in panniers any better than cheap food. Terry and I usually share a dinner when we eat out, partly because we feel stuffed if we each eat a whole dinner, but also because we're cheapskates. If we won a million dollars at the casino, maybe we'd buy more meals, and then just waste more food.

We bypassed the casino.

Traffic on I-90 rumbled past on our right, but Terry and I were on a sweet frontage road that paralleled the freeway. The Clark Fork River also ran parallel, sweeping through a valley of low-lying hills. Overhead, dark gray sky threatened to dump on us at any time.

The billboard just outside of Clinton, Montana, read *World famous festival – Come have a ball!* and featured a drawing of a bull announcing the annual August Testy Festy. So tourists could plan ahead, the billboard also included the festival dates for the next four years.

Not only was Clinton home to the Testicle Festival, but it was also where Terry and I exited our frontage road and entered the Interstate 90 freeway. Our route through rural America would put us on freeways from time to time. A year before, we made a surprising discovery: the rural interstate freeways often felt safer than narrow highways.

I-90 has a wide shoulder and we encountered only moderate traffic. Cars frequently swung into the left lane when passing us, giving us a wide berth. Timing the traffic, I discovered 30-second stretches between many of the vehicles. Cycling on I-90 was a sweet experience compared with many other roads or streets.

We cruised along at fifteen miles per hour, which was lightning speed compared to the previous year when Terry and I struggled against forceful headwinds. I remembered going downhill from Beavertail Hill and pedaling hard, only to be making five miles per hour as my top speed. And that was my fast, downhill section. Going uphill was a different and slower story, and when I crested at one of the hills and met that headwind full on, it completely stopped me, like a giant hand against my chest. My bike shoe was clipped into my pedal, and I yelled a bad word as I frantically struggled to free my foot before falling over. My foot finally released just in time and touched down right before I would have done a total body splat. I did the total body splat in a crowd one time, and it's an awkward thing to suddenly fall over before a group of people just because you can't unlock your feet. People don't know what to make of it. One moment you're upright, and the next moment you're on the pavement at their feet, with your feet still attached to your pedals.

Last year we struggled in the winds, and later learned that those winds flattened 150 trees near Missoula.

But today's trip was a breeze. I couldn't easily read my speedometer, though, because condensation muddled the screen. In fact, I hadn't been able to easily read it for the previous three days. I felt like a bobble-head trying to read mileages or my speed. The bobble-head maneuver definitely wasn't safe while I biked; I reserved it for when I had my feet planted firmly on the ground.

Terry didn't like my odometer, obscured or not. He spoke disparagingly about it because it was in kilometers. It had been in kilometers for a decade, ever since we cycled in the Canadian Rockies. Nobody had been able to get it out of kilometers since, although various people had tried and boasted of success. The screen indicated it was in miles, but the numbers really were in kilometers. It made my high speeds look impressive, as the speedometer would indicate I was going fifty miles per hour, but it was really only thirty-one. My distances for the day would also look good, frequently topping a hundred – although it was really a more modest sixty miles. Calculating kilometers to miles gave me something to do as I pedaled, and over the past ten years, I'd become pretty good at it.

Terry had his own odometer issues; his wasn't working at all. He spurned my odometer but at least mine was working, even with kilometers and condensation.

The gray sky lightened, the temperature climbed, and it was time to shed clothing. There was no place to hide by the freeway shoulder, so I simply parked my bike along I-90, pulled off my long sleeve shirt, bared myself in my bra, and put on a short sleeve shirt. What's a girl to do?

We bounced back and forth between the freeway and frontage road, and contemplated bears. A sign informed us we were in bear country, and we hadn't yet bought any bear spray. That gave us something to think about.

My favorite garbage can from the previous year's bike trip greeted us at a Parking Area. Oregon and Washington have Rest Areas, but this stretch of freeway offered a Parking Area. Instead of trees and grass, the Parking Area provided a big metal can with orange painting that read "Urine Bottles Only." One of the beauties of cycling is that you can often pee wherever and whenever you want. No need to lug around urine bottles destined for garbage cans in Montana.

Back on the frontage road, we competed with fewer vehicles, less noise, and saw better scenery. Pink rocks studded the road, and purple hues ruled the rocks. Cattle and calves fed near the fence by the road's shoulder, and as we drew near, they began to run. Soon the whole crew ran in the same direction we cycled. I love being the reason for a stampede. It's especially exciting when only a flimsy looking barbed-wire is in between.

Bump, bump, bump, bump. Another flat tire – my second of the trip. We were on an uphill curve, which definitely wasn't the best place to stop, but at least the road was quiet and we were semi-protected on a shoulder. First on the agenda: put on rain clothes. The sky darkened, the wind picked up, and the weather taunted Terry while he graciously changed my flat. I couldn't blame the flat on a rooster this time; it was three piercing stubs of copper wire instead.

Five miles later, we headed directly to a café in Drummond. The place was packed with people who knew each other. Noisy conversations flew from one table to another, and each time people entered the café, hearty greetings rang out. Terry and I seemed to be the only strangers—plus the topic of conversation among various tables.

"Where are you spending the night?" one man asked. "There's a cold front coming in."

"We don't know. Maybe the park, maybe a motel," Terry answered.

"It's going to be cold. Best to look at a motel. There's one just down the street." The man pointed his finger back the way we came.

"Looks like it's going to rain hard," another man said.

Sold. Rain had threatened all day, and a soft bed and a warm shower beckoned. That was an easy sell.

Now we just hoped there was an available room at the town's only motel.

There was, and it even had two big beds. We dumped panniers on one bed and saved the other for ourselves. Our room had an awesome toilet, too. Well, the toilet was standard, but the experience was awesome. The toilet faced a long counter, which was only inches from my chest when I sat down. This toilet was not meant for a chunky person. I had to side step in order to get into position, like sidling into an airplane seat. Once seated, I could easily rest my elbows on the counter in front of me. I could have played cards, eaten dinner, worked on a computer – all just inches away, and without ever having to get up from the toilet. You could basically live on that toilet and never have to leave – just have people keep bringing you whatever you want. I wondered if the motel clerk sized up people when they checked in and decided "Special toilet for you" or "No special toilet for you." I'm glad we had the special toilet.

🚲

It didn't rain during the night. Did we cheat by staying in a motel when it didn't rain? Maybe, but I liked writing inside a warm, cozy room. I would have felt better if it had rained, though--that would have justified our decision. *C'est la vie.*

As we headed south on Highway 1, the temperature was 42 degrees and dropping. Snow on the low-lying hills reminded us that we chose mid-May as the start for our trip so we could be well underway before encountering the summer's heat. That theory was right on track--more snow was predicted for Georgetown Lake, up another 2400 feet and thirty-seven miles down the road.

I wore my Vana mitts. Our friend Vana sewed some heavy-weight fleece mittens for me and I was finally using them. After fifteen minutes of wearing my Vana mitts, I had to remove them and switch to my fingerless cycling gloves. The Vana mitts were simply too hot. I loved that problem.

A RV zoomed by us, way too close and ticking me off. Most of the vehicles that came from behind on the two-lane highway veered to the left into the oncoming lane to give us a wider berth. There was no oncoming traffic when this particular RV came up, and it roared past, damn near hitting me. RVs are big and long, and when they nearly hit you at a high speed, bad stuff happens. The gust wobbled my bike, and I fought to keep a firm grip and steady course. It's easy to get sucked in towards a moving hulk. The RV roared by, and then roared by Terry, frightening me as I watched as Terry's bike pitched towards the RV as it barreled through. Terry stopped while I caught up. That was damned scary, and we cursed the driver. Arrogance? Stupidity? I leaned towards arrogance, and I was mad as hell.

A cold headwind gradually cooled my anger and slowed our progress. Snow began swirling before we passed a sign that read *Watch for snow removal equipment next 16 miles.* I hoped that snow removal equipment wouldn't be necessary.

We soon sought refuge in a tavern at Phillipsburg and made ourselves at home. The dark tavern was almost empty, so we draped our wet gear over chairs and settled in for hot food and drinks. I ordered clam chowder, lured by the sign that read *Fresh clams and oysters,* but I wondered how fresh they could really be if Montana was serving them. Living near the ocean, we were accustomed to fresh seafood, but fresh seafood in Montana seemed dubious. Of course, neither one of those "fresh" seafood locations comes even close to a Norwegian friend's definition of "fresh fish." Living on an island near the North Sea, his definition of fresh is if the fish is in your mouth within four hours of catching it.

My clam chowder was still delicious, hot, and thick. Coupled with hot apple cider, we were content to eat, drink, and be warm, watching snow fall outside our tavern window.

Still snowing an hour later, I left the tavern better equipped. Terry found a Thinsulate hat for $4.99 in the grocery section of the tavern, and I was relieved to wear it. It was thin (it lived up to its name), but it covered more of my head than the fleece headband from Kamiah. The two of them made a good head combo. I asked our waitress for a few bread bags. She came back with four plastic bags which I turned into overmitts. One for each hand, and two as spares.

They definitely weren't fancy, permeable Gore-Tex, but they created a barrier between the snow and my fleece mittens. Fleece is fairly water resistant, but I wanted to keep my cozy fleece mittens as dry as possible. I knew condensation would form from the plastic, but the plastic bags were better than nothing.

Terry and I left the comfort of the tavern and headed outside. My finger dexterity was already limited from the mittens, and plastic bags over my mittens didn't help. I struggled to tuck both bags into my coat sleeves. Finally, I put on the first bag and tucked it in with my free fingers, and then asked Terry to help me with the second. With my plastic bags, I could still grip the brakes, and I was set to go.

We escaped the wind as we climbed on the lee side of the pass towards Georgetown Lake. We made easier progress on the 1100-foot ascent than on the flatter, headwind infected road between Drummond and Phillipsburg. During each break, I removed my hands from my mittens and plastic bags. Terry did the final tuck of the second bag into my sleeve again before we resumed cycling, reminding me of childhood days when an adult zips up the snow suit. My Vana mitts were wet on the outside from the condensation of the plastic bag, but my hands were warm and dry inside.

On the wide, snowy 6300-foot summit, we cycled alongside huge Georgetown Lake, past empty summer homes and snow-covered canoes, and headed for the community's Seven Gables Bar. With a tavern for lunch and a bar for the afternoon, Terry and I were anesthetizing our way through the snowy day.

"Georgetown Lake often gets a foot of snow on Memorial Day weekend," the bartender told us.

Indeed, it was the Friday of Memorial Day weekend. And it was snowing, right on schedule. I was happy we weren't in a foot of it yet.

Terry and I spent the night at the Seven Gables the year before, and it was snowing then, too. By the time we arrived at Georgetown Lake a year earlier, Terry wanted to call it a day. A loud, fat man at the bar had asked us about our three-week bike trip. He looked like a pirate with his scraggly beard and patch over one eye. At first, he and his questions were friendly. Later, the pirate became belligerent, and ranted that cyclists don't pay road taxes and that motorists get blamed if cyclists get hit. He went from being Mr. Nice Guy to Mr. Mean Guy. After a final rant, the pirate got up and walked out, and the bartender gave a woman customer a high five.

There weren't any pirates at the bar this time, and we weren't spending the night.

We were headed down the pass to Anaconda, fourteen miles away, where we hoped to escape the snow. We layered up, Terry tucked my second plastic bag into my sleeve, and we ventured out in the swirling snow and wind towards the lake.

Fifteen minutes later, we were in a blizzard. We stopped to get fully decked out, with shoe covers, over-pants, jacket, overmitts (or plastic bags), balaclava, face mask, and dark glasses. I still wished I'd packed snow goggles. As we biked and the snow accumulated against my dark glasses, I also wished for little wiper blades on the glasses.

Down from the blizzard up at Georgetown Lake, Montana

Rather than being a hazmat worker, I gave myself a promotion: Darth Vader, navy-blue style. With my balaclava, face mask, and sunglasses, no eyes or facial skin were visible. I was one big, expressionless, navy blue mask. I breathed like Darth Vader, too, only faster. Stuck inside my face mask, my exhaled breath had nowhere to go but to creep along my cheeks and either drift out some cheek holes or keep going up to my ears. Clad in his extreme weather gear, Terry still looked like a thug.

We descended, sometimes gradually, sometimes steeply, but never quickly. The wind blasted and the snow pelted, making our downhill ride more sluggish than expected. I looked at my speedometer: eight miles an hour on a steep downhill, with me pedaling hard against the relentless wind and snow.

Reflecting on my flat tire from the previous day, I thought, "Please, no flat tire today."

Cars with snow built-up passed us coming down from the summit. Thankfully, as Terry and I dropped elevation, the snow turned to rain. And then the bumps came. Not bumpy road kind of bumps, but flat tire kind of bumps. Cripes. I shouldn't have been thinking about flat tires.

Houses appeared as we neared Anaconda. I wanted a carport or a porch so we could escape the rain to work on the flat. Yesterday's flat had been my back tire, but this one was my front. I'd gone for years without flats, and now had three within two weeks. This wasn't a good trend.

Just then, a pick-up pulled up from behind.

"Where you going?" a grizzled face asked.

"Anaconda," I said.

"That's where I'm going. I can give you a ride," he invited.

Boyd's old, battered pick-up was full of big equipment. By stuffing our panniers into the back corners of the rig, we managed room for two bikes and all our bags. The rain poured, and I was happy for a ride into town.

I slid to the middle of the seat, pulled Boyd's large, skinny dog Squeaky onto my lap, and Terry climbed aboard. Squeaky was clearly excited to have visitors, and kept pawing me, shoving his long nose in my face, and panting.

A small, wiry man in his seventies, Boyd had a grizzled yellow beard and mustache, and long yellowing hair tied back in a pony tail. His wrinkled, sallow face framed yellow teeth – at least the ones that were still there. Boyd wore a short sleeve shirt, showing off an armload of tattoos on either side.

"We ain't got much time – need to be at the pawn shop before four. I think I'll make it. Maybe take you with me."

"How far are we from town?" Terry asked.

"Couple miles."

"Could you drop us off at a motel somewhere?" Terry asked.

"Yeah, there's one by the casino. Maybe after the pawn shop. He closes at four. I got two chain saws in the back I'm gonna sell. They're worth eight hundred bucks but I'm gonna sell 'em for two hundred. Can't get the damn money they're worth. I need money for the weekend."

"Is there a bike shop in Anaconda?" Terry asked, ignoring Boyd's train of thought. "We need to buy some tubes."

"You need some tires or tubes? I live a few miles back there." Boyd pointed his thumb behind us. "Have eight bikes at my place; I got lotsa damn parts if you need some." Boyd was talkative and I liked watching him talk, fascinated by all those missing teeth and his yellowed beard, mustache, and pony tail.

At a motel near the casino, Boyd pulled over. "If you wanna reach me, just go to the casino and ask for Boyd's phone number. I go there every damn day, and they know me well."

Maybe there was a connection between Boyd going to the casino every damn day and him selling his chain saws to the pawn shop for some damn money. But I didn't ask.

Boyd nimbly scrambled up to the back of the pick-up and hefted our heavy panniers and awkward bikes. For a small man, he was strong and energetic. Our bikes and bags piled up on the asphalt while the rain steadily fell on them.

"Thank you so much for the ride!"

"Gotta get to the damn pawn shop. Good luck to you." Boyd nodded to us and drove off.

Goodbye, and a tip of my helmet to Boyd, a kind and grizzled gentleman.

I stayed outside with our bikes and piles of gear while Terry inquired at the motel. No room at the inn. It had been snowing in

Anaconda all day, and the high school girls' softball tournament was postponed due to the snow. Everyone who was supposed to have played and gone home was still there, taking up all the rooms. The motel manager instructed Terry to go to another motel. I was invited to come inside, have some orange juice, and hang out by the flickering fake fire in the lobby.

Terry and I schlepped our stuff under an outside awning and out of the rain. I sat down in a comfy chair inside, plugged in my Blackberry, and wrote while I sipped orange juice by the fire.

Terry finally returned with news. No room at this inn, and no room at any inn in Anaconda. All the motels in town were full. But the manager of the other motel called a woman who owned a B&B. There was no room at the B&B, but the woman also owned a little cottage that was vacant for the night. Sold! We'd get the bed, but not the breakfast. Fine with us – we didn't even need the bed. We just wanted to be inside.

Wydette, the second motel manager, even drove her rig over to haul our gear to the cottage.

"Thank you so much, Wydette! You have been so generous and gone out of your way for us," I said.

"That's how I like to do things. I'm just glad that there is a place for you tonight," Wydette replied.

We waved goodbye as she drove back to her own motel. Small town kindness at its best.

The cottage looked in disrepair from the outside, but was charming on the inside. After being told there was no room in town for us, we felt like we'd just won the jackpot.

We'd made it safely over the snow. Yes, we had a flat tire, but a kind man gave us a ride into town, and more kind people found us lodging. We were safe, warm, and dry inside an old cottage. So lucky we were.

My flat tire was a minor annoyance and could wait until morning.

Terry replaced my tire tube in the warmth of our cottage kitchen after breakfast. A cozy, dry kitchen sure beats a lot of settings for a flat tire repair. A piece of glass was the culprit. So far, I'd had a rooster, three bits of wire, and a piece of glass to blame for my flat tires. Thank goodness for Terry's calm demeanor about changing my flats—he was certainly earning his stripes, but two flat tires within two days had me spooked.

It was 33 degrees when we left Anaconda. The snow was gone from the lawns, piled up in heaps where it had been shoveled. No rain, snow, or wind--what a sweet change. Layers of clothes and my comfy Vana mitts easily handled the chill.

A few miles east brought us to the small town of Opportunity, where we began playing hot potato, cycling between the interstate and frontage road. Here, there, here, there. On the frontage road, cattle noise replaced the noise of the freeway. These cattle weren't interested in stampeding; they just stood and made noise. "The cattle are lowing" jumped into my head. What does that even mean, "The cattle are lowing?" I wasn't sure, but I think these cows were doing it. I had "Away in a Manger" stuck in my head for the rest of the day.

The Grizzly Bike Trail fed us into Butte, where we sought bike tubes, a bike light for Terry, and overmitts for me. The rain returned, and I was back to using plastic bags as covers for my Vana mitts.

While Terry perused the bike shop, I phoned outdoor stores. They were out of overmitts, and I was out of luck. The Continental Divide promised snow, and my plastic bags would have to suffice.

Which route to take? We cycled the Route 2 Highway a year earlier, but two bike shop guys advised the freeway.

"Route 2 is narrow and steep, and there are no shoulders. With the snow, at least you'd have some good shoulders on I-90," one said.

I-90 has a four-mile climb to the summit, while Route 2 is steeper, with only a two-mile climb. I wasn't keen about being on a freeway in the snow, but I wasn't keen about being on a steep, narrow, dangerous highway, either. Terry and I were undecided about what to do. We were familiar with Route 2, as we biked it the previous year. But what if we ran into trouble? Would our phones work? Would there be people who could help? Traffic in the snow might be scary, but at least if we got into trouble and needed help, we could probably get it from freeway drivers. Who knew how much traffic there would be on Route 2?

Neither option was inviting, but we decided to follow the locals' advice. If they felt the freeway was preferable in the snowy conditions, so be it.

At least we had more tire tubes, and I hoped we wouldn't need them any time soon.

I donned my plastic bags, tucking the first one into my sleeve while Terry tucked in my second. The bike shop guys appeared amused. With my stylish plastic bags, we thanked the bike guys for their help and biked away into the rain.

Our climb up Homestake Pass started almost immediately. Cycling in snow and wind on I-90, we soon passed a *Chain Up Area* sign. We had no chains for our bikes, and hoped that neither we nor others would be needing to chain-up soon. The bike shop guys were right about the nice shoulders on I-90, though. Traffic was heavy but the shoulders were wide and acceptable.

Huffing and puffing our way up the four miles, the snow continued to fall, and traffic roared past. Eventually, the snowy, windy uphill came to an end, and the road curved over the summit and started its descent.

I was disappointed there wasn't a sign at the top congratulating us on our achievement of cycling over the Continental Divide. There hadn't been one on Route 2 the previous year, either. But as we crested the divide, I saw it, downhill from the summit and attached to an overpass: *Continental Divide, 6393 feet elevation.* Yay! Our first Continental Divide of the trip, with two more to come. Since the Rockies curve, we'd be crossing three Continental Divides on our way through the range. The next two would be while traversing Yellowstone National Park in Wyoming.

Terry and snow at our first Continental
Divide, Homestake Pass, Montana

Our troubles weren't over, though; in fact, they were just beginning. Going up in snow or rain on bikes is definitely preferable to going down. We had six miles of a 6% downgrade once we crossed the summit of Homestake Pass. My balaclava, face mask, and dark glasses went on for the descent, turning me into Darth Vader once again.

Fortunately, the snow didn't stick, but the surface was wet. The shoulder looked like someone took a giant cleaver and went on a hacking spree, chopping through pavement and giving us a bumpy ride. My hands quickly fatigued from squeezing my brakes. Trucks often flew by close to the shoulder, and consequently close to us. Wind and snow blew, and I needed to stay focused with all the movement, noise, and chaos around me. The snow built up on my dark glasses, but I didn't dare take a hand off of a brake in order to wipe off the snow.

And to think this was the recommended route.

Terry and I took breaks from our braking. We'd move onto a freeway pull-out, wipe the snow from our glasses, and ready ourselves for the next section. My braking became less reliable; a tighter grip on the brakes didn't give me a tighter brake anymore. We were mentally exhausted, too.

Although I appreciated their generous width, the slashed-up shoulders were bumpy or full of potholes, and strewn with gravel and debris. Downright dangerous. I used my bike mirror to see approaching vehicles from behind. If clear, I'd veer to the left and bike in the right lane of traffic instead of the shoulder, but due to the heavy traffic, that didn't happen often enough.

The 6% downgrade finally leveled off. We still had miles of pedaling to get to Whitehall, but at least we were finished with apprehension and constant braking. The snow turned to rain.

Terry and I were ready to be done with the great outdoors.

We pedaled into Whitehall, a small community adjacent to I-90, stopping to get our bearings. A man strode over from a gas station.

"Are you going to Billings?" he asked.

I shook my head.

"I'm a cyclist, too, and I live in Billings. If you are going through Billings, you are welcome to stay at my place."

What a nice offer. He was interested in our trip and said that he had done several cross-country bike trips himself. When he discovered we would end on the east coast, he had another offer.

"I also live in Vermont for half the year, and if you go through Vermont in August, you'd be welcome to stay with me there, too." He gave us his name, phone, and e-mail address.

"Good luck with your trip!" he called as he walked through the rain back to his car.

His generous offer brought a smile to my rain-soaked face. So did our arrival to a cheap motel.

Terry and I made quick work to crank up the heat and renovate the room in our customary style. The dim room, small to begin with, significantly shrunk by the time we added two bicycles and all our stuff. Our bikes crammed into narrow spaces between the bed and wall, and panniers and wet clothing overflowed everywhere else. It was like navigating a mine field to get anywhere.

We had spent the day in the cold, snow, and rain, and eagerly anticipated changing into warm, dry clothes for the evening. I pulled fleece pants from my pannier, aghast to discover they felt wet. No, not wet. Dry, but frozen. With no available floor space, I stood on the bed and slipped on dry, cold clothes. My thick socks and boots felt like heaven, however. Despite their weight and bulk, once again I was happy to have all my extra clothing.

As the evening temperature dropped, the rain turned to snow. Would it stick and pile up overnight? With warm food and drink in our bellies, we didn't care. We could just spend another day in Whitehall. No need to cycle through that blasted snow.

The little bathroom was funky. The sink had two faucets, one for hot water and one for cold. There wasn't a way to get warm water – you either had blasting hot water coming out of the left faucet or cold water coming out of the right. I tried mixing them in the middle to get warm water but all I did was scald one hand and freeze the other. As I fiddled at the sink, something hissed beneath me, like a tire losing air. Much to my relief, it wasn't my bike; it was just the torn and saggy linoleum floor that dipped and hissed.

Snow stuck, the bathroom floor hissed, and we navigated our way over mounds of wet belongings to find our way into bed.

To our relief, the snow didn't pile up overnight; in fact, there was no trace of snow on the streets when we awoke. That soon changed, and a morning snowfall turned to rain as we packed.

My face felt sunburnt, although there hadn't been any sun the day before, just rain and snow. It must have been a wind burn, but I had no idea how it penetrated my face mask and balaclava.

As tempting as it was to stay inside to do our dirty work, we took the bikes out in the rain to grease the chains. I was startled to find a rusty chain – it rusted just in the two days since I had last checked it.

The weather forecast predicted an inch of snow, and soon we pedaled out in the cold rain, pushing east on a quiet highway paralleling the Jefferson River. The river swung south, cutting through rocky cliffs on either side. *Falling Rocks* proclaimed a sign, explaining all the rocks on the road. Just as I was hoping that no rocks would tumble onto us, the noise of falling rock startled me. Fortunately, it was just a small rock, and it neither hit me nor caused an avalanche of other falling rock. Nonetheless, I sped up.

Across the river, a herd of cattle bellowed and I wondered what the ruckus was about. The herd began stampeding the same direction as us, but soon came to a fence, where they turned 90-degrees and ran the other way, still bellowing at full force. I was disappointed. There's nothing like the thrill of causing a stampede and having a bellowing herd of cattle run with you.

It rained, it stopped, it rained, it stopped. The Lewis and Clark Caverns State Park beckoned us from the road. I wanted to see the caverns, but we still had thirty miles to pedal before reaching our friends for the night, and the caverns wouldn't be a quick stop.

"Hey, Kimberley!" I spoke into my phone. "Want to go to the Lewis and Clark Caverns tomorrow? In a car? And to the headwaters of the Missouri River?"

She said yes. So now, not only were Terry and I going to see some sights in the region, but we would see them from the comfort of a car. Splendid. With renewed energy, Terry and I set out towards the dark gray sky that led to our friends.

Heading towards ominous weather near Three Forks, Montana

Our family loves our Montana stops at Kimberley and Robert's. Kimberley and my days stretched back to Portland, where we worked together at Home Infusion. Our children, Erik, Nicci, and Chris, grew up dancing in the *Leikarringen* Norwegian youth folk dancing group, and Erik and Nicci were early dance partners in the Tirolean Dancers. Our families spent many a dance practice and performance together as we watched those children grow. Now we three Rudds kept showing up at their house in Belgrade, Montana.

After dinner, Terry and I zeroed in our on bikes, removing everything. The tent was wet, despite having been wrapped in a garbage bag, so we spread it in the garage. The garbage bags did a better job inside our panniers, though, and clothing was dry, but gritty. The day's damp clothes and the panniers' gritty ones earned a trip to the washer and dryer, and we draped rain gear from the bikes. Sweat turned into sweet, and it was sublime to hold a pile of warm, clean clothes fresh from the dryer.

Molly, one of the three dogs, ran off with a sock. She was just about to blast through the dog door with it when someone nabbed her. Sock crime averted.

Good conversation, stories, laughter, and memories filled our blissful evening.

Slacker Day.
College-age Chris helped pile bikes into the truck and drove us to a Bozeman bike shop, ten miles away. The previous year I descended the Rockies in Yellowstone National Park with worn-out brake pads, and I had no interest in repeating that scary scenario. We had descended in a snow storm, just like yesterday's trip down the Continental Divide. The beauty of experience is if you pay attention, you can learn a thing or two along the way. I learned that I wanted new brake pads this time before entering Yellowstone.

I was obsessed with getting overmitts, too. Plastic bags on my hands weren't going to cut it for the rest of the trip. Although I didn't find overmitts, I did find mittens that claimed to be waterproof.

There was one pair in the store, and they fit. I greedily grabbed them.

We swapped-out children for tourist time. Nicci drove, while Terry and I sat like royalty on our throne of upholstery and steel, skimming the countryside at fifty miles per hour. Soak up the sights on a bicycle, skim them in a car. I loved being a slacker.

Lewis and Clark never saw the Lewis and Clark Caverns, nor were they even aware of their existence, although the Lewis and Clark Corps of Discovery did pass through the area. The Native Americans knew about them and honored the caverns. White men later came and commercialized them, and Lewis and Clark ended up with the glory of the namesake.

The Caverns are spectacular, with gnarled limestone formations reaching out from their uneven ceilings and floors. Led by a guide, we walked, scooted on our rumps, and oohed and ahhed our way through the colorful array. I wondered about early explorers of the caverns, when darkness or primitive light filled the spaces, with the unknown ahead. I marveled at their spirit of adventure.

Thoroughly awed by the caverns, we drove to the Headwaters of the Missouri River. The nearby town of Three Forks is named for the three rivers whose confluence forms the Missouri: the Jefferson, the Madison, and the Gallatin. Lewis and Clark named a river after U.S. president Thomas Jefferson, who initially envisioned their expedition. James Madison, the Secretary of State, and Albert Gallatin, the Secretary of the Treasury who provided expedition funding, gave inspiration for the other rivers' names.

According to a sign at the Headwaters, the 2540-mile long Missouri River is the longest river in the United States. It flows into the Mississippi River about 20 miles north of St. Louis, Missouri. I thought the Mississippi River was the longest river in the U.S., but the Headwaters sign assured me that claim belongs to the Missouri.

A quote from Langston Hughes adorned another sign:

I've known rivers:
I've known rivers ancient as the world and older
than the flow of human blood in human veins.
My soul has grown deep like the river.

Time to pack up the next morning. Everything passed inspection and was dry: tent, sleeping bags, Thermarests, and rain gear. Into their plastic bags and stuff sacks they went. I brought down my pannier junk from upstairs and piled it in a heap by the kitchen, but couldn't find my fanny pack. I was confident that I had brought it downstairs. I searched upstairs in the bedroom, bathroom, on the living room furniture, and in other obvious places. Not there. Did one of the dogs take it?

Kimberley and I went out into the back yard, and sure enough, there was my fanny pack on the grass. Phew. Kimberley and Robert have an acre of land – that could have been problematic to search through a whole acre for one little fanny pack. The fanny pack had my ID, credit cards, money, and Blackberry. Be warned – if a visit is planned to Kimberley and Robert's, hang on to your socks and valuables, out of reach of the dogs.

In addition to all our usual junk, Terry and I acquired more: cans of bear spray. The previous year, Robert lent us two cans of bear spray, required gear by the National Park Service for cyclists through Yellowstone. I'm happy to report that we didn't use them. *Déjà vu*. Robert handed us bear spray, and we each added a can to our gear. Those cans aren't little things. Mine was about six inches long and a few inches round. I stuck it in the mesh side pocket of a rear pannier. Once we'd reach Yellowstone, I'd move it closer.

Goodbye to Kimberley, Robert, Nicci, and Chris, and their fabulous respite for grimy cyclists.

Hello to Belgrade's Urgent Care Clinic, a few miles away.

Terry had been having occasional abdominal pain while back in Portland, which his doctor had evaluated a couple of months before with no results. While at Kimberley and Robert's, Terry showed me a protrusion low on the right side of his abdomen and said that he was having increased pain. Kimberley and I put our Home Confusion heads together and suspected a hernia.

"Yes, you've got yourself a hernia," the Urgent Care doc said, after poking and prodding Terry's groin and abdomen. "The good news is that as long as it doesn't get incarcerated, you should still be able to continue your bike trip."

Incarcerated? That sounded bad, whether you were a hernia or a person. What did that mean, an incarcerated hernia?

"It means that it's trapped and can't be reduced." Reduced? I normally understand doctor-speak, but this doc wasn't speaking my language.

He looked at our worried faces. "Reduction is when you can push it back in place. You will need surgery to repair this hernia, though."

Surgery? No, no, no. We were doing a bike trip—not having an operation.

"I'll show you how to reduce it when it protrudes, and some ibuprofen and ice should help the discomfort," he went on. He showed Terry how to push the offending protrusion in towards his belly and make it disappear. "As long as you can push it back in, you'll be okay." We were relieved, but skeptical.

"But what if he can't push it back in?"

"Emergency surgery." The doctor sounded casual about it, like it wasn't his body or his cross-country bike trip that was being threatened.

This was a new twist to our bike trip, and it could be a game changer. Outside, we slowly unlocked our bikes and looked at each other for the umpteenth time.

"We'll see how far I can go," Terry said.

Terry, his hernia, and I slowly rode our bikes from Belgrade, south on Highway 191 towards Big Sky. We still had thousands of miles to go on our trip and I had no experience in coaxing hernias through a transcontinental bike ride. I didn't know whether to be encouraged or discouraged by the doctor's words. I wavered between both, but discouragement eventually won out. The highway traffic didn't lend itself to side-by-side conversations, so we rode along in our own silent worlds.

We left the Urgent Care in sunshine, and predictably the weather soon turned to cold and rain again. At least we had flat terrain and no headwinds. A Travel Plaza appeared, and some hot cocoa and an inside break from the cold and rain assuaged our troubled minds.

There wasn't much to say to each other than the obvious: we didn't know what was going to happen. We never knew what was going to happen-- and now there was this new possibility that we hadn't anticipated and didn't like.

Drink up the hot chocolate, get on our way, and there would be plenty of time to dwell on it.

As we cycled up towards Big Sky, I also dwelt on something else: the concept of trust.

Trust is the foundation of good healthcare and of a good camp—two entities with which I spend much of my time. A trusting relationship between healthcare worker and patient, between staff and staff, or staff and campers, is the platform from which important work may be started and accomplished. My background as an oncology and hospice nurse primed me to start relationships from a trusting standpoint, and to deviate only when contrary information presents itself... like in working with prison inmates. As a nursing school clinical instructor, I had students doing their clinicals in a penitentiary infirmary, and we were instructed by the prison staff "Don't trust."

For better or worse, when I'm not in a prison, I often trust people. It's my default starting point. I start relationships with an assumed trust—eyes wide open-- and move forward or backward from there.

"The traveler is dependent upon the kindness of strangers" a man once told me. I stood at a street corner, apparently looking lost, and he offered help. I was grateful for his help, and his words have resonated ever since.

Of course, it's foolish to trust everybody, but it's equally foolish to trust no one. Travelers, by virtue of being away from home and known conditions, frequently find themselves in positions of needing assistance.

To trust, or not to trust? That is the question..

On a cold, rainy day in May the previous year, Terry and I also rode our bikes away from Belgrade and towards Big Sky, fifty miles south. I remembered passing a Grizzly Adams-looking guy walking along the road; he was decked out in a hat, fishing vest, and shorts and waders, while I was covered with rain gear.

Terry and I stopped at Greek Creek campground to use their single hole toilets, with one on either side of the highway. Terry went to one side of the road and I went to the other. A car drove up and a guy in his thirties got out.

"Where are you two going?" he asked me in a vaguely Irish sounding brogue, standing outside in the rain with neither hat nor coat.

"Spearfish, South Dakota."

"Where are you planning on spending tonight?" he asked.

"Big Sky, probably."

He handed me a napkin with a name and phone number on it.

"My name's Sean. I live in Big Sky, and you two are welcome to spend the night. I'm a property manager, and you would be welcome to either spend the night on a couch at my place, or I could put you up in an apartment. My brother did some bike touring in Europe, and he told me about the kindness of strangers. I'd like to pay it forward."

Wow.

"I passed you two on the road, and I drove until I found someone with a piece of paper so I could give you my name and number." Even more unexpected.

Sean and I talked; I loved listening to his accent. He was from Isle of Man in the Irish Sea, had been in the states for fifteen years, married with two children. The next week he and his family were going back to Isle of Man for a month.

"If you are interested in spending the night, call me after four. I'll be back in Big Sky by then." Sean drove off.

That was weird, but I had a good feeling about the guy. By the time I'd peed, Terry had pedaled over to my one-holer and I told him about Sean and the offer. Terry, however, did not have a good feeling.

"Some guy just drives up to a woman cyclist and invites her to come spend the night?"

Well... yes.

Terry sounded skeptical.

As we pedaled in the rain, I thought about Sean the Cyclist Stalker. He seemed friendly, and I felt inclined to take him up on his offer. It sounded like a good adventure, and I envisioned interesting conversations with Sean and his wife, as well as a room for the night.

Over 4000 feet higher than Belgrade, the village of Big Sky sits at 7400 feet elevation amidst open land, forests, and beautiful log and stone buildings. After killing time in a restaurant until four o'clock, Terry and I resumed cycling up into the village, and Sean phoned as he pulled up beside us on the road.

The skeptical Terry met the welcoming Sean, and we conversed for several minutes.

"You could either stay at my place, or I can put you up in a condo, whichever you'd like," Sean offered.

I eyeballed Terry, who nodded his head. I guess that meant he didn't feel Sean was a serial killer.

"A condo sounds great. We have a lot of wet stuff and can spread it out to dry," I answered. A condo! "Could we treat you and your family to dinner tonight somewhere in Big Sky?"

"I'll check with my wife – that would be nice. I'll give you the address and directions for the condo, and I'll drive ahead and turn on the heat."

Sean wrote out information and drove off. I was glad that Terry had come around. I would have hated to turn down this adventure that sounded warm, dry, fun, and free. Ten minutes later, Terry and I cycled into a cluster of condos and rode into an empty, heated garage. A heated garage!

"Welcome," Sean greeted us. "I've turned on the heat and laid a fire for you."

Terry and I shed our drenched rain gear in the entry way and entered a beautiful condominium--bright, spacious, warm, and dry. We had arrived at heaven.

The condo had a large main floor, with a kitchen, dining area, and living room all in one open space, and a big stone fireplace in the corner of the living room. A bedroom and bath were on the main floor, and an open staircase led up to two more bedrooms and a bath. From the upstairs landing, we could look down on the spacious area below.

"I feel like Cinderella, and you are my fairy godfather who has just told me I'm going to the ball," I told Sean.

Sean left, and I kept smiling at our good luck. It seemed hard to believe.

After a hot shower and some dry clothes, Terry and I biked to a restaurant to meet Sean and his wife, Tara. The bike without its heavy load was actually hard to navigate at first. It felt like it was made of helium and was ready to drift away without its ballast.

"When I saw you two, I thought of my brother's stories," Sean told us again. "My brother bicycled in Europe several years ago, and he told stories about the unexpected generosity of strangers. When I saw you cycling, I knew this was a good time to pay it forward. I wanted to give you my name and phone number, but I didn't have a piece of paper. I kept on driving until I saw someone and asked him for some paper."

It turned out that the someone was the Grizzly Adams fishing guy. Grizzly gave Sean a napkin, on which Sean wrote his info and gave to me. We had probably passed Grizzly not long before Sean stopped and used Grizzly's napkin.

"Do you remember the green bridge with all of the orange

flagging?" Sean asked us. I didn't remember the green bridge, but I did remember a ton of orange flagging. "Two hikers were mauled by a grizzly bear there earlier this week." A shiver ran through me. I was glad that I didn't know that as we biked through the flagged area.

That great adventure with Sean the Fairy Godfather had been the year before, during Terry's and my bike trip from Missoula over the Rockies towards Spearfish, South Dakota. When Terry and I entered Montana this time, I e-mailed Sean, told him we were cycling again, and asked if we could rent one of the apartments or condos when passing by Big Sky. Sean wrote back that we could stay in the same condo as his treat – such generosity. Terry and I wanted to take Sean and Tara out to dinner again, but the timing didn't work with their family schedule.

Terry and I biked once more towards Big Sky, in rain that was reminiscent of last year's weather. Following the Gallatin River, white crosses decorated the highway's edge.

Montana designates its traffic fatalities with white crosses at the site of the accident, and there were many on this road, especially by the curves. Sobering. Going slowly on the bikes gave time to reflect on lives that ended or changed at those sites. Life can change so quickly.

We passed the green bridge, but the orange flagging had disappeared from the year before. I looked for grizzly bears and was not disappointed that I didn't see any. My bear spray was in the mesh side pocket of a pannier – maybe it was time to promote it to a closer reach. I pulled it out and nestled it under a bungee cord behind my rear end. I hoped that I would be able to quickly grab the bear spray if it was needed.

In Big Sky, we rolled up to our favorite heated garage and entered the condo, once again marveling at Sean's generosity. Sean had already brought in firewood and laid it on the hearth. I nearly cried. Sean's generosity to us once, and then twice, was so kind, thoughtful, and completely unearned. Humbling.

With heat cranked up, we got the fire crackling with pages from a magazine that Terry bought earlier; he burned pages that he didn't want to continue carrying.

It's easy to trash a cramped, dark motel room, but much harder to trash a spacious, beautiful condo. The bikes were in the garage, our wet clothes hung on pegs or were spread over benches in the entry way, and panniers and other gear were on the entry way floor, leaving the remainder of the condo just for our bodies. We lounged and draped ourselves over the furniture, basking in warmth and coziness. My legs were sore – it was only the second time on our trip that I had sore legs. Hot bath, hot fire, and some R&R to the rescue.

In addition to my sore legs, I had a sore brain, and that was more troublesome than the legs. Here we were, living in two opposite worlds. One world was the random kindness and generosity that gave us a warm, beautiful place to spend the night, and the other world was Terry's hernia diagnosis that morning, capable of incapacitating Terry and putting an end to our bicycle adventure at any time.

I just wanted the hernia to go away and for our amazing bicycle adventure to continue.

Our relaxing night was followed by a relaxing morning. Terry built another fire and we hung around like sloths until noon. The fairy tale continued.

But eventually it was time to leave. With a note thanking our fairy godfather, we left the fabulous condo, zoomed downhill from Big Sky to the highway, and then kept our downhill momentum going towards West Yellowstone. Billboards showed splashy rivers, advertising the wonders of river rafting and fly fishing on the Gallatin River. Some catch and release sounded good to me.

Ten miles down the road we stopped at a campground along

the Gallatin. Milky green and glacial, the river tumbled by as we ate lunch. It wasn't sunny, but it wasn't raining either, and for the first time in over a week we enjoyed a break, decent weather, and a river view all at the same time.

Lunch break along the Gallatin River

Back on the bikes, the headwinds returned, blowing over the high plains and low lying, snowy hills. We plodded along the gradually climbing highway. This place was desolate, with few trees and even fewer passing cars. A chill pervaded the open space.

A coyote ran across the road in front, and three elk stood off to the side. One was a baby, looking more like a big dog than an elk.

Out in the middle of nowhere, a sign for Yellowstone National Park welcomed us. Unlike the busy entrances at other sections of the park, Highway 191 dips in and out of Yellowstone for about 20 miles along the northwest fringe. There's no fanfare. Nobody to welcome us, take our money, give us maps, or warn us about bears. Just a big sign. Terry and I wanted a photo of us, our bikes, and the Yellowstone sign, and fortunately a big RV drove up and stopped at the same time. Tit for tat; you take a photo of us, and we take a photo of you.

We still paralleled the Gallatin River, its constant gurgling a companion as we silently pedaled. Tributary creeks shoved their way into the river, including my favorite, Specimen Creek. I loved that name, although as a health care provider, a name like that only made me suspicious of the water.

How can a loaded bike be silent as it goes forward? At times I strained to hear a noise, and there was nothing, unless I was bumping over gravel or having the wind whip my ears.

One might think that I was just mindlessly pedaling, mile after mile. But that wasn't so. I was mindfully pedaling. There was no end to the diverse conversations and scenes that played out in my head as my feet went around and around. I didn't live in Portland anymore; I lived in my mind.

I liked shadow watching. The shadow of myself and my bike on the road would morph from nonexistent to vague to distinct, and back to vague or nonexistent again as clouds moved across the sky.

High on the plateau, I felt like we were on top of the world. Once again Terry and I wore many layers, but this time our layers were due to the chill, and not due to rain. I was a rolling refrigerator. No need to worry about how to keep my yogurt and cheese cool – everything was cool.

The headwinds made for a long day. Although the road climbed slightly uphill, headwinds pushed at us and slowed our speed. Our late start to the day seemed like a good idea at the time, but we hadn't counted on headwinds to slow us down.

We were 18 miles from West Yellowstone, and soon we were on easy street. The road declined and the headwinds abated. Desolation gave way to tall, gray, naked tree limbs, and then some short, bright-green trees – likely a burn area from the 1988 Yellowstone forest fire.

A flashing electric sign blinked *Caution Animals on Roadway Next 10 Miles*. Beyond that we saw another blinking sign: *Bison on Roadway*. Bison, about fifty feet ahead, grazed on the left side of the road. We sped up and zipped away on the right.

Around a corner we met a long line of cars. The cars slowly crept down the middle of the two-lane highway, with about fifteen bison on either side munching grass in the ditches. Terry and I nudged up to a passenger's open window.

"Could we stay right behind you?" I asked. I was glad to be close to a car and some potentially helpful people.

"You can come on in!" the woman told us.

I was sorely tempted.

But we stayed right behind the car, as far away from the bison as possible, which was only about twenty feet. Those things were huge. I felt vulnerable and exposed on the bike. Everybody else hung out their windows, taking photos, but Terry and I just kept a grip on the bikes, and our wary eyes on the bison. We sure weren't pulling out our cameras. The invitation to jump in the car was forefront on my mind. Fortunately, the bison were interested only in eating grass, and didn't seem concerned with either cars or bikes.

Once we passed the bison, Terry and I pulled over and gave each other high fives. My heart hammered.

We had followed the Gallatin River for much of the day, and about three miles from West Yellowstone we crossed the Madison River.

"Want to stay here at this campground?" I asked a mile later.

"No, I want to be closer to town and food." Food ran Terry's life.

Two miles later, our late day netted us a big fat zero for lodging at West Yellowstone's Grizzly RV park. The RV park required a hard-shelled container for lodging as protection from the neighborhood grizzly bears, so our fabric tent didn't qualify. The park had some cute little cabins, but it was after 6 p.m. and the office was closed for the evening. We were too late for a cabin, even though some appeared to be vacant. Dang. It was our last night in Montana, and I realized that Terry and I had biked through Montana without a single night of camping.

We backtracked into town for dinner and rode up just as a costumed group of eight young people exited a restaurant. They were singing and in high spirits. Terry and I walked our bikes outside the restaurant and the group practically enveloped us.

"What are you doing?" a young man asked, looking at us and all of our bike paraphernalia. He wore a striped shirt and his pants were held up with bright red suspenders. Everyone was colorful, and striped or polka dotted.

"We're on a cross-country bike trip," Terry answered.

"What?"

"No way!"

"That's awesome!"

The group was already excited, and this piece of information revved them up even more. Some even jumped up and down, clapping their hands.

"What are *you* doing?" I asked the guy who had asked us that same question. He and his group looked like they were up to something.

"We're in a musical that starts in 45 minutes, around the corner. How about coming to our musical? It's a great show – you should come!"

"Where'd you start?" someone else asked about the biking.

"The Pacific Ocean. We've biked a thousand miles so far," I said. This information just added fuel to the fire.

"Oh, you've got to come!"

"That's so amazing!"

"We'll put you in the front row!"

They were an animated group and their enthusiasm was contagious. At least it was contagious to me. I wanted to bike right up to the musical and plant myself in that front row seat. The cast was loud, boisterous, and fun.

"We need to eat first," Terry informed them. Ah yes, food.

"We'll try to eat fast and get there in time," I promised optimistically.

"Okay, we'll save you two seats!" someone said. "Bye! See you soon!"

Terry and I locked our bikes and went inside the restaurant, hoping for a quick meal. Alas, the restaurant was a hopping place and there was no quick meal for us. It was clear we were going to miss the musical and our newly found musical friends.

After dinner, we found a cheap motel, where a placard in our room stated: *The management wishes you a hearty welcome, a happy stay, and a purposeful departure.* A purposeful departure?

What did that mean? That we wouldn't impulsively run out of the motel in the middle of the night with no place to go? I pondered that for the rest of the evening.

I had sore legs for the second day in a row and noticed that my lower legs were more toned than they had been a thousand miles earlier. It was the end of our third week, and I liked the way my body was changing.

Perhaps I wouldn't put on those 70 pounds after all.

Terry and I did have a purposeful departure the next morning, arriving at the entrance to Yellowstone National Park five minutes later. This time, the entrance felt official. Someone took our money, gave maps, asked if we had bear spray, and wished us good luck.

A few miles later and barely into Yellowstone, we stopped for a break. I held up my can of bear spray and excitedly posed at our new state's sign:

Entering Wyoming.

That's bear spray I'm holding—a mandated item
for cyclists in Yellowstone National Park

CHAPTER 6

Bison and Geysers and Bears, Oh My! — Wyoming

I n a world of warmth and sunshine, I wore cotton capris, a short sleeve shirt, and sunscreen—a trifecta not seen in over a week. I did keep my bike shoes unclipped, just in case of bears.

Established in 1872, Yellowstone is considered the world's first national park. Half of the world's geothermal features and two-thirds of the world's geysers are found within Yellowstone's two million acres.

With cans of bear spray within arms' reach, we pedaled out to explore.

Bison ate, grunted, and sloshed their way through swampy grassland paralleling the Firehole River, with mamas patiently standing as their calves nursed. Fascinated, we gawked for ten minutes.

"Let's take a break," Terry soon said after resuming our cycling.

We just had a break, but we pulled off near the river and Terry lay down on some rocks.

"I'm not feeling good. I'm hurting," he groaned, pointing to his hernia.

It wasn't a pretty picture with him laid out on the rocks looking ill. I fed him ibuprofen and nervously waited. Twenty minutes later, we were back on the bikes.

That was sobering.

Anxiety nags, often relentlessly, and frequently it stems from forces beyond one's control. Our bike trip started back in Oregon with an anxious thought: "What if something bad happens?" I was no stranger to death from bike accidents or car accidents; I lost a childhood friend from a car hitting her while she rode her bike, and lost an aunt to a car accident. It's possible to die on a cross-country bike trip, as many people pointed out before Terry and I started our trip. It's also possible to die in your bathtub at home, as has happened in my family. There's no guarantee to anything, except that a person is going to die sooner or later.

Most of my bike trip anxieties didn't revolve around death. Most revolved around being wet and cold, or wondering where we would sleep—issues that were temporary, and generally far below the severity of death. Still, anxiety gnaws at one's brain, sometimes with subtlety, sometimes with ferocity.

It was clear I had no control over many aspects of our trip, such as Terry's new hernia diagnosis. While I lacked control about much, the pundits informed me I did have control over how I responded. The positive aspect of anxiety is that you can make plans. Have a lot of worries? Make a lot of plans. Anxious about where to sleep? We had tent and sleeping bags for that; we could "stealth camp" if needed. Anxious about being cold and wet? That's why I had a lot of extra clothing with me. Have anxiety about Terry's hernia? There's medical care for that. Anxiety about the trip ending prematurely? I didn't have an easy fix for that one.

Pedaling hour after hour gave me plenty of time to reflect. My brain alternated its management of my anxieties: sometimes it wrestled with them, sometimes it gently massaged, and sometimes it shoved them far from my consciousness.

Mulling over my anxieties, I continued pushing the pedals.

As we pedaled, four bison sauntered down the center of our two-lane road, slowly approaching us. Once again, Terry and I stuck close to a nearby car, keeping it between us and the bison. My heart pounded. The bison didn't pay attention to us, but Terry and I sure paid attention to them. Bison stand five to six feet high, literally weighing a ton. They have big horns and are quick – I doubt it's advisable to be close to them while on a bike.

Clouds of steam rose in the distance—the Lower Geyser Basin. We locked bikes and wandered the boardwalk, which keeps (most) people from falling into the hot springs, geysers, fumaroles, and mud pots along the half-mile boardwalk. My favorites were the mud pots, slurping and throwing mud several feet high, sometimes burping it onto the boardwalk.

Geysers lured me, too, and after a short stint back on the bikes, we pulled into Biscuit Basin for more geyser action. I left my helmet on for an anticipated quick stop. An older woman approached me.

"My husband and I saw you when you were biking up that steep hill back there. We said how spunky you must be, and then we passed you. I said, 'She's got white hair!'"

The woman seemed pretty enthusiastic about that. I wasn't sure about the spunky part; I wasn't feeling particularly spunky, but she did get the white hair part right.

Two other cyclists pulled into Biscuit Basin. Sarah and Lena were six weeks into their trip, cycling three thousand miles from Virginia on their way to Oregon. They did not have white hair. In their 20s, Sarah's dreadlocks fell to her waist.

"Where are you spending the nights here in Yellowstone?" Terry asked them.

"We stayed last night in a campground that hadn't opened yet," Lena replied. "A ranger came at midnight and said we were illegal. At least he didn't make us pack up right then and leave."

And at least a bear didn't visit them. They hadn't hung their food from a tree, and they ate inside their tent. Terry and I were warned that bears will disturb tents that have had food in them, even if the food is no longer there. Because Terry and I had been eating while inside our tent during the last few weeks, we weren't planning to camp in Yellowstone's grizzly country.

We four swapped cycling stories, including information about what lay ahead in either direction. The camaraderie between us was short but high-spirited.

With a friendly wave, they headed off to find another illegal camp spot for the night.

A few miles later, we turned in to the community of Old Faithful. A Visitor Center sign indicated the geyser was to erupt in about fifteen minutes, so we high-tailed it over. Old Faithful erupts about every ninety minutes, give or take ten of them. It's not the highest geyser in Yellowstone, but its claim to fame is its punctuality.

Crowds gathered at Old Faithful's boardwalk, but Terry and I made a beeline for the wooden sign that read *Old Faithful Geyser*. With our loaded bikes to the side, we stood near and waited for Old Faithful to go. Old Faithful's eruptions last from one to five minutes, so there's plenty of time for photos. We accosted a passerby and asked him to snap pictures of us, our bikes, and the erupting Old Faithful in action.

Old Faithful, Yellowstone National Park,
over 1000 miles from our start

It was a grand feeling to realize we biked all the way from the Pacific Ocean to Old Faithful. I was one happy girl, white hair and all.

Terry and I rode to the Old Faithful Snow Lodge, one of three lodges in the area. People stared as Terry and I wheeled our loaded bikes up to the reception counter. I liked arriving with panniers instead of a suitcase.

Hernia pain claimed Terry's energy. My legs ached again, although we rode only thirty miles, and with minimal uphill.

Perhaps I was wearing out, instead of getting stronger.

Slacker Day at Old Faithful and the beginning of a new month: June 1.

Nowhere to go, no hurry, and the bikes stayed put.

At a bear spray demonstration, we learned to spray a "wall" between us and the bear, not just to spray right at the bear. It's the bison who generally injure or kill, four times as often as the bears, but it's the grizzlies who get a bad rap at Yellowstone. A ranger warned that we should stay twenty-five yards away from bison and a hundred yards away from bears. Apparently, the fifteen feet between the bison and us the previous day wasn't recommended. No kidding.

Exhibits, movies, geysers, and tours exquisitely filled our day. I wondered about the early inhabitants of this area. What was it like to discover and explore this land that is so alive?

We loaded up in the morning, rode to Old Faithful for one more eruption, parked our bikes by the sign, and waited. I asked a woman if she could take a photo of Terry and me with our bikes when Old Faithful went off.

"You're hogging the sign," a man on the bench grumpily told me. Clearly, he wasn't impressed by all of our bike paraphernalia. I didn't see anyone else by the sign – did he want us to leave so the sign was all by itself? I biked a thousand miles to get to be by that sign, and I didn't feel like letting anyone tell me where I could or couldn't stand.

"We rode our bikes here from Oregon," I said, like that was a good excuse.

"You're hogging the sign," he repeated.

I ignored him and walked back to the sign, acutely aware we were a blight on his view. I just wanted Old Faithful to erupt as soon as possible so we could get out of there and get away from his penetrating glare. The geyser eventually did erupt, and with Old Faithful blasting away behind us, we smiled broadly at our camera and in the direction of the grumpy man. Then we got the heck out of there.

Temptation lured me to a long, steaming stream by the side of the road just out of the Old Faithful community. The previous year, I dipped my finger in it, knowing full well the warnings against that. It was hot, but my finger didn't dissolve either then or later, so it must not have been one of those flesh-eating pools we'd read about.

I dipped my finger in the same steaming stream. Still hot, and so irresistible.

"Did you have some bike trouble back there?" Terry asked when I caught up.

"No, I just stopped to dip my finger in a hot pool."

Terry gave me a disapproving look. I was getting into trouble all over the place.

We immediately began climbing, and soon encountered snow piles on the roadside. As we rummaged for rain gear in a parking area, a car pulled up and a man's head emerged from the window.

"I just passed you a while ago and had to turn around to hear about what you are doing."

We told him.

"That's just amazing!" he said. "Good luck to you and I hope you have a fine trip!"

He headed down the road, protected in his car from the rain, and we headed up the road, protected in our rain gear. His curiosity and enthusiasm buoyed me as I chugged uphill.

Still raining, we reached our first Continental Divide of the day, Craig Pass, elevation 8262 feet. Cars hurled their splash at us as we enthusiastically stood before the sign.

By the time we reached the day's second Continental Divide, the temperature dropped and snow banks lined the road. Only a hundred feet higher, it was enough to keep the second Divide still looking like winter.

Continental Divide Elevation 8391 read the sign. Another powerful arrival.

It's a great feeling to reach Continental Divides by bike

Terry and I layered up for our descent, dropping six hundred feet to arrive at West Thumb on Yellowstone Lake. Someone tuned in to anatomy named Yellowstone Lake's features; it has West Thumb, South Arm, and Southeast Arm. West Thumb is bigger than either of the two arms, making Yellowstone Lake an anatomical freak.

Back in the 1800's at West Thumb, fish cooked in a lakeshore geyser named Fishing Cone. Mountain man Jim Bridger claimed "A fellow can catch a fish in an icy river, pull it into a boiling pool, and cook his fish without ever taking it off the hook." Known for his tall tales, people didn't believe his outrageous stories about Yellowstone. Other miners and explorers also relayed stories about geysers, mud pots, and scalding pools, and in return were called liars or drunkards.

Steam rising from the ground on both sides of the road made

for eerie cycling along the sunny shoreline. Dead tree trunks and steam jutted up from the gray, baked earth of the lake's banks. In the distance, the blues and whites of lake and sky layered with blue foothills and white bands of snow on the Absaroka Mountains. Someone just turned on the color TV.

Yellowstone is a land of contrasts. Verdant woods stood on the lakeside, and a forest of giant, gray sticks stood to our left, evidence of the massive 1988 fire that burned for months, affecting over a third of the park. A barrier during the fire, 30 feet of road was all that separated a thriving forest from a decimated one. The healthy side smelled of moist dirt, wood, and plants. The burnt side smelled of nothing.

Remnants of Yellowstone's 1988 fire

A traffic jam at Yellowstone means one thing: animals.

"What's out there?" I asked someone peering into a meadow.

"A couple of bears were there," a man pointed. "We watched them for several minutes before they wandered away."

Terry and I just missed seeing bears while on our bikes, and that was fine with me. My goal at Yellowstone was to see geysers from my bike, not grizzlies. I wasn't even slightly disappointed. If we would have been in a car, that would have been different.

The sun shone and the temperature climbed as we neared Lake Village. After adjusting my clothing for the umpteenth time, I breezed along at twenty miles per hour, feeling light, quick, and chipper. I was fast, but I knew the grizzlies were faster; they clock in at thirty miles per hour.

As we moved into our cabin near the imposing Yellowstone Lake Hotel, I reminisced about our previous year's stay in the big hotel. I purchased a can of Chef Boy-ar-dee Beefaroni at the little store nearby, expecting to microwave in the hotel. Nope—the hotel denied having a microwave. Returning to our room, I emptied the Beefaroni into my bowl, draped myself in a plush, white bath towel, and aimed the hotel's blow dryer at my Beefaroni. Dismal progress with low heat; I increased it to medium. Sauce flew everywhere— onto the mirror, sink, counter, floor, and my plush hotel bib. The bib was no longer white, and no longer plush. Furthermore, my Beefaroni didn't heat up.

A year later, I wasn't planning on trying that again.

After a more conventional dinner, Terry and I were grateful to be in a cabin instead of our tent. Rain poured, lightning dazzled, and thunder rattled our world—and all was well inside our cozy cabin.

By morning, the storm wore itself out, and Terry and I walked shoreline. Yellowstone Lake was a gigantic mirror-- reflecting lake, blue sky, and soft white clouds like some kind of surreal painting. Turning my camera upside down taking a photo, I couldn't tell which direction was right side up and which was upside down.

Leaving that fabulous lake and sky abstract, we biked past the ironically named Fishing Bridge, where it is now illegal to fish from the bridge.

At the general store, a three-generation family questioned us about our trip. The teenage daughter listened, eyed my panniers, and asked her mother, "Where does she keep her hair dryer?"

I gave her the unbelievable news that I didn't have a hair dryer, and further shocked her that I packed only three pairs of underwear for the three-month trip. She looked horrified.

"There's no way...," she gasped.

Mom shook her head at our day's plan to ride over 8530-foot Sylvan Pass and down to Cody, nearly eighty miles away.

"That's a lot of work to go up that pass in a car, let alone on a bike. And your bikes look so heavy!"

She was right. It was going to be a lot of work, and our bikes certainly were heavy.

"You two are inspiring!" Grandpa beamed.

Although we stopped at the store for food, we left not only with food, but also with an immense infusion of energy, powered by the support of strangers.

🚲

Terry and I zipped along Yellowstone Lake, coming to a three-foot-high stone wall paralleling the road. A bison stood on the opposite side of the wall, munching grass. A woman and boy approached the bison from the road, and when they were less than ten feet from the bison, it suddenly jumped the wall. We all jumped, especially the foolish woman and her boy. Fortunately, the bison quickly moved away from them, and not the other direction.

🚲

Our ascent of Sylvan Pass began with an electric road sign flashing *Slow*. Did we really need a reminder? As cyclists, we were nothing but compliant.

We passed another burn area, a skeletal forest of gray and

white. A rich, green forest thrived on the opposite side of the road. The road again divided what lived and died.

We began at the lake's 7700-foot elevation, and I huffed and puffed as I slowly pedaled up the winding road. Terry and I turned into a pull-out for a ten-minute break. Just then, a bison came into view, slowly ambling up the road. With no time to jump on our bikes, we used them as barriers between us and the bison. The protection was mostly psychological. My heart thumped, but as usual, the bison didn't pay any attention to us.

Bison and bikes—too close for comfort...

But the bison was going up the road, and that's where we wanted to go, too. We wondered how long to wait to let the bison get ahead. Maybe it would leave the road and we wouldn't have to pass it, but maybe it was taking a long road trip, too. Should we stop for a while? Should we get on the bikes and pass the bison? The road wasn't wide, and to pass that big animal was a daunting thought. We dithered.

After a few minutes of watching it stroll up the road, we took to our bikes with trepidation. Approaching it, we amped up our pedaling as fast as our legs would push. I tried to breathe quietly, but it's difficult when huffing and puffing while trying to pass a bison uphill.

But the bison kept plodding along, uninterested in us. Once past, I looked behind to see if it looked inclined to charge. It looked bored.

After inching our way up to Sylvan Lake and Eleanor Lake, we found ourselves on a downhill slant. Were we beyond the summit of Sylvan Pass? Guess so. No sign marked the summit—it was wiped out in the previous year's avalanche. Terry and I stopped, shook hands, and called it good.

I remembered our Sylvan Pass bike adventure from the year before. Due to a recent avalanche, Sylvan Pass had been closed but was expected to soon open. Terry and I needed to return to our jobs, and that was the best route for us to take to our awaiting rental car in Spearfish, South Dakota. The first day Sylvan Pass reopened, we were on our bikes to head over it.

One problem: it was snowing, and soon became a blizzard.

Slush accumulated on the road in the 30 degrees as we started the climb from Yellowstone Lake. A snow plow passed us, and other cars followed in the blizzard conditions. I kept my eyes on the road, gripping my handlebars. Motorists probably thought Terry and I were fools to be biking in a blizzard – and they were probably right.

Eventually, the snow plow returned, passing us as it drove downhill. Terry and I took that as a good sign. If the driver didn't stop and order us to turn around, we figured it was okay to keep pressing ahead –so we did.

Visibility was piss-poor as the snow swirled. The snow plow passed us again, going up. I liked having the snow plow pass us in the same direction; it scraped away the accumulating slush and snow, giving a brief opportunity for our rubber to meet the road on the freshly exposed pavement.

Eventually, Terry and I sensed we were on the downhill side of snowy Sylvan Pass. There was no fanfare for having reached the road's summit in a blizzard. Going downhill at last, I steered my front tire into the dark parts of the road where car tires had recently been, staying clear of the white slush as much as possible.

Braking on slush sucks.

For nearly a quarter-mile, I clenched my brakes, slowing, but not stopping. I wanted to stop, but couldn't. When my brakes finally gripped enough to sufficiently slow me down, I tried putting my right foot on the ground--but I couldn't get it off the pedal. I wasn't wearing bike shoes – I was wearing boots, without clips, and both boots were frozen to the pedals. Panic set in while I jerked hard with both feet until a foot finally came free. I stood, heart pounding, waiting for Terry to catch up.

The weather gradually improved. It stopped snowing, although the storm blew loose snow off the banks into our faces. In between the gusts of wind and snow, sunshine peeked occasionally through the clouds.

Going down again, I once more fought to control my speed on the steep slush. A sign read *Avalanche Zone Next 2 Miles, No Stopping.* I couldn't have stopped even if I wanted to, and I did want to. I was braking hard down that steep, slushy hill and my brakes squealed in protest. Fortunately with my slower speed, I figured if I wanted to stop badly enough, I could always just fall over.

Going uphill again, I disobeyed the No Stopping sign and did some illegal gazing at the tall, steep snowy slopes on either side of me, bright and beautiful in the sunlight. Avalanche tracks draped the slopes. I resumed cycling before another avalanche appeared.

Soon the slush turned to wet pavement. I stopped at the end of the avalanche zone to wait for Terry. The snow plow appeared again, coming uphill towards me. The driver raised his hand to his forehead as he passed and gave me a salute. Over the five-and-a-half decades of my life, I've received accolades for a variety of accomplishments, but his salute for our bicycle trip over snowy Sylvan Pass was a salute I will never forget.

We stopped at the east entrance to the park. A walking popsicle,

I stomped around the parking lot, trying to bring back feeling into my frozen right foot.

Two women walked over.

"We saw you two up on the pass, and said prayers for you as we came down," one of them told us.

That was nice to hear. I'll take prayers anytime.

That was last year. This year, it was so easy. Go up, come down. Nice and simple. With the good weather, dry pavement, new solid brakes, and minimal traffic, our downhill ride from Sylvan Pass was a recipe for fun.

Goodbye to fantastic Yellowstone.

From the East entrance, we breezed a mile downhill to Pahaska, a tiny blip on the road. The restaurant served Rocky Mountain Oysters as part of its appetizer menu. It took more than being on the appetizer menu for me to believe that Rocky Mountain Oysters were actually appetizing. I ate chili instead.

Our bikes outside the restaurant window generated conversation. Diners plied us with the usual questions.

"Where are you going?"

"Where did you start?"

"When did you start?"

"How long will it take you to get to the Atlantic Ocean?"

"How many miles a day do you do?"

That's the way I like to spend a meal. With enthusiastic questions and listeners, it was hard for Terry and me to eat.

"It's all downhill from here," a man told us.

He was practically right. We biked downstream, paralleling a small flow of water that gained volume and strength from the summit. I liked watching the Shoshone River grow before our eyes, mile after mile. Towering red rocks stood sentinel along the road towards Cody.

I love Wyoming rocks . . . in fact, Wyoming rocks.

A tailwind propelled us. With fifty-three miles between

Yellowstone's East entrance and Cody, the tailwind was a gift as we continued to drop elevation. The forest thinned until it vanished into the open ranch country of Cody, named for William Cody, aka Buffalo Bill. A showman and statesman, Cody was the mastermind of his legendary Buffalo Bill and the Wild West Show of the late 1800s.

"Hi!"

A blond, muscular guy on a loaded bike came from behind as we entered town. With his one-word greeting, he passed us and disappeared.

It had been a long spell of no camping—none in Montana or the grizzled Yellowstone. We pitched our tent in the warm evening air on a green lawn of a RV park. It was good to be living outdoors again.

Evening tent life as Terry studies route information

East of Cody, we aimed for Shell, seventy miles away through the Big Horn Basin. The low land looked brown and thirsty.

Thanks to my shower at the RV park, my wet laundry was primed for the day. I spread a wet shirt under my bungee cords behind my seat. Sunshine would dry it soon, and then I would replace it with the next wet item. Drying laundry while bicycling on a hot, windy day is easy.

A man riding a recumbent zoomed up as I rotated laundry on a break. Andy, in his 70s, was lean, muscular, and on a mission.

"Yeah, the recumbent is lots of fun. I ride several times a week, usually doing about fifty miles each time."

Several minutes later, Andy took off at an impressive speed. In comparison, Terry and I were tortoises.

We met Andy again at the top of a hill where he stopped to break. While we talked, a van stopped from the opposite direction. A man Andy's age got out and looked at Terry and me.

"Are you the ones going to Maine?" he asked.

"Yeah," I said, surprised. "How'd you know?"

"It's all over the news and radio!" he said.

Really?

No.

But Ernie drank coffee that morning with his friend, who had been at Pahaska the day before. His friend sat at a table near two people who were cycling cross-country, headed to Maine. Ernie knew all about it.

"I passed you when I was driving someone home this morning, and then when I saw you the second time, I had to meet you." Ernie drove cancer patients to and from Cody's radiation center.

"I'm also a cyclist," he told us. "When I get off work this morning, I'm gonna go for a twenty-five mile ride."

I told Ernie my nursing background was oncology.

"I absolutely love my job," Ernie said. "I get to meet some of the best people in the world. Other people say to me 'That must be depressing to work with cancer patients', but I get my joy from being around them."

"I know what you mean. I loved oncology," I replied.

"One of my former patients is nearly blind and deaf. Her health is going downhill. I stop to see her nearly every day because she is so upbeat. My life is so enriched because of the patients I've gotten to know." Ernie smiled broadly.

I told him what one of my oncology patients told me long ago. "Every day above ground is a good one." Thanks for that reminder, Joe B.

While we four chatted, another cyclist appeared, a young guy in his thirties. He, Andy, and Ernie greeted each other, chatted about rides, and a few minutes later, the young cyclist took off. I marveled at the connections; this road was one big social machine.

A group of motorcyclists zoomed towards us from the opposite direction, honking their horns and giving us the motorcycle wave. I'd never been the recipient of the motorcycle wave before this trip, and didn't even know it existed until Terry and I hit Montana. When passing us, motorcyclists would often drop their left hands, spread their fingers, and do a low wave. I liked having motorcyclists wave to me, and I started doing it, too. Being an honorary member of the motorcycle club felt great.

Shortly after the friendly motorcyclists, a driver came from behind with an entirely different greeting: a long, frightening horn blast as he passed close by at a rip-roaring speed. There was room for him to go to the left and put a wider berth between us, but he didn't. Behavior like that ticks me off.

We left the bulk of the Rocky Mountains behind us, cycling in flat open land, a lull before the Big Horn Mountains to our east. With one more mountain range to cross, we'd soon be in the midwest, done with high mountains. We could ditch our cold weather clothes, significantly lightening our pannier load and bulk. All that stood between us and a lighter load was Granite Pass, elevation 9033 feet. That, and some serious headwinds.

While we took a break at a pull-out, a motorcyclist joined us.

"You two are really something," he said. "I'm having problems with these headwinds, and I'm on my motorcycle. You're amazing to be doing this on your bicycles."

We didn't feel amazing; we just felt hot, tired, and droopy.

"I'm from this area," he said, "and the winds are fickle. They can change direction at any time."

I was ready for them to change direction right then. But the headwinds didn't cease – they just kept wearing us down.

By mid-afternoon we met Sam, the big, blond cyclist who passed us in Cody at the end of the previous day, said "Hi!" and cycled past. This time he stopped to chat. Welsh and in his 30s, Sam was cycling cross-country too, with some extra hundreds of miles thrown in along the Pacific Coast just for fun. He started in Vancouver, British Columbia, biked to California, back into Oregon, and then headed east. On his way to New York, he just left Yellowstone. His gigantic calves displayed colorful tattoos.

"It's been a rough go today with the headwinds," Sam said. I liked hearing him say it had been a rough day; I liked hearing him say anything. His Welsh accent charmed me. Hearing him say that it had been a rough go for him made me feel less wimpy.

Sam's plans were to camp for the night at Shell, too.

"See you there," I called as Sam cycled away.

Passing through Embler, population ten, Terry and I found a tiny post office. Closed for the day, its public lobby was unlocked. We withered to the floor, happy to find refuge from the hot, windy day.

As we reluctantly left the building, Terry noticed the jewel of the post office: a vending machine in the parking lot. Dusty, with faded pictures of beverages, the machine looked ignored and abandoned. Our hopes dashed.

A long tail caught Terry's eye; an electrical cord ran from the machine to an outlet on a pole. Our hopes rose.

Terry fished out quarters, fed the machine, and pressed the button for a can of pop. Nothing. He pressed another button. Nothing. He pressed another. Something rattled inside and down dropped a can of orange pop. It was cold – nothing short of miraculous.

We fed the machine more quarters, but the machine refused to give up more orange pop. We tried other buttons; it was like playing vending machine roulette. Finally, out came a cold Mountain Dew. Elated, we returned inside to savor our cold drinks.

Once back in the heat, we wilted again.

Houses were scarce since leaving Cody. Seeing a woman in her garden, I stopped, grabbed an empty water bottle, and approached.

"May I please fill up a water bottle?" I asked, holding out my empty plastic bottle.

She said nothing; I don't think she understood English.

She looked at my empty water bottle and turned on the hose. I smiled while my bottle filled.

"*Gracias,*" guessing at her language. "*Adiós.*"

"*Adiós,*" she replied.

I was grateful for the water. I'd drunk five liters since the morning, but the day pulled fluids out of me faster than I put them in.

Gracias.

Sing along now to the Beach Boys' tune:
"Good, good, good, good hydration!"

An afternoon storm brewed. The sun disappeared and dark gray clouds filled the sky. My wish was granted as headwinds abated, but crazy winds replaced them. Terry and I struggled to negotiate the bikes in the gusts. Heads low, we steered with determination as crosswinds threatened to knock us off our bikes.

An oncoming pickup stopped across the road, and a young man leaned out the window.

"Looks like you're having trouble with these winds," he shouted. "Would you like a lift to Greybull?"

I straddled my bike with my feet on the ground. While Terry and the driver talked, a gust walloped my bike, nearly blowing it over and taking me with it. I staggered to keep from falling.

Smart move to escape the wind. As we loaded bikes into the back of Curt's pickup, another gust nearly blew me over. I heard a tree branch crack; the world was getting wild. With gray skies and whirling wind, I felt like we were smack dab in the middle of the cyclone scene in *The Wizard of Oz*.

We headed towards Greybull.

"Yeah, I passed you. I could see you were having problems with the wind, so I turned around to see if you wanted some help."

That was darn nice, and it spooked me to think what would have happened without him.

Curt kept a tight grip on his steering wheel as wind buffeted the pickup. Five miles brought us into Greybull and a KOA campground. Big trees waved wildly and the little ones bent sideways. Branches were strewn everywhere.

Falling branches don't make for safe tent camping, so a little cabin became ours.

"Thank you so much, Curt!" His kindness in delivering us to safety was a gift.

Power was out for twenty miles, the KOA owner said. Two hours later it returned, and Terry and I sat outside enjoying the absurdly gentle evening air.

Another hot day lay ahead of us, with most of its 5000-foot elevation gain slated for the hottest part of the afternoon. Fifteen miles later, we arrived to the tiny town of Shell, named for the abundance of sea shells and fossils discovered in the area. The town could have just as easily been named Dinosaur. Highway 14 is replete with signs indicating dinosaurs roamed the area long ago.

Red rocks ruled the land, and we could almost touch them as we pedaled through a narrow canyon alongside Shell Creek. The temperature dropped as a welcome breeze blew through. Leaving the corridor, the grandeur of distant rocks greeted us, every bit as spectacular as the snow-covered mountains and wild rivers of Yellowstone.

The Big Horn Mountains rose up with their mesa flat tops. They looked appealing from a distance, but that would change in the coming heat of the day.

The road up Granite Pass appeared to have black snakes all over it, which turned out to be lines of tar plugging the cracks caused by the cold winters. The gooey tar melted in the heat, and parallel tar cracks powerfully gripped my tires. Whenever my front tire sank into the tar, I'd jerk on my handlebars and vigorously pedal to get free. Fortunately, most of the tar lay at angles.

Sam passed us right before Shell Creek Falls, and we swapped storm stories at the thundering water.

"I just finished cycling through Greybull yesterday when the winds went crazy," Sam told us in his beguiling Welsh accent. "I biked back to Greybull to wait out the storm, and then biked to Shell. I spent the evening in the bar and camped behind it."

I liked listening to Sam's accent, and I liked looking at the Celtic tattoos on his big, muscular calves. Sam was a complete entertainment package. He said he usually slept until 11 a.m. and then would start to cycle. So different from us. We typically had an early start but were often still cycling late in the day. That's the difference between a Ferrari (Sam) and clunker models (us).

We took off, knowing that Sam would power past us soon. The welcome breeze from Shell Canyon became an aggressive headwind, and at one point I couldn't propel myself forward due to the force. Instead, I fell over sideways--fortunately, I didn't have my bike shoes clipped to my pedals.

Sam joined us near Granite Pass summit, elevation 9033 feet, and the highest point of our transcontinental trip. Piles of snow intermittently lined the road. Terry and I played leapfrog with Sam on the descent: descend, take a break, get overpassed by Sam, and then overpass Sam while he took a break. After one more uphill workout, I looked down from the summit, feeling detached from the flat, green land below, as if I were in a spaceship looking down at earth.

An eleven-mile, eight percent downgrade rolled us into Dayton, where we arrived after dark and checked into the motel that was attached to a campground. Terry was shot from the long descent. Although a perfect night for camping, there was no denying that a motel was simpler.

At Dayton's café for breakfast, two groups told Terry they'd watched us ride in to town the night before. That seemed weird; we weren't used to being monitored.

"I've lived here in Dayton for 70 years," one man reported. "It's the best town in the world. There's no gangs or hoodlums here."

Departing the best town in the world, we headed into spectacular scenery: green fields, snow-capped mountains, blue sky, and a dry twenty-five miles between Dayton and Sheridan.

With a population of 17,000, Sheridan was a big town compared with most on our trip. I mailed the bear spray back to Robert, while Terry shopped for running shoes to replace the boots he'd no longer need.

At the post office, I unloaded my four panniers on the sidewalk. By the time Terry arrived, I had a pile to send home: boots, a warm jacket, heavy rain pants, my Vana mitts, and maps. Curious people stopped to talk. I had plenty of time to tell stories as I dropped items into piles either to keep or mail. I easily rid myself of five pounds without exercising or dieting – I just mailed it home. Easiest weight loss program ever.

While Terry mailed our boxes, I waited outside. A young man with a camera around his neck walked up, looked at the bikes, and looked at me.

"Do you know whose bikes these are?" he asked.

"Yeah, one is mine and the other is my husband's," I replied.

Someone phoned the Sheridan Press newspaper with a hot tip and the Press dispatched Nick to get a photo. We arranged the bikes with the *Sheridan, WY Post Office* lettering visible behind them. Terry came out, and Nick took his photos of us with the bikes. We felt like celebrities.

We found Sam outside the grocery store. This was our fourth day in a row playing leap frog with him and I loved that. Sadly, this would likely be the last time we'd see him. Terry and I planned to bike to Ucross, twenty-five miles away, while Sam aimed for Gillette, a hundred miles from Sheridan. Good bye to Sam.

Using directions given to Terry at the store, we cycled looking for Highway 14's intersection. No go. We checked our map, and retraced our route to try again. Finally on Highway 14, I rounded a curve and startled twenty antelope. Other animals run, but antelope spring, bounce, and boing when they get spooked.

Terry called for a break at the top of an unpaved road intersecting with the highway. While we ate and drank, a car drove to the turn-off and a woman rolled down her window.

"Hey, I just passed you a while ago on another road and now I'm seeing you here! This is the top of my road." She pointed down the gravel road.

"We took the wrong road from Sheridan and had to reverse. We're on the right road now –we think."

"I passed another cyclist behind you and stopped and talked with him," she said.

"Oh, that's Sam! He's doing his own trip and we've been leap frogging for the past four days since Cody."

"Would you like to spend the night with us? We live on that

farm and my husband would love to meet you. He's training for a triathlon and would love to talk with cyclists."

Dana radiated friendliness and enthusiasm. While we spoke, Sam arrived. He had already declined Dana's invitation, saying he wanted to get to Gillette for the night. Finding Terry and me, he changed his mind.

Dana brought home three guests and surprised her husband, John. He seemed to take the surprise pretty well –Dana's enthusiasm and energy undoubtedly meant frequent surprises in John's life.

The ranch was an old sheep farm set among broad, undulating hills. The original farm house, a white cottage with a picket fence, was ours for the night. Our fairy godparent appeared again, giving us unexpected hospitality in such friendly and beautiful surroundings.

Across from the cottage was John and Dana's new house, a barn-like structure with abundant windows and amazing views.

"We drew up our house designs on a restaurant's sugar packets," Dana explained. Their house design included a fire pole inside, which Dana's two sons used as a quick descent from the second floor to the first.

"Sometimes I use the fire pole, too," John said with a smile.

We piled in their pickup for dinner in Sheridan. Stories flew about bike adventures and Ironman Triathlons. John thought our cross-country bike trips sounded impressive, but swimming 2.2 miles, biking 112 miles, and then running 26.2 miles sounded not only impressive to me, but crazy. Also a nurse, Dana enthusiastically hatched plans with me to bring her family to camp in Switzerland the following summer, where we planned to work together.

Animated conversations continued back at the ranch. Hearing of Warmshowers, the couch-surfing organization for cyclists, Dana immediately planned to sign up as a host.

Dana and John's darling daughter, Thea, at seven months was already worldly for someone so young. Her egg mother lived in the Czech Republic, her surrogate pregnancy mother lived in

Oregon, and her loving parents Dana and John were raising her in Wyoming. Amazing technology and globalization.

Being so warmly welcomed into Dana and John's family filled me with joy and gratitude. It was another unforeseen adventure of our trip. Once again, I felt humbled by the kindness of strangers.

By breakfast, John was cycling towards Gillette as part of his upcoming Ironman training. Sam still slept, but we knew he would overtake us somewhere on the road to Gillette.

Good bye to Dana and Thea – many thanks for a wonderful time together. The moral of this story: be open to random relationships that can begin near driveways.

Predictably, it began to rain. Lightning flashed ahead of us, but unlike a couple of weeks earlier, I wasn't spooked. After all, lightning hadn't hit us yet.

Sam caught up at a little store in Clearmont, twenty-five miles from Dana and John's. It was our fifth day seeing him. Once again, I figured it was our last Sam sighting, as he planned to push all the way to Devils Tower, while Terry and I were stopping at Gillette. Terry and I left Clearmont and Sam soon overtook us. Goodbye, Sam! Good luck!

Playing leapfrog with Sam at Clearmont, Wyoming

We slogged our way through a day of headwinds. By 7:30 p.m., we clearly weren't going to get to Gillette by dark, or any time soon after that. We kept cycling, considering options. We could cycle in the dark with our bike lights. We could pitch the tent along the side of the road, or go up to a house and ask if we could pitch our tent on their property. Or we could ignore the problem and wish it would go away. We ignored it until 9:30.

Arriving at a little community fifteen miles from Gillette, we eyeballed houses and buildings, looking for protection from the wind where we could pitch the tent. We decided to go up to a house that was lit and ask if we could pitch our tent in the yard.

We rang the bell.

A man wearing a Seattle Space Needle T-shirt answered and I was immediately optimistic. Seattle is in our neck of the woods back home. He was older than us and had a friendly look to him.

"Hi. We're cycling and aren't going to make it to Gillette tonight due to the headwinds. We're wondering if we could pitch our tent in your side yard for the night."

"What?" He looked confused.

I tried it again. It's probably the kind of request that doesn't immediately sink in the first time.

"Well, we have a room downstairs you could use. We've had rain and hail the last two nights, and it would be a lot more comfortable than a tent."

A woman popped her head from behind him. She heard the situation, looked upwards, and said "Dad sent them."

Darrell and Becky graciously invited us into their home for the night.

Becky went downstairs to get the room ready and Darrell invited us into their living room. He told us about living so close to Gillette's big coal mine.

"We're just a few miles from it," Darrell explained. "Sometimes the explosions wake me up, and sometimes they rock the house. We have a lot of cracks in our house from the mine explosions."

Becky reappeared and sat down. I asked about her comment that "Dad sent them."

"My dad died a couple years ago. He frequently invited people that he saw on the road up to the house for food and drink."

"Yeah, Bob was always inviting people up," Darrell agreed.

Thanks, Bob, for sending us.

Darrell and Becky were hunters. Their living room had His and Her corners, with mounted chests and heads of deer that each of them shot.

Becky led us to their basement. The main room was practically a museum of animal parts, with almost a dozen racks of deer, elk, and moose, as well as a bear's head and a stuffed bobcat. The bobcat looked ready to pounce. Another wall displayed a turkey, and a buffalo skin lay on the floor.

Terry and I would certainly have a lot of company for the night.

After showers, we went to bed clean and comfy in the bedroom, away from the false eyes of all those staring animals.

Such a radical change. Only an hour earlier we were on our bikes, anxious about the approaching darkness and the need to find a place for our tent. Now we were in a bed in a house, at the kind invitation of people we didn't even know.

Two nights in a row of such generosity and radical hospitality.

Goodbye to Becky and Darrell and their kindness. Their warm hospitality and fascinating stories sure beat a pitched tent off the side of a highway in the dark.

Sharp pain put Terry on the highway's grass five minutes later. Ibuprofen, food, and rest put him back in the saddle twenty minutes later, although pedaling slowly. Hernia pain and headwinds made for a slow go.

Down again, up again, went Terry and his hernia, for the second, third, and fourth time in close succession. Close to the Gillette airport, we pedaled to the terminal to get out of the wind and sun.

We stayed for two hours as Terry rested, ate, and eventually felt better. He wanted a motel at Gillette. Okay. Half hour later, he wanted to keep cycling. Okay. Each day of our trip was different from the others, but this day was the most sobering yet. We worried.

The wind quieted and we made it to Gillette, rolling into a bike shop so someone could look at Terry's brakes.

And there was Sam. He'd made it past Gillette, but spokes, axel, and ball bearing problems forced him back. Now we were all behind schedule as we waited at the bike shop together.

Thank goodness for bike shops and bike mechanics, who play a huge role in long distance touring. Without them, a trip of this magnitude would be nearly impossible. A tip of our helmets to all the bike mechanics of the world.

Both bikes were finished at the same time. Terry felt better after his long rest and wanted to keeping cycling, so we three pedaled off together. Sam, a veteran of the side road towards Moorcroft, advised us to take the freeway instead—less miles and less bumpy.

We three briefly rode together before Sam kicked up his pace to Sam Speed. Goodbye once again to Sam, and best wishes!

Freeway cycling would never go well in Portland, but rural Montana and Wyoming played by different rules. With a decent shoulder and light traffic, twenty-eight miles of freeway cycling to Moorcroft felt pretty sweet. By mid-afternoon, the hernia pain disappeared as mysteriously as it arrived, but by our arrival at Moorcroft, Terry was wiped out. An air-conditioned motel partially revived him, and a postcard I purchased for him did the rest. The postcard showed a bison layered in snow and ice, with the heading *Wyoming's Not for Wimps*.

That was for sure. Headwinds, hernia, and hurt—be gone.

With Devils Tower only forty miles away, we earned a lazy start.

Our winds changed to crosswinds—better than headwinds, but still problematic. A stiff crosswind can shove you sideways – either into the path of speeding cars or off the shoulder. I didn't like either option.

Halfway to Devils Tower, we caught sight of it, jutting up like a knob from the flat plain. That was our one and only sighting of Devils Tower the previous year.

Long story short-- the prior year, Terry crashed while going downhill on that same road, presumably from some rumble strips. Motorists stopped to help, gave us and our bikes a ride to the closest emergency room, from which Terry was transferred to Spearfish Regional Hospital in South Dakota. A lacerated liver earned him time in the intensive care unit, and that was the end of our three-week bicycle trip. We were planning to end in Spearfish, anyway-- just not via ambulance.

But that was last year, and this was this year. A year after his accident, Terry was back on his bike with a nicely-healed liver.

Things looked familiar. We scouted the road for the scene of the accident, and finally entered new territory.

Down, up, down, up. Crosswind, headwind. We lost sight of Devils Tower. Up another long hill we suddenly had another Tower sighting. This time it was much closer.

Devils Tower is a gigantic brown rock that pokes up 867 feet from the flat landscape, like a giant plug on the Wyoming plains. Scientists used to think that Devils Tower was the core of an ancient volcano, but now they think it's an igneous intrusion – whatever that is.

Devils Tower, Wyoming

Devils Tower was designated the first national monument in 1906. The state of Wyoming is home to both the first national park, Yellowstone, and the first national monument. President

Teddy Roosevelt's influence was huge in protecting some alluring U.S. land from commercial exploitation.

Less than two miles from the Tower, Terry and I stopped at a restaurant. As we locked our bikes before heading in, a woman left the restaurant and stopped to talk. She knew the area and we questioned her about the best route to Mt. Rushmore.

Delpha invited us in for dinner, and back inside she went. With her contagious enthusiasm, we quickly warmed up to storytelling. She told us stories, too.

"I've been a special ed. teacher, a hippie, a photographer, and a freelance writer. I don't do anything for over five years, and then I move on to something new. Right now, my plans are to move to the Oregon coast, live in a trailer, and monitor for tsunamis."

Goodbye and thank you to Delpha—we hoped our paths would cross again when we were all back in Oregon.

As we unlocked our bikes, a motorcyclist complained about his day on his motorcycle.

"It's been a hard day for riding with all these winds," he said.

Oh yeah, tell us about it. And he was on a motorcycle.

"The tent sites are the best in the campground," the KOA receptionist informed us a short time later. "They are right on the edge of the property, and you'll look out at Devils Tower. You'll like it. The film *Close Encounters of the Third Kind* is showing right now, but it's already started. Some of the filming was done here at Devils Tower. Be aware that a storm is predicted for tonight. Expect thunder and lightning."

That sounded like a Close Encounter I wanted to avoid. Perhaps I'd be spending my night in the bathroom instead of my tent.

Nothing obstructed our view of Devils Tower, where it stood imposingly about a mile from our tent. What an amazing tent site. A million-dollar view from the open flap of our tent, all for a few bucks at KOA.

With three campgrounds near Devils Tower, we figured Sam was at one of the other two. Like us, he planned to see Mt. Rushmore next, but there were multiple ways to get there. When we three talked in Gillette, Sam hadn't yet chosen his route.

Terry and I basked in our twilight view of Devils Tower and eventually closed our tent flap.

Nighty night, aliens.

⨂

After forests and back in ranch land, we stopped next to a cattle guard. A few cattle milled near us on their side. Those cattle were magnets, and within ten minutes, thirty head of cattle gathered on their side, all standing and staring at us. Close Encounters of the Cow Kind. One began to bellow. Unfortunately for me, it was only one. Sometimes one bellowing steer would start a chain reaction, igniting a mass of bellowing. I liked that kind of chaos. Too bad that this time, other cattle weren't in the mood.

My cattle jollies came a couple hours later. Cycling by a ranch, a few cattle started running parallel to us along the fence line. Some bellowing started, more cattle joined in the run, more bellowing followed, and then we had a herd of stampeding, bellowing cattle joining our ride. I loved the ruckus of bellowing, stampeding cattle--as long as they weren't stampeding over me.

We climbed again, to the Black Hills National Forest. I thought the Black Hills were in South Dakota, which they are, but it turns out that Wyoming claims them too. From a distance, the pine and spruce covered hills did indeed look black.

Gazing at ice cream and hardware in Aladdin's ancient general store, Terry and I saw something even better saunter through the door: Sam.

"I was at the National Park Service campground, and spent the whole day yesterday sleeping in my hammock," he told us. "I couldn't sleep last night, though, with all the thunder and lightning."

Terry and I must have really been out of it to have slept through a thunder and lightning storm.

Heading to Spearfish and then to Mt. Rushmore, leapfrogging with Sam once again became my favorite activity.

Descending a steep downgrade, gravity and tailwinds pushed us to a welcoming sign with the four familiar faces of Mt. Rushmore. Another state and its accompanying state of happiness and sense of accomplishment was ours as we read the greeting:

South Dakota—Great Faces, Great Places.

CHAPTER 7

Endurance—
South Dakota

Twenty easy miles later we breezed into Belle Fourche, whose claim to fame is being the geographic center of the United States. Actually, someone's farmland twenty miles north of Belle Fourche is the real center, but Belle Fourche has received the glory ever since Alaska and Hawaii joined the Union in 1959. Terry and I shoved our bikes onto a large granite map of the U.S., while fifty colorful flags flapped around us.

Geographic Center of the Nation Monument,
Belle Fourche, South Dakota

We arrived at Spearfish, grateful to have made it on our bikes this time instead of in an ambulance. We loaded up with cans of Almond Roca and thank you cards to deliver to the hospital units where Terry received care the year before. As a nurse, I know healthcare staff are always happy to receive candy and appreciative notes--even when it's a year late.

Terry and I shouted to hear each other over the turbulent wind at the campground.

As I walked into the bathroom, I glanced at a sign and was puzzled to read "Spearfish doesn't usually have tomatoes. In the event of a tomato warning...."

A tomato warning? What the heck? I read again, more carefully.

Tornadoes, not "tomatoes. Evidently this area did get some turbulent wind at times.

As Terry and I packed up in the morning, a campground worker wandered over.

"I saw another touring cyclist last night when I was at Safeway. A guy with tattooed legs."

A Sam sighting! That was great to know. Sam was probably still asleep somewhere and would zoom past us in a couple of hours.

In town after breakfast, a man stopped to ask questions. Throughout the entire conversation, he scowled.

"Leave me your address. I'll send you a sympathy card."

A minute later, another man came over, asking the same questions.

"You ought to be commended," he said.

Or did he say, "You ought to be committed"?

With those two opposing opinions, Terry and I pedaled from Spearfish towards Deadwood, trading tailwinds for crosswinds after turning south. Bellowing cows gave me a mental boost, balancing the fulcrum.

A vehicle passed us with a sign *Paint Striper Ahead*. I double checked and confirmed with Terry. After my tomato/tornado confusion back at the campground, I didn't trust my eyesight. Paint Striper? What did that mean? Shouldn't it be Stripe Painter? That bothered me grammatically. It bothered me all the way up the long hill towards Deadwood, and then it bothered me down the hill into town. Meanwhile, while I was bothered by the grammar, a vehicle passed us, painting a stripe on the right side of the road.

With the discovery of gold near a gulch of dead trees in 1876, Deadwood became the site of the last great gold rush in the lower United States. All Terry and I wanted was a grocery store, but Deadwood didn't appear to have one. It had a lot of casinos instead.

Not finding a grocery store, we ate at a café, attracting the usual attention. A man told us about the Mickelson Bike Trail, a converted rail line.

"It starts here at Deadwood and goes over a hundred miles to the south. It's packed with fine gravel, which makes it more suitable for mountain bikes than touring bikes, but it will get you off the highway. This highway doesn't have shoulders, and your bikes will do fine on the trail."

I wanted to give it a try. Terry was hesitant.

"It's not going to be as fast," he stalled.

"Let's give it a try. We can always change our minds," I countered.

We gave it a try. Our skinny road bike tires sank into the finely crushed gravel, requiring us to push our pedals harder to keep the momentum going. But it was beautiful and the going wasn't too tough. We pushed our way up, paralleling a creek that splashed down through rocks and vegetation, past walls of rock that butted up to the creek, past slabs of wood that formed mysterious structures, and through dense pine forests. Soon we left civilization and paved roads behind, and it was just the two of us out under blue sky and beside green trees. I loved it.

On the trail about an hour, I stopped for Terry to catch up. I relished being out in the serene beauty.

Terry crunched through the gravel to where I sat on a rock in the sunshine.

"Let's go back," he said.

"Why?" I was disappointed – this was exactly the kind of setting that I loved.

"I don't want to eat my lunch food for dinner."

What?

"This trail is going to take a long time. I don't have dinner food, and I don't want to eat my lunch food for dinner."

You've got to be kidding, I thought. Terry looked grumpy, and certainly didn't sound like he was kidding. We'd been together for thirty-two years, and I knew everything he did began with the end point in mind: food.

"I don't want to eat my lunch food for dinner," he repeated.

I knew Terry well, but I evidently didn't know him well enough. I could hardly believe it. I didn't want to believe it. I didn't say anything, expecting that Terry would realize the idiocy of his statement and say something more reasonable. He didn't.

"What? But this area is so beautiful. We can pitch our tent anywhere and be out in the wilderness. We can get back on the road tomorrow if you don't like this trail."

"I don't have dinner food with me. I want dinner food; I don't want to be eating my lunch food, Mari!" He raised his voice.

It was a lost battle before it even began.

I knew that Terry's dietary habits were deeply ingrained in him. He ate the same thing for breakfast every day and wanted his three meals on schedule even if the world was turning upside down. At home, I was accustomed to his regimen, but we weren't at home. We were on a cross-country bike trip, for cripe's sake.

Couldn't there be some flexibility with a couple of meals so we could be on this lovely bike trail for a hundred miles, or at least the day?

Apparently not.

I wasn't about to turn around and lead us back down the trail, so I waited for Terry to do it. I just stared at him, fuming, ready to explode. Oblivious to my anger or ignoring it, he pulled out some food, sat down on the ground, and ate. I said nothing. He said nothing. He chewed and I stared. When he finished, he got to his feet, rummaged in his panniers, and turned his bike around.

"Ready?" he asked.

No, I wasn't, and I wasn't going to be.

He began pedaling back down the trail and I reluctantly followed him, boring my eyes into his helmeted head and wanting to scream.

We turned off the trail towards Lead, the town with a big, air-conditioned grocery store near Deadwood. I loaded up with my usual grocery fare, paying no attention to what Terry was buying that would constitute an acceptable dinner.

Terry also bought two ice cream bars, which we ate while sitting on a bench outside the store. I wasn't in the mood for ice cream, but it's not the kind of thing you can tuck into a pannier on a hot day and eat later when you finally are in the mood. We sat by our loaded bikes. I wasn't in the mood to cheerfully answer people's questions about our bike trip, either – but I did. I refrained from shouting that we had just been on the Mickelson Bike Trail, a great trail, and that we weren't on it anymore because Terry refused to eat his lunch food for dinner.

We backtracked to Deadwood, descending elevation that we worked so hard to climb. Once there, we cut over and began our ascent on Highway 385 again, where we'd been two hours earlier. I was mad all over again.

Sometimes there are headwinds in marriage, too.

On the other side of the hill, we entered birch country. Peeling the papery bark from a birch tree was a childhood joy, but in spite of the pick-me-up from the trees, I still wasn't talking much. I resumed my usual position in front, and my anger drove my bike pedals with a furor that shot me far in front of Terry. I'd stop and wait for him to catch up, say as little as possible while he rested, and then get on my bike and shoot down the road some more. The biking conditions were perfect: good temperatures through the forest, no wind, lots of trees and sky, and decent traffic and road shoulders. The only thing that wasn't perfect was my sour mood.

Having lost two hours before getting on Highway 385 again, we ran out of time to make it to Keystone, the town near Mt. Rushmore. Terry hit the wall near the Silver City turnoff, so we stopped with hours left of daylight.

At Whispering Pines campground, I didn't hear any pines whispering; my head was still full of silent shouting.

"Are you going to stay mad about this for the rest of the trip?"

How do you respond to a question like that? I'd cooled somewhat, but I was still angry. Maybe I would stay mad about it for the rest of the trip, maybe not.

I sighed.

"Maybe," I lied.

It's no fun being angry for hours. I walked off to the shower and forced my crabby disposition down the drain, returning with a clean body and softer attitude. We broke camp, and instead of my piercing stare, I made regular eye contact. I said normal things like "Let's shake the ground cloth" instead of deliberately being silent.

I still had a ways to go but it was a good start. "Fake it 'til you make it", as my student nurses would say. At least I had entered the faking it stage. Faking it gradually changed as the day progressed – bit by stubborn bit.

We rolled through lush green meadows and scattered pine, passing Pactola Lake. Fresh piles of sawdust along the side of the road smelled like maple syrup.

Gravity did the work as we coasted into Keystone, the gateway to Mt. Rushmore. Nearing the bottom of the two-mile-steep descent, my phone beeped with three messages.

The first message was from Clifton, Erik's college friend from Penn State. Clifton was now my friend too, through a summer and a January of working together at Concordia Language Villages' camps in Switzerland and Brazil. For the past two years, Clifton had been teaching at Pine Ridge Indian Reservation for Teach for America, our next stop after Mt. Rushmore. Clifton was excited to introduce us to his Lakota Native American community, and we were excited to visit.

But things change. Clifton's message told me his brother was hospitalized, and he'd be hitting the road back to Philadelphia in the morning, two weeks earlier than planned.

The second message was from Bethany, our house sitter, with questions.

The third message was from Terry, a mile behind me, fixing a flat.

Back up the steep hill I went until I saw Terry fitting a new tube into his tire. While Terry worked, I phoned Clifton.

"Parsley!" he exclaimed, using my camp name. Clifton's upbeat spirit radiated through the phone.

Since he was only twenty miles away in Rapid City, he offered to come to Keystone so we could visit. That was a generous offer on Clifton's part – he still had to pack, load his car, and get on the road in the morning.

Phone call number two was to Bethany, who had a simple question about our house. After telling her about Terry's flat tire, she reminded me that now Terry could get a milkshake. I'd forgotten about that rule: fix a flat, get a milkshake.

Our 1500-mile bike trip barely prepared me to bike up the long, steep driveway of our hotel. It took everything I had to push my pedals and heavy bike up that driveway. Terry gave up and walked. I still huffed and puffed while walking into the reception, realizing that was the steepest and hardest ascent of our bike trip so far.

Our two-hour dinner with Clifton flew by. Upbeat, generous, and curious as always, South Dakota's loss would be Pennsylvania's gain.

🚲

While Clifton burned the rubber towards Pennsylvania, Terry and I spent a Slacker Day at Mt. Rushmore National Memorial, cycling a whopping eight miles on our nearly naked bikes.

Mt. Rushmore through my bike frame

The six-story high sculpted heads of George Washington, Thomas Jefferson, Theodore Roosevelt, and Abraham Lincoln amazed me. Gutzon Borglum and four hundred other workers dynamited, drilled, and carved the granite between 1927-1941, with dynamite blasting the initial 90% of the work. Jefferson started out on Washington's right cheek, but due to crowding, ended up behind his left ear.

Posing with our bikes before the four presidents, one strong spit from George would have hit us. A familiar feeling of amazement flooded me. We rode those bikes from the Pacific Ocean. Without loaded panniers, our bikes didn't look intriguing anymore. They looked like regular bikes, and we looked like regular tourists out for a day ride.

But we knew better.

The Visitor Center, Borglum's studio, and the massive granite heads filled me with wonder. What a mind boggling project. It's a good thing I wasn't in charge; things certainly wouldn't have turned out this well. I can barely draw a stick figure.

Our fifth week ended with our excellent Slacker Day, and 1500 miles under our pedals.

Terry's replacement tire tube came with a cost more than dollars: a detour twenty miles north to Rapid City, and several hours of errands and congestion in town. With much restraint, I kept my mouth shut; I was still trying to be a nicer version of myself than I felt.

Frenzied downtown traffic prompted a brief respite at a gas station, where a police officer asked if he could help. Jim, a crash investigation officer, recommended a route through town. Following his advice, we ruefully found ourselves in road construction, where cars sped by alarmingly close to us. It felt far more dangerous than I 90 ever did, and we hoped to avoid seeing Jim in his professional role as a crash investigation officer.

Hours later on the frontage road, we stood with a farmer, anomalies among the prairie grass as the tallest things around.

"Down the road is a church that is always open," he told us. "You can go inside for shade and water—you can even spend the night if you want. It's always open; you just go on in."

Miles of heat and headwinds later, we came to our oasis: Wicksville Community Church. The doors indeed were open, and we stepped into the cool, dark, and empty sanctuary – a sanctuary both spiritually and from the heat.

Sitting quietly in the dark sanctuary, I attended my spiritual state. I was grateful: for the hospitality of this congregation for keeping their doors open to wandering strangers, for this bike trip, for my health, for the relationships that surrounded my life and let me know I was valued and loved. I contemplated how I could be more supportive to Terry and others, and less absorbed with my own interests.

Terry and I left feeling renewed-- not a bad outcome for a visit to a church.

Headwinds and heat zapped Terry's strength, prompting an early end at Wasta to our day, fifteen miles short of our destination of Wall. Equally weary, most businesses were either closed or empty. Two young women sat outside the little town's bar in the heat, smoking and looking bored.

With low expectations for our night, a few minutes brought us to a green RV park. We'd seen few trees since the morning, but green grass and large trees thrived in the RV campground, and the shower was a revival.

Wasta's first impression sucked--good thing for second chances.

The day's menu started with a long, steep decline to the Cheyenne River.

"A cyclist once reached a speed of ninety miles an hour coming down it," the Rapid City bike shop employee had told us.

That seemed preposterous, especially given the conditions we encountered: headwinds so strong that I pedaled hard just to go seven miles an hour. Such a waste of a downhill.

I slowly churned my way uphill and retreated into the short vegetation to hide from the wind. It didn't work. I tried to write on my Blackberry, but the letters once again blew around from the gusts. The alphabet randomly set up home in other words, making a mess of what I already wrote. Bah.

Terry finally showed up, exhausted from the hill and constant headwind. After a long break we continued east, making paltry progress against the wind and 94 degree heat.

Our day was headed nowhere by the time we reached Wall. Lightning, thunder, and hail were in the afternoon's forecast. We sure weren't heading into the isolated Badlands in those conditions.

A major roadside attraction in the U.S., Wall Drug's humble beginnings started with a pharmacist and his wife in 1931. Business was poor, and they began advertising free ice water for passing motorists. With their humorous road signs, business picked up—to the point that the drug store can now seat 530 people in its restaurant section. The drug store still exists, as well as over a dozen other specialty areas inside the Wall Drug complex. The tourist trap worked, capturing Terry and me for a few refreshing, air-conditioned hours.

At our campground, I escaped to the laundry room, where the washing machine violently beat our clothes and I wrote with my Blackberry plugged into the wall.

I checked the odometer. Our grand total for the day: fifteen hard-earned, wind blasted miles, painstakingly drawn out during three hours of cycling.

Well rested and stocked with water, we stopped at the sign: *Entering the Badlands.*

A car drove up and a guy in his 30s jumped out.

"Hey, could I take a photo for you?" he asked. Sure—he read our minds.

Like so many people, Paul was full of questions, and probably the most enthusiastic person about our trip that we had yet met. He wanted stories, so we told him about cycling in the snow in Montana, our free condo in Big Sky, Yellowstone, leap-frogging with Sam, staying with Dana and family near Sheridan, asking for tent space and being offered indoor lodging near Gillette.

While we told stories, Paul opened his cooler.

"Want some cold root beer? How about some string cheese?"

Paul probably had no idea how gratifying it was to be offered cold refreshments on a hot day. Our cold refreshments came from a business, not our panniers. With no businesses around, a cold root beer in the heat of the day at the Badlands was incredible.

And it didn't stop there.

"Need any toothpaste or tooth brushes? My mom's a dental hygienist and she loads me up."

Yes indeed, I did want a little tube of toothpaste, and while I was at it, a new toothbrush sounded great, too.

What a joy to be the recipients of Paul's generous hospitality. Between his enthusiasm and the boost from the cold root beer, I was ready to take on the Badlands in any kind of heat.

"Be safe and have a wonderful trip! It was fantastic meeting you two!"

"Thank you so much!"

The Lakota Native Americans named the area *Mako Sica*, meaning Land Bad. Desolate and lacking water, the land is difficult to traverse. One can't argue the name, but the Badlands are also stunning in their beauty.

We paralleled canyons and rocks, old buffalo jumps, and mama antelopes nursing newborns. Once covered by the sea, Badlands fossils are 25 million years old-- camels, crocodiles, dinosaurs, rhinos, and more. The prehistoric creatures now rest in the earthy mounds of yellow and red hues –colors of fossil soils.

The Badlands felt like Goodlands, though. A pleasant breeze appeared before noon. With light traffic and tremendous views, we gawked at the stunning scenery. I effortlessly rode along at sixteen miles per hour--such a change from the day before when headwinds made cycling even seven miles an hour a struggle. Life was good and easy.

And it got better. As Terry and I gazed from an overlook, a couple walked up to us.

"Where are you two going?" the woman asked. "We saw you back there and passed you in our van."

We told them our story – or at least part of it. Stories, questions, and answers filled the next ten minutes.

"That's fantastic," the man said. "I was curious about you when we passed you, and I'm so glad we had the chance to talk. Good luck with the rest of your trip!"

The two of them walked away. Minutes later, the woman returned with two big oranges in her outstretched hands.

"It's a hot day and you probably could use something juicy. Would you like some oranges?" she asked.

Wow, more gifts from kind people. A gift of oranges, on top of our gifts of root beer, string cheese, toothpaste, and a toothbrush. It was like winning the sweepstakes.

"Oh yeah! Thank you so much – this is such a treat!" Terry and I gratefully took the treasures.

"Enjoy them, and you two be safe," the woman replied. She turned to walk back to the RV.

That day's hospitality became a highlight of the trip. The kindness of strangers, giving us simple gifts of cold drink and refreshing oranges on a hot day, impacted me greatly. I'm sure people had no idea that a small amount of food and drink would stand out in my mind for the rest of the trip, and for years to come. I learned something important: small acts of kindness can have a huge impact. A couple cans of root beer and a couple oranges probably didn't even dent their provisions, and maybe the people thought nothing of it. But I felt the significance of it. The physical refreshment touched my body and the emotional refreshment touched my psyche.

It doesn't take much to bring kindness to a touring cyclist, and it can be done on the road, in a campground, outside of a café, outside of an outhouse. Our bike trip had many highlights, but our day of root beer and oranges was near the top of my list. I vowed to offer similar hospitality to cyclists and adventurers, surprising them with random acts of kindness. I knew how the root beer and oranges surprised and affected me.

A brilliant blue sky contrasted with formations around us. Craggy rocks, with upturned peaks like a stiff meringue, looked like you could cut yourself on the pointed spires. Other rocks were rounded, with muted colors—old dinosaurs fading away.

Exploring the Badlands, South Dakota

The Visitor Center offered respite from the heat with exhibits, films, and the best part of all, air conditioning. We considered repeatedly watching the same film, just to stay in the air-conditioned theater.

At Cedar Pass campground, I parked myself inside the bathroom for a writing and charging marathon, staying past dark. Standing by the sink, tethered to the wall and writing on my Blackberry, I became a bathroom fixture and startled visitors.

We'd lost sight of Sam long ago, but were now e-mailing with him. He wrote that a frontage road paralleled I-90 all the way from the Badlands to Sioux Falls—fabulous news for traffic, lodging, and food.

We were soon on it, and into a swarm of grasshoppers. They filled the air, covered the pavement, and stung our sweaty skin. Good thing for dark glasses, otherwise they would have bounced off eyeballs, too. I spit a few out of my mouth and firmly clamped my lips shut. Fortunately, none flew up my nose.

Fifty large white boxes dotted a small field. Too late we recognized them as beehives; we closed our mouths and pedaled hard. Like the grasshoppers, bees smacked me and bounced off. My heart raced, and I pushed those pedals hard to escape the swarm. Terry had a sting on his face, but only one. We came out of that one pretty lucky. And now we knew what bee boxes looked like.

Heading east, the hot crosswinds blew from the north, bending grass to my right. My helmet brim obscured my vision, and my helmet shoved itself painfully into my right ear.

It was like the plague: grasshoppers, bees, heat, and wind, one after the other.

The prairie lay before us from the top of a hill. Dark green corn fields grew beside grassy fields of golden yellow. It was a beautiful sight, as long as you weren't looking for shade. The tallest things around were the emerald corn fields, and they were only knee high.

Shade and shadows. I'd been shadow watching all afternoon— my companion on this trip when the sun was shining. My shadow attached me to the ground at my bike tires. On clear mornings, the rising sun painted its first shadow to my west, a giant asphalt version of me.

Shadow watching

My shadow transformed dramatically throughout the day. At times, my shadow could be flattering, showing an elegant silhouette of body, bike, and compact gear, an advertisement for a life well lived. At noon, the shadow took a siesta and was practically gone from sight. Then it would appear in the latter part of the day. With the sun behind me, the shadow could be disconcerting, with a long upper torso and hips that bulged out in a horrifying manner. They weren't really my hips, they were my stuffed panniers, but the sun painted them on the road as my hips. I looked like a traveling freak show.

The small town of Murdo blessed us with a shady campground, an air-conditioned diner, plus jumping an hour forward into the Central Time Zone.

One small step for our watches, one giant leap for our minds.

With a clear night and bright stars, I again marveled at our good fortune to be cycling and camping our way across the states.

Rain woke me during the night, but by 7:30 a.m., the temperature already had climbed into the 70s, and was destined for far higher.

From Murdo, the prairie seemed to stretch forever, its monotony broken only by an occasional tree or lonely farmhouse off in the distance, far from the road and miles from the next one. If a person wanted social interaction, best to move beyond the prairie.

As the sun blasted us, my formerly accursed helmet brim garnered accolades. Without strong wind or steep hills, the brim offered great sun protection for my eyes and neck.

An afternoon of loving my helmet brim

In the distance, a tiny wall of deep, dark shadow rose up. We knew what to do with that – get there as soon as possible. We luxuriated in the shade on someone's driveway. Although technically trespassing, we weren't inclined to leave. How could the owners mind us stealing some shade?

A pickup pulled into the driveway. Busted! A middle-aged man leaned through the open passenger window.

"If you are thirsty, you are welcome to help yourself to water from the pump. It's up by the house and it'll be some nice cold water for you. I can't stay but have some water if you want."

With that, the truck drove to the house. The man went inside, immediately returned, and drove back down the driveway. Waving to us, he turned onto the road and disappeared.

It was a bit surreal. I no longer felt badly about stealing his shade.

Refreshed, we continued east and soon I saw three shapes on the road in the distance. Cyclists? Stray bison? The three shapes drew closer – three young men, loaded for touring, and none of whom wore helmets, although one helmet dangled from some gear. Ah, youth.

Nate, Henry, and Julien were college students on a bike tour two weeks out from Chicago. Ride to Portland, take a left, and end in San Francisco. None of them had done bike touring before – why not start with a couple thousand-mile trip as the first one? It seemed to be working for them. Young and muscular, they cycled about a hundred miles a day. I felt old and slow with our paltry sixty mile a day average.

"It's fun to see you—we haven't seen many other cyclists since we started our trip back in Oregon."

"We saw one other guy yesterday, but we haven't seen many either."

"Was the guy going east?" I asked.

"Yeah. Big blond guy with an accent."

Another Sam sighting. Fun to know Sam was still out there, not far ahead of us.

These guys were sleeker than us. Only one bike had front panniers, but another had a trailer. Thirty years ago, my bike trips looked sleeker, too. I either didn't know about equipment or couldn't afford it, so there was much less to haul.

"You're headed to Portland? That's where we live. Want to stay at our place when you arrive?"

"Sure. That would be great!"

Warmshowers with a twist. Bethany came every other day to

feed our cat and bring in the mail. Hopefully, she would be willing to hang around for a night and host three cyclists.

🚲

We left the prairie grasslands, entering farm country. Grain silos jutted into the air, high enough to give us shade if they'd been nearer.

Hello, Missouri River. It grew in the three weeks since leaving its headwaters back in Montana. Here it was, big and wide, resembling the Columbia River back home. The Mighty Mo.

A big sign advertising *Al's Oasis* in Oacoma lured us in with its promise of air-conditioning. Terry ordered a milkshake, only to be informed the Oasis didn't serve them. An oasis without milkshakes—how could that be?

🚲

"There's a cold front coming in," someone warned us the next morning.

Cold front? Two days before, the temperature here was 106 degrees. What did it mean that a cold front was coming in? We already mailed home our snow clothes – was that a mistake? It was 9 a.m. and already hot and muggy.

A cold front sounded positively delightful.

We sought it, but the morning temperature relentlessly climbed as the hours slowly progressed. Resolutely, we pushed ourselves onward for miles under the blistering sun. We laboriously advanced, while the heat melted our energy and spirits.

Endurance. The very word exhausts me, conjuring up memories of barely hanging in there, from sweltering or freezing mountain climbing trips, to intensely discouraging times of juggling school, work, and unexpected family obligations, and then choosing to quit school because I couldn't do it all. Endurance is always a marathon—sometimes physical, sometimes emotional, and never easy.

It's difficult to endure in challenging circumstances. Endurance is an acquired habit, and the more successful practice one acquires with it, the more likely one will persevere through the challenges. Life teaches lessons, and with multiple decades of lessons behind me, I have incrementally realized the rewards of endurance. Sometimes it keeps me moving, physically or mentally, despite exhaustion and despair. I've learned, however, that sometimes endurance is found in simply letting time move forward, as in times of grief. No matter what the problems are, I have realized that the sun does indeed rise the next day, and gives another chance.

South Dakota was testing our endurance, and giving us more chances, every day.

When our frontage road unexpectedly ended, we sought refuge in the shade of a cemetery as we searched for a route other than the I-90 freeway. My Blackberry didn't give up its secrets, and neither did the dead. Back to the freeway for the next eleven miles.

By the next exit, all we wanted was to escape the sun and savor a cold beverage. Terry tried to get a chocolate milkshake for the third day in a row. Two days earlier, the waitress told him her diner didn't serve milkshakes when they were busy, and she brought him sour milk instead. The next day, we learned the Oasis never serves milkshakes. And this day, Terry ordered a chocolate milkshake, but the waitress brought strawberry instead. At least it was progress. Who knew it was so difficult to get a chocolate milkshake in South Dakota?

"The Midwest is as flat as a pancake."

I've heard that saying a jillion times, sure that people were exaggerating. How could that be? South Dakota turned me into a believer. Sure, some trees poked up, but even a hint of hill or slope became nonexistent.

It didn't last long. Within ten miles, hills and dips returned, and then the trees came back – big green trees surrounding houses and yards. With the open prairie behind us, we entered a new world, like coming into Oz's Emerald City, and entered the green town of Mitchell.

Cycling by the ubiquitous corn fields of eastern South Dakota

Arriving at its campground in 99-degree heat, Terry and I were a dripping, sweaty mess. No camping for us; Terry was all about the air-conditioned cabin.

Good thing Terry wanted a cabin instead of the tent. A storm rolled in, bellowing through the night with lightning and thunder, rain and wind. We would have been floating inside our tent, and probably scared out of our wits. Instead, we stayed warm and cozy inside a dry cabin.

Warm and cozy—those were words I hadn't strung together for a while. Warm and miserable had been more like it. The cold front finally came, dropping the temperature 40 degrees overnight. At 59 degrees outside, I donned long pants, long sleeves, and layers. Crazy.

Passing by a checkerboard world of gold and green, the golden knee-high wheat neighbored with dark green corn fields. Wheat was green back at the Palouse in Washington, but this wheat looked like braids of golden hair, rippling in the wind. Terry and I had a front row seat watching the crops mature as we biked across the land.

The cold front delivered, and so did the rain; we dug deep into our panniers to haul out our neglected rain gear. Lightning flashed in the distance – five Mississippis' worth of distance. That's close enough to be uncomfortable when out on a bicycle surrounded by knee-high vegetation.

With two nights planned in Sioux Falls, we checked in to a big-box hotel chain, promoting ourselves from our usual flea bag motel fare. It was the end of our sixth week, with 2000 miles behind us. From Sioux Falls, we were off to the north.

Slacker Day.

We leisurely roamed through the morning and afternoon.

While cycling through a residential neighborhood towards Falls Park, a Santa Claus look-alike, sans costume, called to us from his porch.

"Would you like some water?"

"Sure! Yes, please!" I called back. Terry and I just ate lunch and we didn't need water, but who were we to pass up an interesting diversion? Santa Claus went inside, returning moments later with bottles of water.

"Here, have a seat here in the shade," he said, handing us water and pointing to chairs on his front lawn. Santa had another name-- Jeff.

Jeff asked the usual questions. As Terry and I told stories, Jeff became increasingly enthusiastic. "You should go by the news station and tell them you're here. They'd love it! You're going to bike right by them on your way to the Falls. I'm going to give them a call and tell them to watch out for you!"

Ten minutes and a wonderful visit later, Terry and I cycled away. We made it to the street corner and stopped.

"Do you want to do the TV thing?" I asked Terry.

"Not really."

"Neither do I."

That was the end of that.

⚛

Until this bike trip, I never gave thought to the name "Sioux Falls" and how the name was derived. But there is a waterfall, and the town is its namesake. Waterfalls in the Pacific Northwest are often high, majestic, and frequently flowing through forests. It's different at Falls Park. The Big Sioux River (which really isn't very big at this point) stair-steps over a series of small falls and flows through an open area of gray and beige rocks. The biggest drop manages only 20 feet, max.

People crowded by the falls, giving the impression of a major spectacle. To Terry and I, used to much grander waterfalls, these falls seemed an odd tourist spot. But as I reconsidered, I realized we had seen neither much water nor elevation while traversing South Dakota, and that this little area with both a flowing river and a drop in elevation was indeed a spectacular sight. Accustomed to tall waterfalls tumbling through old-growth forests, it was time for me to appreciate a waterfall of a different nature.

So much of life is about gaining perspective.

Joining the crowd, we asked a couple of women to take photos of us and our loaded bikes at the falls. They asked questions, and as usual, I happily answered.

"You look healthy," one woman remarked near the end.

"Yeah, I feel healthy, and strong," I added.

How terrific was that, to feel healthy and strong? What a powerful combination. And not only was I feeling healthy and strong, but also content.

South Dakota had been wearing us out with its winds and sun, but all things considered, Terry and I were doing well. The hernia pain that plagued him in Montana and Wyoming was nowhere to be seen in South Dakota. For all the other challenges the state gave us, hernia pain wasn't one of them.

Day after day, I felt strong. My legs displayed a muscled look that didn't exist at the Pacific Ocean six weeks earlier, and they consistently pushed me through the country. A good night's rest replenished energy that depleted during the day, and I began my mornings restored with strength.

Yes, I did feel healthy and strong. And ever so grateful.

Zigging and zagging our way north the next morning, we pursued a patchwork of paved and gravel roads on alternating sides of the I-29 freeway. The gravel road's lumps and bumps definitely were not hernia friendly for Terry, nor for our skinny bike tires. Terry and I were both grumpy about the gravel road--Terry because of its jerkiness, and me because of its slowness. I was in a hurry to get to Brookings.

I didn't know Pastor Russ Stewart of the Brookings United Methodist Church, but I already knew that I liked him.

Five months earlier, our 24-year-old son, Erik, drove from Portland to northern Minnesota and ran into problems on his way. Before leaving Portland, Erik mailed a check to his bank to cover his travel expenses but something happened to his deposit – namely, nothing. He had no money left in his debit card account, and he didn't own a credit card. He borrowed money from Clifton when he passed through Pine Ridge, but by the time Erik made it to Brookings, both money and gas were on fumes. Erik found himself in Brookings at 4 p.m. on a snowy January day with an almost empty gas tank. It was soon to be dark, and Erik was still far from his job at Bemidji, Minnesota.

Erik phoned me and I suggested he find a church, explain his situation, and ask to borrow money to get him to Bemidji. I knew our church in Portland has funds for those kinds of emergencies, and I hoped Erik could find help before his gas ran out. We hung up.

And then I worried. I was already worried about Erik driving alone from Portland to Bemidji in January, and now I had more to worry about.

Erik phoned a couple hours later. He found a church, explained his situation, and was turned down. He then found Brookings United Methodist Church, and was referred to Pastor Russ Stewart. Pastor Russ invited Erik to join the weekly Wednesday night potluck, where Erik ate and talked with friendly folks. One woman was interested in language camps, and picked Erik's brain about Concordia Language Villages in Bemidji. After dinner, Erik talked with university students and discovered a young man who had studied in Norway, as had Erik. Good bye to English, hello to Norwegian.

Pastor Russ invited Erik to spend the night with his friendly, welcoming family. Meanwhile, the snow continued; Erik was grateful not to be stranded in his car. In the morning, Pastor Russ gave Erik gas vouchers and money to get him to Bemidji. Positive and influential, Brookings Methodist church and its pastor gifted Erik with not only food, lodging, and gas, but a huge emotional boost.

Pastor Russ and the Brookings United Methodist Church saved Erik's bacon, and I wanted to meet Pastor Russ to say thank you from one grateful mother. Terry and I knew he wouldn't be there that day, but the website indicated the church office was open until 4:30. We planned to leave a note for Pastor Russ and a donation to the church.

We cycled by a sign for another church, West Nidaros Lutheran Church. Ahh, Nidaros. The famous Nidaros Cathedral in Trondheim, Norway, has many namesakes, including a Norwegian heritage youth camp in Oregon. Camp Nidaros started our family's interest in Norwegian, and was the reason that Terry and I were now headed to Bemidji, Minnesota. Fluent from his year in Norway, Erik was spending his second summer as teacher and counselor at

Skogfjorden (SKOOG-fyord-en), the Norwegian language camp at Concordia Language Villages.

Arriving at the Methodist church in Brookings, Terry and I discovered the office closed that day. Disappointed, I wrote a note to Pastor Russ, wrote a check for giving assistance when people ask for help, and slipped the envelope under the office door.

That still felt great.

The good feeling continued at a burger joint, where Terry finally drank the chocolate milkshake that eluded him for much of South Dakota. Dick, the owner and a triathlete, gave us his card after hearing about our trip.

"You two just give me a call if you need anything," Dick offered as we ate and talked. Terry and I continued to experience such kindness.

We were on a roll. While we registered at Oakwoods Lakes State Park after dinner, the man at the desk noticed our bikes.

"The Bike Fairy has already paid your camping cost for the night," he said.

The Bike Fairy?

Later, I researched the park's information, expecting to read about bikes being free. It didn't say that. Apparently, the Bike Fairy really had paid a visit after all. I'd never heard of the Bike Fairy before, but I immediately became a believer.

I liked the Bike Fairy, and I wanted to be one too.

We awoke to wind and rain, so we just stayed in the tent until the rain stopped. You can do that in South Dakota. If you tried that in Oregon, you might be in your tent for days.

We zipped along the road in an *après storm* bliss. The bliss ended as not only the headwinds returned, but a truck loaded with white bee boxes passed us. I warily watched it, as an accident promised to be a grim experience. I gladly saw the truck disappear from sight.

Beyond Lake Poinsett, the rain clouds disappeared and the heat cranked up. A country store's electric sign advertised *Milk and Guns*. We were definitely in the Midwest.

Cycling towards Summit, our campground destination, I pondered its suspicious sounding name. I need not have worried, as we pedaled on the meekest upgrade through acres of corn. On arrival, we stood only about ten feet higher than the neighboring corn fields. I figured someone with a warped sense of humor named that town.

"We're the highest point between the Appalachians and South Dakota's Black Hills," the camp manager explained to me in the morning.

I stopped snickering, conceding that the name was probably deserved. Still, looking down ten feet to the "valley" below made me smile.

A sweet tailwind pushed us for miles to a commanding view of plains and farmland far below to the east. I felt badly for having scoffed at Summit.

Tailwinds became crosswinds, and crosswinds became headwinds. Terry strained against them all, awakening his hernia pain. When we reached Sisseton, he was more than ready for a motel.

My phone rang.

"Mari, this is Bethany." Our house sitter spoke in a soft voice. "I have some sad news. Karl found Tango lying in the backyard, dead. There wasn't any sign of injury. We don't know why she died."

Sweet, fat Tango – gone. Our previous cat died while Terry and I were on a bike trip, too, several years before. It was a sad homecoming without our cat, and we knew it would be another sad homecoming without Tango.

Terry and I went to bed with heavy hearts. Sleep eluded me.

It was morning, and it was time to shit or get off the pot.

Due to Terry's hernia pain, we managed only 39 miles the previous day, leaving over a hundred miles to get to Moorhead, Minnesota, by day's end. If we were going to see Carl-Martin and his wife Martha, we needed to arrive before evening.

As head of Concordia Language Villages international programs, Carl-Martin was a Big Cheese at CLV. His turf included Hometown Europe and Hometown Brazil, the English language camps in Switzerland and Brazil where I worked for five of the previous six summers. He was heading to Bemidji the next morning, and if I wanted to visit him, Terry and I needed to hoof it to his house that day.

South Dakota had been practically devoid of water between the Badlands and Sioux Falls, but as we traveled north, a plethora of lakes appeared, sparkling in the sunlight. Adjacent to the lakes, corn fields thrived. A week earlier, the South Dakotan corn was knee high, but now it rose above my waist.

South Dakota was a rough state for Terry and me. We entered it with gracious tailwinds from Wyoming, but heat and headwinds bullied us for most of the state. In fact, South Dakota and headwinds were synonymous in my brain.

But the Wind God finally smiled on a day we needed to do a century of miles, and our gentle morning headwind swished around and began pushing us from behind. That tailwind pushed us north, where we excitedly read the greeting from a new road sign:

Welcome to North Dakota – Discover the Spirit.

CHAPTER 8

Tailwinds— North Dakota

Cemeteries punctuated the morning, having passed our fourth one. Old cemeteries are a magnet for me, with the tombstones prompting questions about the lives underneath. With a hundred miles to bike, however, cemeteries weren't on our agenda. We were too busy living to have time for the dead.

A kind tailwind pushed us north until we turned east towards Wahpeton.

Unlike South Dakota, which nearly did us in mentally and physically, our time in North Dakota could only be described as sweet and placid. Granted, our experience with the entire state was limited to four hours and a narrow sliver of its southeastern corner, but it was a marvelous four hours of green land, blue sky, and serenity.

Sometimes life is easy--embrace the tailwinds while you can.

Change is inevitable.

With neither fanfare nor a welcoming sign, we crossed over the Red River into Minnesota.

CHAPTER 9

The Uninvited—
Minnesota

I felt cheated.

No announcement. No welcome. No sign at all to assure us we had made it to Minnesota.

Across the river border, the town of Breckenridge posted other signs: *No Parking, Stop,* and *No Left Turn.* Only the sign on the post office confirmed that we were actually in Minnesota.

Barely a foot of shoulder on northbound Highway 75 separated us from busy traffic and the coarse gravel to our right. The road, in poor condition, forced us to bounce over the choppy pavement. I wondered how long Terry and his hernia would last—we still had another forty-five miles until Moorhead.

The emerald-green farmlands sprouted celery. A canopy of leafy foliage hid the prize underneath. Brazen after stealing so much shade in South Dakota, I helped myself to a celery stalk, too.

We rolled into Moorhead around eight o'clock, completing our 105-mile day. Carl-Martin told us Martha was at a book group.

While unloading my panniers in their garage, I noticed a woman standing on the driveway looking at me. A car idled behind her as she slowly made her way towards me.

"Are you Martha?" I asked.

She looked at me and suddenly grinned.

"Yes, I am Martha," she laughed. "I just came back from a book club meeting. We read *Babette's Feast*, and we just had our own feast, with lots of wine. When I saw you, I couldn't figure things out. I forgot you were coming. I wasn't even sure if I was at the right house. It looked like mine, but with a stranger in my garage."

Martha's friend in the car was a school psychologist and asked her "Do you feel safe?" about going up to her house. Martha had to think about that, but determined she felt safe enough to walk to the garage with her friend watching. Once I introduced myself, she remembered through her fog of wine that Terry and I were coming.

That's how our hostess met me. "Do you feel safe?"

Their daughter was at El Lago del Bosque, Concordia Language Village's Spanish camp. In her room, I saw a paper listing eight languages. English was checked off, and the remaining seven were languages taught at Concordia Language Villages summer camps. I theorized she wanted to study them all. I wanted to do that, too.

I not only showered, but washed clothes and filled my water bottles with bleach to soak overnight. I was going for a total makeover.

⚲

Our night at Carl-Martin and Martha's house was welcoming (once Martha decided I wasn't dangerous), and luxurious. The CLV vibe pulsed stronger.

⚲

First order of the day: bike to Concordia College and the office of Concordia Language Villages. While CLV's camp action primarily occurs in Bemidji, 130 miles away, Concordia College in Moorhead is the mother ship that provides the steam for it all.

The previous summer, CLV celebrated fifty years of language immersion camps. A German professor at Concordia College watched international children play, noticing how quickly they acquired new language. The professor surmised that a language immersion camp, with games, songs, and sports in the foreign language, would be a natural way for language learning. His experimental two-week German immersion camp in 1961 had seventy-five campers, which paved the way for future camps.

The year of our bike trip, CLV offered immersion camps in fifteen languages, with about 4000 annual campers. English is a relatively recent addition, for non-native English speaking children.

Northeast of Bemidji, six "villages" now inhabit shoreline on Turtle River Lake. Each village is architecturally authentic to its language, and most village names translate to "Forest Lake" or "Lake of the Woods." Villages at the lake include German, Norwegian, French, Spanish, Finnish, and Russian.

Having spent five summers with CLV camps, I wanted to see the mothership. Not surprisingly, the CLV main office wasn't camplike at all, other than showcasing great photos from its camps.

Strong crosswinds pummeled us after a leisurely morning of tourist life in Moorhead. Those winds—invisible, and yet so influential. My cursing of the crosswinds brought results. they changed to headwinds.

Evening found us at the Hitterdal tavern, where a man brought his beer and joined us.

"The name's Pickles. What are you folks doin' in these parts?"

We told him.

"I'm 62 an' I been livin' here a long time. It's a good place."

We chatted a while, then Pickles leaned in towards us. "You're gonna pass through the White Earth Indian Reservation. You gotta be careful. You got a gun?"

"No," Terry replied.

"Well, that's too bad. You should have a gun," Pickles admonished.

We biked over 2000 miles without a gun and hadn't missed it yet. I didn't even think about bringing a gun until a month before we started our trip, when someone asked if we were going to bring one. No, hadn't even thought about it. She said she would be afraid to be on a two-person bike trip without one. Really?

Twice more during our fifteen-minute conversation, Pickles repeated that was a mistake not to have a gun, but we didn't ask why. As we left the tavern, Pickles laid it out one more time.

"Yes, I don't want to scare you, but that was a mistake not to bring a gun."

Great. I was nothing but nervous as Terry and I rode to the city park.

The little park looked peaceful enough, with the exception of the strong wind outside the tent, and the anxiety inside. Between the tent flapping and Pickle's warning, sleep didn't come easily. We didn't have a gun, but we did have dog zappers. Sleep with one eye open?

Nope. We closed both eyes and fell into the world of oblivion.

Terry and I were still alive in the morning, as were the headwinds. Pushing hard on the Minnesota flats wasn't an encouraging sign. Neither was Terry's hernia pain, which returned as he laboriously forced himself against the wind.

A man walked towards us on the highway, hauling a cart. Short and skinny, he wore a floppy hat, dirty shorts, and a dirty short sleeve shirt, exposing his tan and weather-beaten skin. With taut muscles, his veins bulged like those of a young man, but he was decades older. Without making eye contact, his eyes went immediately to my front pannier.

"Do you have any pop?" he asked.

"No."

"Are you going to Detroit?" he continued.

"No, I'm going to Bemidji."

"The gophers aren't popping out this morning."

"What?" I asked.

"People pay me for gophers," he said, "but they aren't out today."

This was Larry the Gopher Killer, who was missing front teeth. When he spoke, foamy drool fell to the asphalt with a remarkable plop. Friendly and simple.

"On a good day, I can trap two gophers, ja." He spoke with a little intake of air at the end, giving hint of Scandinavian roots.

Larry pointed inside his cart to an array of metal contraptions with sharp prongs and chains.

"What do people do with the gophers? Do they eat them?" I asked.

"Oh no, I just kill them, *ja*."

"No, what do the people who buy your gophers do with them? Do they eat them?"

"Oh, no, *ja*".

He never did tell me what people did with them, and I wondered about the going rate for dead gophers. Larry stood with his gopher traps and cart, with a puddle of white foamy drool at his feet.

"Well, good luck to you," I said as I pedaled away.

That gave me something to think about.

Terry and I stopped at the Two Inlets Country Store to buy food and investigate camping options.

"There aren't campgrounds nearby on paved roads," the owner confirmed. "If you'd like, you could pitch your tent for free in our backyard and spend the night there. There's a cottage in the back and you could use the bathroom there."

Wow, what a gracious offer.

With our tent pitched in Lou and Tim's big, park-like backyard, Terry and I lazily lay on the grass under a starry sky and beautiful moon, listening to the night sounds.

The end of our seventh week, we had over 2500 miles behind us, and were two days away from Skogfjorden.

🚲

Terry and I ate inside the grocery store the next morning.

"Did you hear our dog barking during the night?" Lou asked.

"Yeah, we did," I answered.

"There might have been a black bear around. There was one in our backyard a couple weeks ago but I didn't tell you about it because I didn't want to scare you. I didn't think it would be a problem. But since our dog was barking last night, maybe the bear came back."

Ahhhh.

Bear or no bear, we were grateful to Lou and Tim for the hospitality of their backyard, and grateful that we didn't know about a bear during the middle of the night. Whoever said ignorance is bliss had that one right.

🚲

"Hey Mom! Where are you now?" Erik asked through the phone.

"Almost to Lake Itasca!"

"Cool! People are excited that you're coming. What names do you want on your name tags? Someone artistic is going to make you and Dad each a cool looking *navneskilt*."

"Wow, that's great!"

Everyone at Skogfjorden picks a Norwegian name and wears a name tag. A cool looking *navneskilt*? I relished that thought. My artistic skills are nonexistent, and my name tags usually look like they've been made by a kindergartner.

"I don't know," I mused. "Who should I be? When I was a nurse at Skogfjorden, I was Mari, but I've been Parsley at Hometown. How do you say "parsley" in Norwegian?"

"I'll find out. Do you want Parsley *på norsk* if it's a good one?"

"Sure."

"Does Dad want to be Terje?" That was Terry's name at Camp Nidaros.

Ja, sure, Terry wanted to be Terje again.

"Dad will be sleeping in my cabin and you'll be in one of the girls' cabins."

Right in the thick of things-- exactly where I wanted to be.

"Okay, I gotta go. Be here by 9:30 tomorrow morning, in time for *Allsang*," he said. "*Jeg elsker deg! Ha det!*" I love you. Bye.

At Itasca State Park, Terry and I ditched our bikes to walk across the (faux) Mississippi Headwaters. A camp friend, Webster, reports the genuine headwaters are upstream in a marsh, and the faux site was created to keep people from tramping through the real thing.

It still worked for me.

Terry and I gingerly followed people walking on large, slippery rocks, and a minute later, we'd walked across the Mississippi River. Since starting our trip, we'd been at the mouth of the Columbia and the headwaters of the Missouri and Mississippi—all legendary rivers.

The river's Native American name is *Misi-ziibi*, meaning Great River, but it really didn't look so great on its way to Bemidji. Barely five feet wide in many places, it looked insignificant, but it was just gearing up for its 2500-mile journey to the Gulf of Mexico.

Five miles from Bemidji, we stopped to steal someone's shade. A few minutes later, a woman and a young girl brought two water bottles from their house.

"My daughter saw you and thought you would probably like some water on this hot day," the woman said. The girl hid behind her mother's legs and peeked out at us.

"Wow, yes, you are right. It is hot and we would love some water. That is so thoughtful of you." I knelt down to the girl's level. "What's your name?"

"Aubrey," she whispered.

"How old are you, Aubrey?"

"Seven."

"Well, Aubrey, thank you very much. You are very kind. This water is just what we need to give us more energy for our biking."

Aubrey smiled shyly and squirmed behind her mother.

"Enjoy the water," the mom said.

"Thank you!" we called out as Aubrey and her mom walked back to the house hand in hand.

Aubrey may have been shy, but she knew how to help someone on a hot day. Once again, our bodies were nurtured and our spirits boosted by a someone's unexpected kindness. I loved it that a seven-year-old suggested to her mom that we be offered water. That mom was raising that girl up right.

Camp reunion with Webster! With bikes parked near our patio table, a restaurant staff member plied us with questions.

"I'm so impressed with what you've done," she said before heading back into the restaurant.

A warm brownie with hot fudge and ice cream unexpectedly appeared after diner, compliments of the manager, the one who inquired about our trip. Gifts of water from Aubrey and dessert from the restaurant manager—such kind surprises.

Surprises happen. They're on the menu for a long bike trip, but you never know what you'll be served, or when. Good surprises? They're delicious, welcome, and are some of the joys of bike touring. Bad surprises? They're like mushrooms, which I try to avoid, but they often show up anyway, in either small or large pieces. For mushrooms, I prefer big ones because they're easier to eliminate. For bad surprises, I prefer little ones. Usually, however, I have no say in the size of either mushrooms or bad surprises.

Our panniers were laden with gear for all kinds of surprises. We had clothes for heat, cold, rain, and snow, tubes and tools for flat tires, first aid kits for injuries. My umbrella could protect me under a beating sun or in a pouring rain.

The contents of our panniers could fix a lot of surprises... but as we soon discovered, not all of them.

Terry and I worked off our dinner with a sunset bike ride around Lake Bemidji to the state park campground. Only seven miles from *Skogfjorden*, excitement reigned.

Allsang would begin at 9:30 a.m. I wanted to surprise Erik early, so we rolled out at 7:30 to begin our seven-mile trip.

Ten minutes later on shoulderless Highway 20, a car sped past me with only two feet to spare. I've never had a speeding car that close, and it frightened me. Terry shouted, and I thought it was because of the close call.

I thought it was all about me, but it turned out to be all about Terry.

I spun around as Terry slowly arose from the ground, limping, shouting, and swearing. Two panniers lay several feet away from his overturned bike. The speeding car still sped away.

"I think I was hit!" Terry panted between shouting and swearing.

A car stopped behind us, and my first thought was to ask the driver to follow the speeding car and get a license plate number. I thought this was a hit and run. Up ahead, though, I saw that the car pulled over.

"I saw that car hit you," the driver said.

"Are you hurt?" I asked Terry.

"My elbow," Terry grunted, holding his left arm. He shuffled off the road and sat down on the grass. I took his pulse and began assessing for damages. Meanwhile, the car reversed, parked, and the driver approached. He was a young man, shaken and stuttering.

"I-I didn't see you. I-I was watching the oncoming traffic. I-I'm sorry for the accident."

I returned to my bike to get paper and pen, and the witness driver drove away, telling Terry he needed to get his son to a sports practice. Unfortunately, our one witness left before any contact information could be obtained.

Tim, age 33, was a local.

"My parents own a mechanic business and can fix your bike. I'll pay for anything," he told us.

Terry lay down. Pain radiated from his left elbow and his upper arm. Nothing bled or looked disfigured and he moved his left arm gingerly. He winced and cried out when I pressed on his arm. Fortunately, his long sleeve shirt and long pants prevented painful road rash.

"We were so close to camp," he said, cradling his arm.

"I can drive you to your camp," Tim offered.

"No, no, no!" my brain screamed. We didn't bike all that way just to be driven in someone's car for the last seven miles to *Skogfjorden*. My brain screamed, but the rest of me stayed silent.

"That would be good," Terry responded.

Crap, no!

"How about if you take some ibuprofen and let's wait twenty minutes to see how you're feeling." I didn't want Terry to give in yet.

Terry took three ibuprofen, laid on the grass, and we waited. No one said much. Tim occasionally repeat his assertion, "I didn't see you." Terry rested with his eyes closed, Tim looked uncomfortable, and I remained quietly agitated. I hoped that a little rest would do the trick.

Twenty minutes passed.

"How are you feeling now?" I asked.

"Better. I'm feeling okay enough to bike in to camp."

Those were golden words and a big relief.

With one last apology for hitting Terry, Tim drove off. With Tim gone, Terry and I could freely talk about what happened. Tim had repeatedly said he didn't see Terry. With the highway speed of 55 miles per hour, this accident could have been so much worse.

Attempting to load Terry's fallen panniers back on his bike, I discovered their attachments were gone. I jerry-rigged one pannier to Terry's bike, and added his second to my already big pile of stuff behind my seat.

It appeared Tim's car plowed into the rear left pannier, completely shearing both left panniers off the bike.

Terry's bike was now lopsided with uneven weight distribution, increasing his challenge of biking with a painful left arm. At 8:30 a.m., he set off in the lead, still with six miles of the shoulderless highway to maneuver before turning off for another mile to Concordia Language Villages.

Seven miles to contemplate the *what ifs*. It was easy imagining this scenario leaving Terry gravely injured or dead. It could have wiped us both out, since the car came so close to me, too.

Slowly cycling, we finally arrived at *Skogfjorden's* entrance. Erik! It was 9:15. Erik expected us by 9:30, and came out to greet us.

Erik looked casual and campy, wearing a huge smile. We hadn't seen him in five months, and his hair had grown – not so much down, but certainly out. Planning to donate his hair for wigs for children who have lost hair to cancer, his head was a mass of burgeoning curls.

With hugs and news of Terry's accident, ours was a happy and sobering reunion all rolled into one.

"Here is your *navneskilt*," Erik said, handing us beautiful wooden name tags on a looped string. "Dina made these for you."

I had never seen such amazing name tags, beautifully decorated by a wood burning pen and a skilled hand. "Terje" lay next to a burnt silhouette of a man riding a bike—a man carrying a pair of skis on his back while he rode his bike. Brilliant.

My name tag showed "Mari" outlined over parsley leaves.

"Mom, Dina is making you another name tag that says *Pernille*, the Norwegian word for parsley."

I hung my beautiful name tag around my neck, now an official part of the *Skogfjorden* community.

Tove, dean of *Skogfjorden*, came to greet us and meet Terry. Petite, blonde, and welcoming, Tove looked more like a high school camper herself than a dean with over twenty-five years' experience of directing *Skogfjorden*.

Terry, on the other hand, looked pale and pained as he sat against a wall ten minutes later. He certainly didn't look like a guest of honor – more like something the cat dragged in. Tove, Erik, and other musicians stood in front, while campers gathered and sat on the concrete slab. I sat near our bikes, filled with a mix of excitement and anxiety as *Allsang* gradually took shape.

Allsang is *Skogfjorden*'s singing time, my favorite part of camp. Some songs are goofy, some are tender, some are loud, some are quiet. Normally, *Allsang* fills me with joy, but my brain was stuck on auto-loop, continuously replaying the morning's sobering events.

Meanwhile, Tove lead a song about the stomach—one of the goofy songs. After a rousing time singing about stomach life, Tove stretched out her arm towards Terry and me.

"*Vi har gjester med oss, Mari og Terje, mammaen og pappaen til Hans Erik.*" We have guests with us, Mari and Terry, the mama and papa of Hans Erik.

My turn next. Speaking in my elementary Norwegian, I pointed to our bikes, saying we came from the Pacific Ocean (I had to get help from Tove with that name – *Stillehavet)*, cycling over 2600 miles. I kept it nice and short, saying nothing about the bike accident. I could see some campers' eyes get big at the mention of biking 2600 miles--those were the campers whose Norwegian was good enough to understand big numbers. People clapped and wah-hoo'ed while Erik nodded and grinned. I felt good.

Tove reviewed the song *Du Er Den Fineste,* You Are the Finest, one of my favorite songs. Tove and camp sang the first verse to Terry and me. I was touched. It reminded me of Camp Nidaros days, when staff and campers would dedicate that song to our directors. That would make them cry, and I wasn't far from crying myself as *Skogfjorden* sang to us.

As a parent, there's nothing like seeing your offspring thrive. Erik thrived at *Skogfjorden,* playing his guitar, singing, making goofy faces at campers and smiling broadly at Terry and me. We sang a song with a short waltz as its refrain; everyone jumped up, grabbed someone, and waltzed for ten seconds between the many verses. Erik ran over to me for a waltz, his guitar hanging from his back by the strap. Waltzing with Erik was always good – we had been waltzing together since he was three years old.

I waltzed with Tove, counselors, and campers. Terry did one waltz, and then stayed fixed to the ground, protective of his arm and looking wan.

After *Allsang,* Terry and I strategized a game plan. Reluctantly leaving Erik's folkdance activity midway through, I waited with Terry while he spoke on the phone with Tim's insurance company.

"Hey, Bob!" I shouted as someone bicycled near.

Bob did a double take. "Hey, Parsley!"

A Brazilian, Bob and I knew each other from working at Hometown Brazil, CLV's English language camp near São Paulo, Brazil. This summer, Bob was driving for all the lakeside camps, and all CLV staff who weren't tied to one particular camp ate lunch at *Skogfjorden* an hour before the campers. Perfect—we could eat and visit with Bob, then focus on Terry's painful arm.

Linda, CLV's head honcho for healthcare, spied us at lunch. I worked under Linda's direction for portions of five of the six previous years while I was the healthcare provider for Hometown Europe and Hometown Brazil. Not licensed to practice nursing outside of the United States, CLV's solution was to call me a *healthcare provider* and leave the licensure out it. I loved my blended roles at Hometown teaching English, leading programs, being a counselor, and doing healthcare.

"Mari!" Linda's big smile and open arms embraced me. "Welcome!"

Bingo—I happily visited with two CLV friends right off the bat. Unlike me, Terry didn't have a great lunch. Painful, not hungry for once, and uninterested in socializing with people he didn't know, he just wanted to get to the urgent care clinic.

Terry wasn't the only one needing urgent care—so did his bike and saddle bags. I loaded up and drove us to Bemidji in Erik's car. After seven weeks on the bike, I was impressed that I still remembered how to drive.

I mused that my first afternoon at camp wasn't turning out to even be at camp. How different things were than I anticipated. When Terry and I left our campground that morning, my only concern was hoping we wouldn't get a flat tire, delaying our arrival time for *Allsang*. I didn't think about cars speeding by and clipping one of us.

Arriving at urgent care, a physician's assistant listened about our bike trip and Terry being hit. Terry went off for an X-ray, returned, and soon the physician's assistant returned, too.

"I have bad news," she gently said. "Terry has a hairline fracture near the elbow. This will require six weeks in a sling." She looked at us and paused. "This is the end of your bike trip."

My gut twisted.

Silence.

A broken arm for Terry. A broken dream for me.

My brain blew apart while she gave instructions.

Terry and I walked out in silence.

Our first day at Skogfjorden. Our last day of the bike trip. Neither one turned out the way I anticipated.

But there was nothing we could do. After fifty-one days and over 2600 miles on our bikes, our bike trip had come to an abrupt and painful end.

CHAPTER 10

Processing— Skogfjorden

We left urgent care and moved on to the orthopedic clinic. We said little while Terry was outfitted with a sling. We said little while getting Vicodin from the pharmacy. We had nothing good to say. The threatening question of "What now?" roared in my head, but I wasn't ready to let it out.

Back at the car, I finally spoke.

"Let's finish this trip sometime when we can." That was the most I could muster without bursting into tears.

"Yeah, I want that, too," Terry replied. He wasn't too chatty either.

My words were more optimistic than I felt. Dance and band commitments for the Oktoberfest season already filled our calendars, and I had already given a verbal commitment for camp in Switzerland the following summer. Waiting two years to complete our bike trip seemed pointless; too many unknowns between now and then. No version of my three-decade-old dream of cycling cross-country included stopping halfway.

Terry downed his Vicodin. As long as he didn't move his arm, he had no pain. Little movements caused a little pain; big movements caused big pain. The physician's assistant told us that with a radial head hairline fracture, the treatment of choice is a sling that still allows some movement, versus a cast that completely immobilizes the arm.

Next stop, urgent care for Terry's bike. Although the urgency was now gone, it made sense to get repairs done and billed to Tim's insurance.

Silence filled our drive back to *Skogfjorden.* "What now?" I repeatedly asked myself.

We found Erik and Tove in the staff office during a break. They looked at us expectantly.

"Terry's arm is broken. Our bike trip is over," I said quietly.

The tears that had been dammed began to flow. Erik enveloped me in a long hug while I cried. After Erik and I finally released each other, I had a long hug with Tove while I cried some more.

"You are welcome to stay here as long as you want," Tove gently told us. I couldn't speak through the tears, but I knew that *Skogfjorden* was a good place for our healing to begin. With Tove's open invitation, that just made me cry some more.

More staff hugged us, my tears momentarily quelled, and someone asked the Big Question: "What are you going to do?"

I shook my head and looked at Terry.

"We don't know; we haven't talked about it yet."

What were we going to do? We had a rental mini-van reserved in Portland, Maine for an August 11th pick up, six weeks away. So much for that. Now we needed something to get us home from Minnesota.

Just the day before, Terry and I learned we would be in the campers' cabins. To be in a *hytta* was unexpected and happy news. I'd get to spend more time with campers and staff, which I wanted. This would be my first summer in 15 years to miss camp, trading it for our long-awaited bike adventure.

But that was yesterday. Everything changed since then. We had so many decisions to make, and noisy, laughing campers were the last thing I wanted. I worried that I wouldn't be able to keep my tears in check. Terry's broken arm meant he would need some help. Staying in a *hytta* with campers suddenly felt intrusive and wrong.

I left Terry to his own thoughts as I rode my bike through camp. A cabin nestled in the woods above the lake, where a dozen towels and bits of bikinis hung over the rails of the large deck. My new home.

"Hello?"

Nobody answered. All the campers were at their language classes. I had the place to myself.

The clutter of teenage girls and their counselors littered the table, and shoes were strewn all over the floor. Three little side rooms hosted bunk beds, with clothes casually tossed everywhere.

I took the cabin's one empty bunk. As I unloaded gear, I heard voices from the doorway.

"*Hei!*"

"*Velkommen til Bodø!*" Welcome to Bodø.

"Wow, it's just amazing that you rode your bikes from Oregon!"

The campers returned. They introduced themselves, chatted with each other and me, and I felt my spirits rising.

My spirits sank again by dinner, my head spinning with a constant barrage of thoughts. Terry still looked wan. The sling kept his left arm captive, impairing his ability to cut food. It didn't matter much; neither of us were hungry.

People asked about our trip, not knowing that Terry's arm was broken and our bike trip was over. Only hours before, we arrived as bike sojourners, but now, what were we? Frauds? It was all so new and raw.

As news of Terry's broken arm circulated the room, the questions changed.

"What are you going to do now?"

"We'll get a rental car and drive home." That much we knew. Terry wanted his hernia surgery and to start recovering.

Dinner concluded with singing *Takk for Maten*, Thanks for

the Food, to the cooks, who shouted back from the kitchen *Vel Bekomme,* You're Welcome. Outside, a few campers lowered the flag while everyone sang *Aftensolen Smiler,* The Evening Sun Smiles, a quiet song about the evening sun and nature resting in sacred peace.

There was no sacred peace for me.

But camp activities continued, this time with a troll wedding. Under normal circumstances, a troll wedding would be just the fun I had been anticipating at *Skogfjorden.* But with Terry's fatigue and pain, he just wanted to escape to his *hytta.* I was conflicted. Should I join the fun, or send out e-mails?

In the end, I did neither.

Bob returned, snagging a late dinner. We talked for more than an hour. His smile, teasing, and sense of humor was a balm for my worried mind.

I returned to the *hytta* in time for *En God Ting,* One Good Thing. After each person told about her favorite part of the day, I told about Terry's broken arm and the end of our bike trip. That definitely was not my *En God Ting.* I did have *En God Ting,* though, and it was just to be at *Skogfjorden* and to be with Hans Erik (Erik). I barely made it through without crying.

Erik arrived just before bedtime, and we talked on the darkened steps for an hour. The mournful song of the loons rippled across the lake, matching my mood.

Sadness eclipsed everything. With tears never far from the surface, I managed to smile, sing, dance, and converse my way through the day, all the while dragging my invisible anchor behind me. After Erik left, I wandered into the woods and cried, cried, cried. The grief was enormous.

But I was thankful, too. If our bike trip had to abruptly end somewhere other than the Atlantic Ocean, we couldn't have picked a better place than *Skogfjorden.*

Just to be at *Skogfjorden* was *En God Ting.*

I awoke at 4 a.m. with that familiar flash of excitement to bike and cover our next quota of miles. For fifty-one days I'd done that, but then I remembered, and the flash dissolved into the bitter, bleak reality of the broken dream.

In the dark *hytta*, I groped through my panniers for clothes, brushing against items I no longer needed: spare tubes and that damn sun brim for my helmet. It was a kick in the gut.

I walked through woods and found a quiet room in which to write. Before breakfast, I joined camp at the flag pole for flag raising and the Norwegian national anthem.

Terry stood on the side, protecting his arm and looking less pale than the previous day.

"How are you?" I asked.

"Okay. Sometimes there's a lot of pain, but most of the time it feels okay. I loaded up on Vicodin last night, crawled into my sleeping bag, and tried not to move."

For Terry, life was in slow motion-- slow motion shower, shave, and dressing. A camper tied Terry's shoe laces for him.

"The *hytta* boys are very friendly and helpful," he said. "It's a nice group. I managed to put deodorant under my left arm, but I didn't want to ask anybody to put it under my right arm. I can't reach that with my good hand." That was good to know – best to sit on Terry's left side rather than his right.

Déjà vu of *Allsang* for a second day; I still felt disconnected while we sang. While Tove masterfully taught in Norwegian, using pictures, gestures, and simple vocabulary, my mind drifted back to our shattered trip and Terry's broken arm. I considered a variety of options, none of which I liked. The only plan I did like was the one before the car hit Terry.

All the other possibilities were crap.

We had instructions to make an appointment with an orthopedist in a week, but we didn't know where we would be. Originally, we planned to stay at *Skogfjorden* for two or three days. Should we stay in Bemidji and see an orthopedist there? Should we hit the road, guess where we'd be, and try to get a referral for somewhere in a week?

Terry also wanted his hernia surgery done so he could recover before our Oktoberfest dance season. Hopefully, he could recover from the hernia surgery and the broken arm at the same time.

We needed a car and were in luck; we could rent a van from Bemidji to Portland.

I wandered to the lake and stared at the still waters until I grew weary of staring and moping. I returned to the *hytta's* deck, where girls sang and played guitar during their break. I joined in with harmony, feeling welcomed and included--much better than staring and moping at the lake.

Terry and I headed to Erik's language class as guest speakers. On our way, Dina gave me a second wood-burnt name tag, inscribed with *Pernille*, and a drawing of a woman playing the accordion. What a work of art. I couldn't decide which name tag to choose, so I wore them both.

Our fabulous *Skogfjorden* nametags

Spreading out our U.S. map, we told stories of our trip. We told of dipping rear tires in the Pacific, and how we'd hoped to dip front ones in the Atlantic. We told of Yellowstone, and of blizzards, wind, and sun. We told of kindness. We told of the car accident, Terry's broken arm, and the end of the bike trip.

The phrase *bucket list* came up and Erik asked everyone to share their bucket lists. One boy wanted to go to the deepest part of the ocean and also climb Mount Everest—visit the lowest and the highest places on earth.

Number one on my bucket list was to finish our cross-country bike trip.

As class ended, I realized I was energized by their questions, and that I enjoyed talking about our trip. I wasn't threatened by tears every minute. Healing was starting.

Terry loaded up on more Vicodin.

"You now have a daughter, Ann." Erik crouched beside us at lunch, whispering his secret. "She's another counselor and we say we're brother and sister." Without another word, he vanished as quickly as he appeared.

Thirty seconds later, a camper approached our table.

"Is Ann really your daughter?" he asked me.

"Oh, yes," I replied.

The boy looked at Terry.

"*Det stemmer,*" Terry said. That's right.

"Are you pulling my leg?" the boy asked.

"No!" I lied, keeping a straight face.

The boy went back to Erik's table and exclaimed "It's true! They are brother and sister!"

It was a good thing the boy didn't ask any questions about Ann, like "When is her birthday?" We had no clue *who* Ann was, much less when she was born.

Erik introduced us after lunch. Ann and Erik both had curly hair, impish expressions, and played musical instruments. Apparently, that was enough to be brother and sister.

"I told that boy that you don't like Ann," Erik told Terry and me. "That's why you didn't acknowledge her yesterday when you arrived and were introduced at *Allsang*."

Oh no – that was harsh.

"Yeah, she's the daughter we never talk about," I said. Classic camp. Create a camp world that may or may not reflect the real world. But I was happy to have a daughter.

Afternoon came and went with activities, free time, and language classes for *Skogfjorden*, but I wrote and mused.

Erik skipped *Skogfjorden's* evening program and we drove to Bemidji, spending the evening with Eddy, the leader of the year-round German and environmental programs. Erik was Eddy's sidekick and German intern for the previous five months.

Webster joined us, along with Martin and Lisa. Martin was another CLV Big Cheese, in charge of the year-round language programs. Martin and Lisa's son co-counseled with Erik in their *hytta,* and their nephew and Erik worked together the previous summer. The stories were flying.

What an evening of laughter and stories. What a great group of people. I felt fortunate to be associated with all of them and with CLV.

We returned late to *Skogfjorden*. Once again, I was alone in the dark. The night before, I disappeared into the woods to bare my soul and release my tears. This night was different. I felt buoyed by the spirits of my CLV friends, and it was clear that the abrupt end of Terry's and my bike trip couldn't steal the joy I felt being surrounded by community.

Yes, healing was happening.

I woke up early with that familiar flash of excitement to get on the bikes. "Wake up!" my mind shouted. "You're on your bike trip!"

Except that I no longer was.

I lay on my dark bunk for an hour, listening to the call of the loons. It was a haunting call whose pitch started low and climbed high, like the howl of lonely dogs.

But some of the despair was gone, thanks to the energy from Eddy's gathering. Remarkable people, whose creativity and passion for learning flowed through CLV, and flowed into me. I felt welcomed, loved, and inspired.

If Terry's accident had happened on a desolate road, our trip might have ended alone at a flea bag motel. Things could have felt a lot worse. Things could have *been* a lot worse. Terry could have died.

I reflected on what we accomplished. We biked over 2600 miles from the Pacific Ocean to Minnesota. Seven weeks of adventures on our bikes. We came through snow, rain, wind, and heat, and met some marvelous people along the way.

We saw amazing places: Yellowstone, the Badlands, the Lewis and Clark Caverns. We watched the country turn from forested land at the mouth of the Columbia River to open, dry farmland. We crossed the Rocky Mountains, witnessed the wonders of geysers and mud pots, discovered the red rocks of Wyoming, and crossed the plains and prairies of South Dakota to arrive at the lakes and woods of Minnesota.

We experienced kindness and generosity from so many people, both people we knew before and strangers we met along the way.

We experienced excitement, enthusiasm, weariness, frustration, disappointment, and through it all, persistence.

We saw and experienced all of that from our bikes, up close and personal. Our trip from the Pacific to Minnesota was a worthy adventure, and it deserved a celebration.

I wanted to celebrate what Terry and I did accomplish, and not just turn our backs on what we didn't.

What I really wanted was to stick to Terry's and my original route and continue to southern Ontario, Canada, to see my cousin Jody. And if we saw Jody and David, we might as well keep going to Niagara Falls. And if we went to Niagara Falls, we might as well keep going to the Atlantic Ocean. It wouldn't take that long, and we could still return to Portland with time for Terry's hernia surgery.

I liked the shape of this plan.

But when to finish the bike trip? Terry's arm needed six weeks in the sling. That would take him to mid-August, and then in mid-September we would start our Oktoberfest dance and music commitments. If we waited until after our Oktoberfest season, we'd resume our bike ride in northern Minnesota in mid-October, finishing in November on the east coast. Could be tricky timing for weather, or it might be okay.

I listened to the loons. Optimism grew.

I quietly left the *hytta* and walked to the lake, continuing my planning and writing.

Terry looked and felt better at breakfast. I told him my idea, which turned out to be an easier sell job than I expected. I asked Erik about having an all-camp tire dipping ceremony at the lake. He liked the idea.

We caught Tove. I told her that I spent my early morning listening to the loons and thinking. She was immediately supportive of the idea. I don't know if she actually thought it was a good idea, or if she was supportive because I cried as I spoke. At any rate, she suggested doing the tire dip during the camp's mid-afternoon break, and said she wanted to say something at the ceremony.

Our bike trip ended at *Skogfjorden,* and it felt right to include the whole *Skogfjorden* community in the ceremony. We could teach campers about the tradition of tire dipping, as well as teach that Terry and I were celebrating what we did accomplish, even though the ending turned out differently than we hoped.

I walked five minutes to Linda's house to borrow her accordion and found her at home. I flopped in a chair, telling her about Terry's hairline fracture and the end of our bike trip. The fracture diagnosis was no surprise to her. We talked about the old plan and the new.

Linda fed my soul. I left her house with not only a heavy accordion, but also with a lighter spirit, excited for the upcoming tire-dipping ceremony. A trip to the bike shop netted Terry's bike.

We parked our bikes and bodies at the lakeside firepit, joined by a hundred campers and staff. Tove motioned Terry, Erik, and me to stand.

"We've gathered here for a ceremony to celebrate with Mari Pernille and Terje."

Presumably, the English was for Terry's and my benefit, since *Skogfjorden* normally operates in Norwegian. I was glad for the English; it was our ceremony, and if part of it was in English, we could at least understand more of it. Tove motioned for us to take over.

Terry started out in Norwegian, made it through a few sentences, then switched to English.

"There's a tradition among cyclists who are doing cross country trips to dip their back tires in the ocean where they start, and then dip their front tires in the next ocean when they get there. Mari and I started our bike trip on May 10th at the Pacific Ocean, and we stood in the ocean and dipped our rear tires. We were planning to bike from the Pacific to the Atlantic, and were planning to dip our front tires in the Atlantic. But the first part of our bike trip ended here at *Skogfjorden*, and we'll dip our front tires here at the lake. We'll come back in October, dip our back tires, and start the second part of our trip, to the Atlantic Ocean. When we get to the Atlantic, we'll dip our front tires there."

Terry turned it over to me.

I took the easy way out. *"Jeg skal snakker på engelsk."* I shall speak in English. "When we arrived two days ago, most of you didn't know that Terje was hit by a car on our way to *Skogfjorden* that morning. He was in a lot of pain when we arrived for *Allsang,* and we didn't know until that afternoon that Terry's arm had actually been broken. We were seven miles from *Skogfjorden* when he was hit by the car, and he rode his bike those seven miles with a broken arm."

The camp burst into applause and whistling. Terje the Biking Viking, riding into *Skogfjorden* with a broken arm.

"Because of Terje's broken arm," I continued, "Part One of our bike trip is over. We want *Skogfjorden* to celebrate with us the completion of over 2600 miles from the Pacific Ocean to *Skogfjorden*." I cut it off because I was going to cry.

Erik saved me and called out in Norwegian, "Come down to the water, everyone!"

Erik and I rolled the bikes to the water's edge, lifted them to our shoulders, and carried them five feet out into the lake. Terry walked out with us. Tove stood on the dock and the rest of *Skogfjorden* gathered on the sandy shore. Terry, Erik, and I stood and faced campers and staff.

"*En, to, tre!*" One, two, three! Erik and I lowered the front of the bikes to dip the front tires in the water.

Terry, me, and Erik dipping front tires in Turtle River
Lake, *Skogfjorden*, near Bemidji, Minnesota

Unbeknownst to Terry and me, Tove created a certificate for us, which she read in Norwegian and English as she stood out on the swimming dock:

> *With this diploma we mark Mari Pernille and Terje's bicycle arrival to Kilden – generally known as Mjøsa and Turtle River Lake, near a geologic and metaphoric phenomenon at the Laurentian Continental Divide.*

Mari Pernille and Terje started at the Pacific Ocean, and here they stopped at Kilden in northern Minnesota. Kilden lies near the northern Continental Divide. From here water runs in three different directions: Towards Hudson's Bay 1900 miles north, towards the Gulf of Mexico 3200 miles south, and towards the Atlantic Ocean and half the continent to the east.

Before arriving here, Mari Pernille and Terje bicycled 51 days from Portland, Oregon. Here was a heartfelt reunion with their dear son, Hans Erik. In addition, here they were received by their big and admiring CLV family.

Mari Pernille and Terje stand here today to mark a personal crossroad. The loons whispered in their ears after they arrived, and together they decided to dip their bike tires in Lake Mjøsa to end Part I of their journey. In one respect, they mark that they have completed the water which runs behind them towards the Pacific Ocean.

They will start Part II of their tour at a later opportunity when the loons take to wings and leave from here. At that time the loons will follow the wind, and Mari Pernille and Terje will follow the water which runs towards the east. At that time, they will leave again towards their final destination to Portland, Maine—a place at the awaited Atlantic Ocean which whispers their names even more.

With this diploma we note that it is life's journey as much as life's destination which counts. Surprises come. Plans change. Follow the heart. Listen to what whispers your name.

Once again, tears filled my eyes and my voice was stilled. There was nothing left to say. Tove had said it all and said it so elegantly. I was glad to be right where I was, holding my bike out in the water with Terry and Erik, and in the company of Tove, and our big CLV family. We were so lucky to be at *Skogfjorden*.

Erik, Terry, me, and Tove at *Skogfjorden*

Terry napped in his *hytta* while *Skogfjorden* played, and I practiced the accordion in the sunshine.

As evening descended, we made our way to vespers. A counselor stood by the forest path, with fingers to his lips. He allowed one person at a time to enter in silence, quietly walking through the silent forest to *Bukkesjoen*, Buck Lake.

I've spent many hours hiking with a knapsack or backpack, but a silent hike with an accordion on my back was a new experience. I felt like a minstrel from centuries past.

The path opened to a spacious forest canopy. Much of camp was already there, in small groups or as individuals, spread out and sitting on the ground. I felt conspicuous with the accordion, but now there was no turning back on my decision to play.

We sat quietly in the forest until Tove's voice broke the silence. I couldn't see her; she spoke for several minutes and then there was silence again. Two people stood, read a poem, and sat. More silence, and then a counselor played the guitar and sang. Silence.

I hoisted the accordion to my shoulders while the girls from my *hytta* smiled and gave me a thumbs up.

I began playing *Emma*, a hauntingly beautiful Swedish waltz. I played it without screwing up, much to my relief. I ended the waltz, froze in place so as to not disturb the new silence, and the trio of my *hytta* girls gave me another thumbs up. Others nodded and smiled. I quietly set the accordion at my feet.

Sounds of a cello wafted through the woods.

The tranquility of vespers enveloped me, my day, my week, my journey. Once again, I felt healing occurring within me, gradual and invisible. There was no doubt about it. Terry and I were fortunate to be where we were.

🚲

As usual, I awoke with the familiar flash, which immediately changed to the somber reality. Today was the day Terry and I would have left *Skogfjorden* on our bikes. It wasn't going to happen that way.

Again, the loons whispered my name. I lay on my bunk, listening.

🚲

As lunch ended, Terry and I stood.

"*Mange takk for alt,*" I started. "Thank you for being so welcoming to Terje and me. We felt welcomed into your *hytter*, classes, and activities. You made some tough days for us easier with your welcome and support. You already know what a special place *Skogfjorden* is, and it is all of you who make it so special. We will take you with us in our hearts."

I stopped talking so I wouldn't cry. Terry took over, expressing his thanks, and doing so without blathering. The room gave us a round of applause.

"*Mange takk og ha det bra!*" Many thanks and have it good!

Terry, Erik, and I walked to the car.

"Everyone loved your music last night, Mom," Erik said. "A lot of people told me how cool it was that you played at vespers, and how beautiful that song was. Thanks for playing."

Don't cry, Mari.

Tove came over with hugs.

Ha det bra to Erik, Tove, and *Skogfjorden. Vi skal komme tilbakke igjen.* We shall come back again.

Good bye to *Skogfjorden* and Erik

Loaded in the van, we set off with the bikes getting a ride from us, instead of the other way around.

We made it as far as Eddy's in Bemidji, where we hoped for a roundup of more CLV friends who couldn't attend Eddy's first gathering.

Two hours later, the radio warned of a coming storm, with strong winds from different directions. Bemidji was the center of the convergence. Lightning cracked, thunder roared, the rains poured down, and the winds grew wild. I initially watched from Eddy's porch, until the storm moved closer and better sense prevailed. From inside, I watched the darkening world like it was a black and white TV show.

Branches blew through the park and big trees waved wildly, sometimes dropping off parts as we watched. The rain blew sideways and slammed heavily into the windows, like we were in car wash.

Water filled Eddie's street until we couldn't see the pavement. A parade of downed tree branches flowed past, leaves waving at us.

The power flickered and vanished. I hung my headlamp over the table while we ate our dinner in the shadowy light.

Police cars drove back and forth with their flashing lights. The lightning became bigger, badder, closer, and the thunder roared alarmingly close.

"You're putting on quite a show for us, Eddy," I complimented him.

Eddy and I both liked wild weather, and this was my wildest weather yet. Eddie's upstairs neighbor Rachel came down.

"The radio's saying not to go outside for the next twelve hours, due to downed power lines and falling trees," she announced.

It was good that Terry and I weren't on our bikes or camped at Bemidji State Park. Our initial plan, before Terry's broken arm, was to bike from *Skogfjorden* and spend another night at the campground before leaving town. According to that plan, we would have been at the park during the storm with our bikes and tent, neither of which are recommended for lightning storms.

"You would have been herded into the Severe Weather Building," Eddy told us. That would have been good for our bodies, but we would have left our bikes, tent, and gear at the camp site. Based on the wild winds we saw, I doubt there would have been much left of our stuff after the storm.

I wondered what was happening at camp. Where was everybody? Were they safe?

I watched more branches as they rapidly flowed by on the main street. They went through the intersection and soon were out of sight.

Eddy's landlord showed up. "There are small trees bent over so much from the wind that they are actually touching the ground."

"It's really unusual for a storm to last this long," Eddie reflected as the wind and rain persisted in their intensity. We stood at windows, watching the wild show.

After forty-five minutes, the lightning and wind decreased, but the rain continued, unabated. Window visibility improved enough that we could see two huge evergreen trees down on the ground across the street. Enormous white caps topped the lake. Sirens and lights broke the gloom as emergency vehicles splashed by.

Rachel reported radio news.

"Seventy five percent of the trees at Bemidji State campus have blown down," she announced. "The winds were between 75 and 105 miles per hour."

The thought of being out in the storm on our bikes was sobering.

The evening's excitement finally wound down, and all that remained was the now quiet, dark night. Without electricity, the fans didn't work, and the room was hot, humid, and stagnant. One window was stuck shut and the other only opened two inches.

We sweltered all night long.

歳

I didn't sleep well and awoke early, curious to explore the park. Four huge evergreen trees had toppled, their giant roots exposed. Big branches were strewn around the park, all lying the same direction. It was easy to tell which way the wind blew when they came down.

One tree stayed upright, sort of. It would have fallen over, but it fell against another tree. The authorities warned people to stay inside because trees could still fall over and hit people. I decided to be a good girl, and reluctantly left the park.

Eddy's wife, Laura, came by.

"We've got a tree down back at the house. The lightning hit it last night and now it's on the ground, split, and has a big black, charred area where it was struck."

Yikes.

"I drove by the Dairy Queen, and its big sign is gone," she continued. "So is the sign from the business next door. I think their signs are now in the lake."

Power returned mid-morning. News reported that winds reached over eighty miles per hour and the storm covered an area of more than 1000 square miles. Thousands of trees ripped out or snapped. Amazingly no deaths or significant injuries were reported.

One resident was quoted as saying this was the "greatest" storm she and her husband ever experienced. I wasn't sure what she meant by greatest—but I had to agree.

Utility lines suffered extensive damage and thousands of homes lacked power. Residents were asked not to travel due to the storm's damage.

Terry and I weren't residents, though, and we decided to take our chances with our road trip.

Vielen dank, Eddy! *Tschüss,* and see you in October!

CHAPTER 11

Resilience–Van Life

I didn't want to be in the van. I wanted to be on our bikes. I flew along at sixty miles an hour, but I wanted to be going twelve. I didn't want to get somewhere the quick way. I wanted to get there the slow way. My way, on a bike.

Not even cherries tasted as good in the car as they did on my bike.

Bemidji looked like a disaster area. Trees lay where they shouldn't be--primarily on the ground, but also slammed against houses, electricity poles, and other trees. A downed power line lay across a road like a venomous snake. With chain saws in hand, work crews and homeowners gawked at the incredible mess.

Once again, I wondered what might have happened to Terry and me, our bikes, and gear if our plans unfolded as expected.

Seventy miles east of Bemidji, the storm's destruction continued to unfold. Mile after mile, residents armed with chain saws assailed fallen trees.

My mind was still in bike mode. I'd see a billboard advertising camping or a motel, and automatically calculate how long it might take us to get there based on our bicycle timing. How many hours would it take for us to cover those miles? Could we spend the night there?

We crossed into Wisconsin, where a welcome sign greeted us at the border. No exhilaration. Crossing a state border in a car was not the same as crossing it on a bike.

Lake Superior boasted lovely campgrounds. Conditions were perfect for camping, but not surprisingly, Terry didn't want to crawl in and out of a tent with his broken arm. As we checked into a hotel, my beloved camping became a memory of the past.

The hotel served a big breakfast of yogurt, bagels, fruit, and juice. On the bikes, I would have absconded with the treats, stuffing my panniers for long distances between stores and restaurants. Now, we could easily drive to towns stocked with food. Now we had a car and a cooler. Now I wouldn't have to forage for food anymore.

Damn it.

I'd been sad, but now I was getting mad. I wanted to be loading our bikes that morning, not loading the car. We were still living out of our panniers. Every time I reached into my pannier, it triggered the bike spot of my brain. I couldn't stop thinking about being on the bikes.

It was the Fourth of July. I automatically thought like a cyclist, imagining long distances for food or lodging, and realizing many stores would be closed for the holiday. Maybe we'd have trouble finding food. Then I remembered we had a car; it would be easy to drive to food and lodging on the Fourth of July. Back in the car, my mind switched back to cyclist mode, and I instinctively calculated arrival times based on bike mileage.

A mind is hard to change.

Five days into Terry's broken arm, gravity still frequently

dragged it from his sling, causing gasps and jerks. Vicodin remained Terry's best friend, and he popped that stuff on a regular basis.

We talked in the car, something we couldn't easily do while biking. Cycling single file for most of the trip, it was generally hard to hear each other. Now we sat side by side in the car, and I asked about Terry's perspectives on the accident.

"I'm lucky to have come out of this with just a broken arm," Terry mused. "It could have been so much worse. *Skogfjorden* was a good place to begin the healing, and people were so kind. There are a lot of great people there, like Tove and Eddy. Many people gave me help, asked if I needed help, and asked how I was doing. I felt a lot of sympathy and kindness."

"I've been thinking about the crash I had near Devils Tower last year," he continued. "Last year, that accident was my fault. This year a car hit me, and it wasn't my fault."

He switched gears, like he was in front of a microphone, addressing an audience.

"To lead an adventurous life, you have to expect to take a fall once in a while. I've had two set-backs while biking, and I don't want a third one. I'm up for the next round. I want to finish this trip and get to the Atlantic. We're over halfway through, and I'm looking forward to Part Two."

Cut to black, with a soaring crescendo that carries you away.

We drove into Michigan on Highway 2, oblivious to much of the outside environment. With a push of a button, the air-conditioning kept us comfortable. We weren't seeking shade for our breaks, nor were we seeking water to drink or dump on our heads and shirts. The air flow from the air-conditioning was our only wind-- no headwinds inside the car.

I did, however, notice the road conditions. Those roads were possibilities for October's bike ride. One road had good shoulders intermittently, and another road had none. I was now more leery of roads without shoulders.

We stopped at campgrounds to inquire about October conditions. Most would be closed by mid-October, our intended start time. Northern nights would be cold. That wasn't appealing. I wanted cozy, warm nights in our tent, not long, cold nights.

Daylight would be limited, too. Two years earlier, Terry and I biked in October and November in northern California, getting a lesson in restricted daylight. It was dark before 8 a.m. and after 5 p.m., or 4 p.m. if the fog rolled in. In contrast, our July light shone from 4:30 a.m. until 9 p.m., giving us a huge window of cycling possibilities. We'd lose eight hours of daylight by biking in November.

We would need to carefully maximize daylight when returning in the fall. By 3 p.m., it would be time to start zeroing in on lodging possibilities so we could be off the road before dark. We would likely cover fewer miles per day, so the second half of our trip might take even longer than the first.

Shorter days, closed campgrounds with fewer lodging options, colder temperatures, and the likelihood of October and November rain and snow. Bah. The second half of our trip was going to have a very different feel to it.

Before the accident, Terry and I discussed how much easier our bike trip was getting to be. We'd left the Rockies far behind and we were on the flats. We'd left the headwinds of the prairie and were back into land with protective trees. We were done with sparsely populated states and huge distances between food, services, and towns, and we were getting into areas with easier access to services. From Bemidji State Park, our prospect of cycling east from Minnesota looked downright easy compared with what we had already done.

Once again, I felt robbed. I wanted to be biking and camping now, during the summer.

I already missed the simplicity of life on the bikes. Now that we had a car, we had a myriad of choices regarding which roads to take, which towns to visit, where to eat and spend the night. On the bikes, we had a focused destination in mind.

I couldn't help myself. Even in the car, I found myself scanning the highway, inspecting inclines, declines, shoulders, and road conditions.

We sped past advertisements for homemade pasties. I did a doubletake. *Pasties*, not pastries. My knowledge of pasties was limited to artsy nipple covers worn by strippers. It was curious that so many Michigan restaurants advertised homemade nipple covers.

We drove into the evening, towards a spectacular full moon of pink and orange coming up just over the horizon. I wanted to be camping underneath that amazing moon.

In our motel at Gaylord, I searched the definition of *pastie*, something that weighed on my mind all afternoon and evening. According to Wikipedia, a pastie is a decorative covering for the nipple worn by a stripper, or a folded pastry case filled with seasoned meat and vegetables.

I realized that if I ever ordered pasties of either kind, I would need to be specific.

Just south of Gaylord, a highway sign proclaimed we were at the 45th Parallel, halfway between the Equator and the North Pole. There is a sign like that just north of Salem, Oregon-- my favorite sign in the world. My second favorite sign is a Portland city sign, giving the Pothole Hotline phone number. The Pothole Hotline makes potholes sound important.

It began raining. If we were on the bikes, we would stop to put on rain gear. It would probably take five minutes just to find all the stuff, and usually it meant that five minutes later, the rain would stop, and all the rain gear would come off again. That ate up a lot of our time. In the van, I didn't care if it rained or not, once I discovered where the windshield wipers were.

Terry and I were getting sloppy. We could just toss stuff around, not needing to carefully put things away. On our bikes, everything had to be contained in the panniers or bungeed down on the bike rack. One develops organization and junk management when living from a bike. Living from the car, we were just disorganized slobs.

I drove, and Terry made phone calls. Two days earlier, he left messages at orthopedic offices in Flint and Port Huron, Michigan, hoping he could be seen for a one-week follow-up of his broken arm. Nobody returned his calls, and we were now barreling down the highway at sixty miles per hour, closing in on both towns.

Port Huron phoned. Could we be there by 1 o'clock? Yep. Great!

On the bikes, I fantasized about how wonderful it would be to drive home after reaching the Atlantic Ocean. I figured we'd take our time, relaxing with the drive. I planned to read between shifts of driving, savoring the luxury of traveling in a car. But now driving was stressful. Terry had driven three times since his broken arm, but the resulting pain put the kibosh on that plan. There was no reading time for me, and any writing time came at the expense of a good night's sleep. I was tired.

I sped to the clinic.

It was our lucky day for a random, one-time appointment. Dr. K, an orthopedic surgeon with thirty-three years of experience, evaluated Terry.

"How'd this injury happen?" he asked. Terry explained about our cross-country bike trip and the accident.

"I think you'll win the prize for the best story of the day," Dr. K said. "You certainly are a Viking to have ridden your bike seven miles to camp after breaking your arm."

Dr. K zeroed in on Terry's wrist pain, looked at the X-ray we brought from Bemidji, and ordered more. He discovered Terry didn't have just one fracture, he had two, including a crack at his wrist that was overlooked by Bemidji urgent care. Dr. K explained that a common fracture duo is the elbow (proximal head of the radius) and the wrist (scaphoid) when a crash landing occurs like Terry's. He said that radiologists often miss detecting the scaphoid wrist crack. A short time later, a snazzy blue cast adorned Terry's left arm from his palm to his elbow.

It's always nice to be in the hands of a specialist.

Goodbye to Dr. K, and goodbye to the United States as we drove across the Blue Water Bridge into Sarnia, Ontario, Canada.

O Canada, where life is measured in kilometers instead of miles.

Through golden wheat and corn we headed 120 kilometers (75 miles) towards St. Marys and the home of my cousin Jody and her husband, David. South Dakotan wheat had been green, Minnesotan wheat had been green and golden, and Canadian wheat was now pure gold. The corn was higher than my shoulders. Our eastward migration measured time by the maturing of the crops.

I scouted road conditions for our October ride. Verdict: crappy. Large sections of Highway 22 had no shoulders. We'd certainly be looking for an alternate route on our bikes.

Laughter is good medicine, and we found plenty of it at Jody and David's. Although cousins on our fathers' side, Jody was more like a sister. As children in Oregon, our families grew grapes, made wine, and hunted deer together. I'd seen Jody only three times in the previous twenty years, but it was as if we'd only been apart for weeks. We conjured up family lore and laughter, savoring our two days together.

Parting was easy. Terry and I would return in October, for Round Two of Family Lore and Laughter, and we'd do it all again.

Two hours later, Terry and I stared in wonder at Niagara Falls.

Niagara Falls actually consists of three waterfalls, not just one. Water flowing north from Lake Erie feeds the Niagara River, which spectacularly plunges over three sections of cliff. The largest is Horseshoe Falls on the Canadian side, at a half mile wide and 160 feet tall. It's not the highest waterfall on earth, but by volume it is the largest. Aptly named, it's shaped liked a horseshoe. A colossal mist rises from the bottom of the falls, obscuring its center.

American Falls, on the U.S. side of things, is about 1000 feet wide and nearly the same height, but in two parts. The first plunges straight down a cliff, and then cascades over a diagonal slope to the river below. The third waterfall on the American side, Bridal Veil Falls, is a morsel in comparison.

We wrapped Terry's cast in a garbage bag and became tourists on a boat to the bottom of the waterfalls. Surrounded by towering cascades on three sides, we seemed small and insignificant.

Incredible. The word means unbelievable, magnificent, extraordinary. Niagara Falls was all of that. It was thrilling to be at the bottom of the falls, experiencing the roar and surge of power all around us. There are some moments in life when nature is so grand that it practically overwhelms, and that was one of them.

Although going over the falls almost always ends in tragedy, in 1960, a seven-year-old boy accidentally went over Horseshoe Falls when his boat overturned upstream. The boy plunged over the falls wearing his life vest and was rescued. The boy survived, but most people do not. It's a pretty effective way to commit suicide, proven by about thirty people per year. Thrill seekers have used barrels, a kayak (didn't work), or a jet ski (also didn't work). If you want to go over the falls and survive, your best hope is in a high-tech barrel but be prepared to pay a $5000 fine and spend six months in jail once you are pulled from the water. That is, if you survive.

Our best view came after the boat ride, standing twenty feet above the crest of Horseshoe Falls. The water shot by, roaring in a display of power that made me impressively dizzy.

We spent an amazing two days at Niagara Falls, and I was in love with all of them.

For the first time since Terry's accident, I awoke without an immediate sense of excitement to get on the bikes. I managed to pack my panniers without the nearly overwhelming sadness I'd known for the past week. I was looking forward, not back. Grief about the bike trip's sudden ending gradually inched towards anticipation about our bike adventure that still lay ahead, three months away.

I thought about resilience. At a staff training exercise at camp one time, we were asked to describe another staff member with three words. Someone described me as "consistent, cheerful, and positive." That's how someone saw me, on the outside. I would describe myself, however, as "resilient", an inner and invisible trait. The work is done on the inside, unbeknownst to most of the world.

Grief, anger, and loss are universal experiences. Sometimes people are permanently incapacitated by their negative experiences, while others are remarkably resilient after incomprehensible loss. Most people are in the middle, including me. My childhood was sandwiched between significant family health problems and the loss of important relationships through death, divorce, and estrangement. A resilience emerged—a resilience that has carried me through the toughest times in my life.

I'm grateful for resilience—grateful for past ability to gradually transcend grief, anger, and loss, and I hope that this resilience will continue in my life. Each experience brings something to learn, and I've come to understand that my past experiences provide me strength and wisdom to better prepare me for the future—whatever it may be.

🚲

My appetite for adventure was incrementally returning. Ontario gave us a thin, but tasty, international filling in our North American sandwich. Hungry for more, Terry and I drove across the bridge into the United States and New York.

🚲

Resuming van life, we drove sixty miles along the southern shore of Lake Ontario, which looked more like an ocean instead of a lake. Campgrounds teased us, but we discovered they would all be closed by October. Motels, not camping, looked to be our future for October and November.

Nearing the Adirondack Mountains and the Appalachians, the van easily rolled up the road's incline. I wondered if Terry's and my bike legs would have rebelled after hundreds of miles of flat mid-west cycling.

I stood beneath the starry night at a lakeside inn, hearing the haunting call of the loons. Tove's words echoed and I absorbed their tranquility: "Listen to what whispers your name."

I listened.

🚲

Terry and I walked to the lake before breakfast and met a father and son donning wet suits, training for a triathlon. The dad was in his sixties, lean, silvery, and muscular. His son was a thirty-year younger twin, minus the silvery hair.

"What are weather conditions generally like here in November?" I asked. Terry and I told them about our bike ride.

"Well, last year it snowed two inches on October 10th," the father told us. "You could be in for a harsh ride."

"Or it could be mild," the son countered. "You just never know around here. Generally, though, the snow doesn't stick until Thanksgiving."

The son buckled a stiff, orange flag on his back. He resembled a shark as he and his dad waded into the lake. Wishing each other luck in our endeavors, father and shark swam off.

Terry and I pondered. Veering south looked increasingly prudent.

🚲

The Fort Ticonderoga Ferry, established in 1759, is still going strong. I fantasized how Terry's and my loaded bikes would look on that ferry, instead of our loaded car.

Seven minutes later, we drove off the ferry and into Vermont.

🚲

Stopping at a church established in 1785, we wandered in its cemetery. Thin headstones, so worn that some were barely legible, hinted at long-forgotten stories. One displayed three names: a man and his two wives. The first wife died at age sixteen, perhaps from childbirth? What was that story? What were any of these stories? How different life was then, and how much tougher people must have been just to get through their daily life, week after week, year after year.

Meanwhile, Terry and I snacked on store-bought treats in our air-conditioned van, effortlessly driving along paved roads from one town to another.

Vermont acquired its name from the French *Verd Mont*, or Green Mountain. Known as the Green Mountain state, Vermont is indeed green, hilly, and gorgeous. Its roads weren't gorgeous, though.

Following our Adventure Cycling bike map on the recommended bike route towards Maine and the Atlantic, I wondered how these roads could be recommended for cyclists. They were choppy, narrow, and a crappy ride even in a car. If they were the best cycling roads that Vermont had to offer, I thought it might be best just to skip Vermont completely.

Later, I learned that it wasn't Vermont's fault. Hurricane Irene blew through ten months earlier, causing widespread destruction from St. Croix up through Vermont and New Hampshire. As the seventh costliest hurricane in the United States by 2012, it appeared Vermont ran out of money for continued road repair. Still, the idea of cycling on Vermont's choppy roads did not rate a thumbs up from me, Hurricane Irene or not.

The crummy roads in Vermont led to more crummy roads in New Hampshire. By luck, we ended our day at a motel that blended indoor lodging and camping into one lovely evening. At North Woodstock, people gathered around a campfire only fifty feet from a splashing brook. As the fire crackled, Terry and I joined the group, and were soon enfolded into their conversation.

"Where are you from?" someone asked.

"Oregon."

"You're a long way from home."

That launched us into the story of our bike trip. Terry showed off his cast, which always prompted sympathy.

"We're planning to finish our trip in the fall after my arm has healed. What's the weather like around here in November?"

"It's damn cold and icy," a man said. "You'd probably break your other arm."

We heard it from the local experts around the campfire. New Hampshire and Connecticut chimed in, and they knew their autumnal weather conditions. Finding a more southerly bike route was the way to go, if Terry and I insisted on biking that late in the year. However, nobody indicated that a bike ride in November to the east coast sounded like a reasonable idea in the first place.

In the morning, what would have been a cause for celebration on the bikes twisted into familiar heartache as we crossed into Maine, our final state. Soon we reached Portland, our original destination. Our hometown, Portland, Oregon, was named for Maine's Portland in 1845. A coin toss decreed the name, and if the coin would have landed on the other side, Terry and I would be claiming our hometown as Boston, Oregon, instead.

Despite all indications contrary, I still hadn't entirely given up on ending our autumn bike trip in Portland, Maine.

"How do we get to a sandy beach?" I asked at the Visitor Center.

"A sandy beach?" an elderly man mused. "We don't really have that around here. We have a lot of rock."

Unlike Oregon and unbeknownst to me, sandy beaches aren't Maine's thing—only two percent of Maine's shoreline is sand. The rest is rock and eroding bluffs.

Ten miles to the south lay some sand, and off we went to an inn near Higgins Beach. The inn was open for the summer, but would be closed in October, as would be most of Maine's coastal lodging due to the coming storms and snow. An increasing dose of reality replaced our initial ignorance. The more we learned about late fall in the northeastern United States, the more we realized it was foolish to think we could return in October and November on our bikes.

Emotions invaded all over again.

Terry and I walked from the inn to the crowded beach. There was no way around it; I felt depressed. It depressed me to arrive at the Atlantic by car and not on our bikes. Gazing at the ocean, the best I could muster was apathy. The whole arrival at the Atlantic was anti-climactic.

Nonetheless, Terry and I dipped our feet in the Atlantic, and someone took a photo. It wasn't the same as a bike tire dip, but there we were. I followed that with a whole-body dip, and cold waves knocked some sense into me. We experienced an amazing cross-country trip, no matter what our transportation mode had been. How lucky we were, despite Terry's accident. How lucky we were that Terry was still alive, with only cracked bones.

It hadn't turned out the way we expected, but it was still an incredible adventure.

Time heals.

I've heard it, and I believe it. As we drove west, the heavy load of disappointment lightened every day.

Approaching Wyoming's Teton Mountains, we spied two loaded bicycles leaning against Togwotee Lodge, with two cyclists seeking respite in the shade. I braked, and Terry and I climbed the porch steps to join them.

"Okay, tell us your story," I said as Terry and I sat down uninvited and looked at them.

The girl laughed. "What kind of a story?" she asked.

The guy pulled food from his panniers. At their feet were apples, jelly beans, Nutella, raisins, and dirty plastic bags. It looked so familiar.

Josh and Laura were students at MIT. That meant that not only were they adventurous with their bikes, but really smart too. Cycling from New York, they planned to meet family in Seattle and return to school in a month. Several minutes into our conversation, two more cyclists rode up. Oregonian college students Ben and Skot biked the opposite direction, on their way to Virginia. Skot's tattooed right arm was almost as colorful as his vibrant, multi-colored cycling jersey with *Oregon* blazoned across his shoulders.

Skot and Ben pulled up chairs and the cycling talk flowed.

"I'm going inside to buy some chocolate milk," Ben said a few minutes later, starting to get up.

"Oh, wait, we have some in our cooler," I told him.

I returned with an unopened half-gallon of chocolate milk and a new bag of chocolate chip cookies. I set them on the floor between us.

"What a treat!" Ben exclaimed.

The surprise of being offered an unexpected gift. I knew it well and could appreciate what it meant to the four cyclists. For the first time on this trip, I could also appreciate how it felt to be the person offering, instead of receiving.

We swapped stories.

"We've been hanging out in bars for most of the evenings," Skot said. "Lots of times, people invite us to their places for the night. We've hardly spent any money on campgrounds on this trip and we've met a lot of really cool people."

"There was that one guy, though," Ben said, looking at Skot. "One guy had been telling us all about his criminal history, and then he invited us to come stay at his place. We said no to that one."

The chocolate milk and cookies quickly disappeared, and I returned to the van for reinforcements. Good thing we had so many treats from Maine, and too bad that some of our friends back home weren't going to get them. I brought a fancy package of blueberry truffles back to the cyclists.

"A toast to our friend, Bethany," I told the group. "She's house sitting for us in Portland, and tonight she's hosting three cyclists at our place whom Terry and I met in South Dakota. Bethany, these blueberry truffles were intended for you, but we are eating them in your honor instead." I raised the package, and then we all devoured the blueberry truffles. Better luck next time, Bethany.

We also ate a package of chocolate covered blueberries that were accidentally pierced in the sloppy organization of our van. Those were intended for Karl, our summer lawn mower. Too bad, so sad. They tasted really good, too.

The six of us had much in common, and we swapped stories of the challenges and adventures of a cross country bike trip – the heat, being lost, getting wrong directions from people, living out of panniers, and more. We talked of the kindness and generosity that we all experienced, agreeing that a bike tour was a terrific way to meet so many great people. Our conversation could have continued for hours, but the cyclists still had miles to go in their opposite directions.

Rather than feeling despondent that I wasn't cycling, I felt jazzed, and realized that I was buoyed by the friendly kinship I experienced with these cyclists. We were all part of a corps, a small band of adventurers linked to one another with common challenges, joys, and discoveries. All six of us wanted more.

I awoke during the night thinking about the cyclists. My heart pounded, engulfed by disappointment and stress. I felt so happy and energized during our time with the four cyclists, but that was now replaced by envy. How does one control a sad, mad, and envious brain? I had yet to learn.

A cyclist passed us going east. Not only did he have panniers and gear on his bike, but he also carried a full guitar case on his back as he pedaled.

We easily zoomed up Homestake Pass and the Continental Divide near Butte, Montana, remembering our dangerous bicycle descent in the snowstorm seven weeks earlier. Instead of snow, we looked out on a warm, sunny day.

A few days earlier, I felt excited to be returning home, but now that it loomed so close, I had second thoughts. The nomadic lifestyle suited me with its discoveries and adventures, even in a car. I wasn't quite ready for all of that to end.

Having come full circle, we drove on Washington's Highway 14 along the Columbia River, where we biked during our first week of the trip. We passed areas where we camped, remembered where we stopped for clothing adjustments, places we took breaks. I even remembered where I pee'd. We went through tunnels, including the one where we both forgot to remove our sunglasses and were surprised how dark the tunnel was. We remembered the heat of the gorge that wilted us that first week; it was just a teaser for the mid-west heat to come.

The Columbia River Gorge is stunning, and it welcomed us in style. Colorful sails from wind surfers and wind kites skimmed the water. Mount Hood grew as we neared, and then gradually shrank as we overtook it. The world looked greener and fluffier than when we left in May. Flowers bloomed that hadn't yet appeared on our eastward journey. It was like going to sleep in black and white, and waking up in color.

As we neared cloudy Portland, Terry and I dug through our panniers for long sleeve shirts, something we hadn't worn for weeks.

And then, we were home again. There was no Tango to welcome us, but a neighbor did. A note from the three cyclists brought a smile to my face with their funny comments and drawings. I was glad they came.

Terry and I experienced an extraordinary ten weeks of a cross-country trip by bike and car, covering over 2500 miles by bikes in the first seven weeks, and over 5800 miles by car in the following three weeks. Over 8300 miles of adventures, and we were alive.

Terry acquired a hernia and a couple of cracks along the way. We both acquired memories.

We were supported physically and emotionally by so many people, both those we knew before we began our ride and those we met along the way. We were grateful for the e-mails, Facebook interactions, and phone calls from family and friends as we journeyed through the good times and the bad.

After Terry's accident, many people gave their two cents' worth about our bike-to-car transition. Someone encouraged me to work at *Skogfjorden* for six weeks while Terry's arm healed, and then resume the ride. Another advised finishing up our trip on a tandem. Not all the suggestions were encouraging. Some told me to find another dream, or that perhaps God was trying to tell me something. But my favorite suggested I ride while Terry drove. He could be my sag wagon, drive ahead, set up the tent, and have dinner ready when I arrived. I loved that one.

Anticipation. Participation. Recollection.

A dying man once told me life consists of these three experiences. Anticipation is imagination, aiming at hope, dread, or something in-between. Excitement and great satisfaction can occur when anticipating something desired. Sometimes you get lucky, and whatever has been eagerly anticipated actually happens, leading to participation. Sometimes the event doesn't happen, but there is still the enjoyment of the time spent anticipating it. Recollection is the memory of both anticipation and participation.

Anticipation. I anticipated this cross-country bike trip for thirty-two years.

Participation. Terry and I were fortunate to have participated. In our seven weeks of cycling, we biked over 2500 miles.

Recollection. We had memories of our time together, and of family, friends, and strangers. We had memories of discoveries we made about ourselves and about each other.

My recollection was captured not only in memories and photos, but also within my written words. Perhaps someday, if age and disease dim my memory and ability to read for myself, someone will read my story to me, so that I can recall it all over again.

Anticipation. Participation. Recollection.

Every day's a crap shoot. Take your chances.

Meanwhile, our anticipation again began.

CHAPTER 12

Waiting

Terry and I had no control over his healing; we just needed to wait and allow healing to happen on its own schedule, something that couldn't be prodded even by modern technology.

We waited for time to speed up—unsuccessfully.

Some of the toughest times in life are spent in the Waiting Zone—waiting for biopsy reports, waiting for news of a missing person, waiting for dysfunction to turn to function.

Our goal of the Atlantic remained, and we made adjustments. Some aspects were in our control, such as our route, equipment for increased wet and cold, and expectations for more indoor lodging. Other aspects were out of our control, such as our time commitments that stretched into October.

Between the polar opposites of Control and No Control, we waited.

July 22 through October 9, 2012
Arrived home July 22.
Terry's to Do List:

✓ Hernia operation, July 31. Check.
✓ Sufficiently heal two cracked bones in order to resume bike trip, September. Check.
✓ Buy recumbent bike, September. Check.

Terry's and my To Do List:

✓ Oktoberfest dance and band season, September 15 through October 7. Check.
✓ Catch red eye plane to Bemidji, Minnesota, October 7. Check.
✓ Resume cycling, October 9. Check.

Part 2

CHAPTER 13

Back in the Saddle – Minnesota Resumed

"**A**re you f—ing crazy?" Our friend Knut gave his not so delicate response to our plan to resume our cross-country bike trip in October. We had received the same reaction, minus the expletive, multiple times in the preceding three months.

Maybe we were crazy, and maybe we weren't. We just hoped we weren't foolish. It was a tossup which kind of weather we'd encounter. Of course, we hoped for a chunk of good weather, but we had hoped to cross the country in one go. We knew how those plans worked out.

"Are you trying to kill Terry?" That was another common question. Friends and family knew of his lacerated liver a year before, and this trip featured a broken elbow and wrist. However, I claimed no responsibility for either, so the answer to that question was a definite "No."

Despite the skepticism, we pressed forward with plans, and Terry's included switching to a recumbent bicycle.

The recumbent generated enthusiasm from Terry for two reasons: there'd be no pressure on his left arm, and there'd be a shorter distance to the ground if he fell. In the end, he bought the recumbent off Craig's List before his arm healed, and with only six days of practice, we resumed the trip. By the sixth day, he wasn't as wobbly as the first.

"Our bodies were finely tuned a few months ago, but they're sure out of tune now," Terry ruefully noted. We trained a whopping total of three days before flying out. Back in May, we were physically well prepared, but this time... not so much. We'd have to get in shape as we rode.

Arriving home Sunday evening after our last Oktoberfest performance, Terry and I dumped the lederhosen, dirndl, accordion, and clarinet, and replaced them with our heavy duffel bags. Crammed inside each bag were four tightly-packed panniers and our camping and biking gear. My duffel bag weighed in at exactly 50.0 pounds – a packing achievement probably never to be repeated.

By midnight, Terry and I were on a plane.

Reunited with Erik, Paul Bunyan, and Babe
the Blue Ox at Bemidji, Minnesota

One sleepless night later, we arrived at Bemidji. Erik drove us to the bike shop where our bikes were shipped two weeks earlier, and after a short test drive, we muscled them into the van. I peered impassively at the scene of Terry's accident as we drove by.

Skogfjorden was cold and empty. Barefoot with rolled up pants, Terry and I stood in frigid Turtle River Lake, dipping our rear tires while Erik took photos. Brr.

Rear tire dip in Turtle River Lake at *Skogfjorden*,
near Bemidji, Minnesota

My fortune cookie that evening knew something was up:

*A journey of a thousand miles begins with a single
step. Take that step today.*

Skogfjorden in the autumn chill

At first glance, Terry's recumbent looked more like a motorcycle than a bicycle, with its long, low base and tall protective windshield. My bike was unchanged, with four panniers and camping gear bungeed to the rack behind my seat.

"This is crazy, but great," someone at breakfast pronounced. "Did you know that we had snow on the ground four days ago?"

No, we didn't know that. We knew it felt damn cold, though, just standing inside an open door of a building.

Terry, Erik, and I stood outside under an archway at *Waldsee*, the German village where Erik worked during the school-year. Protected from the cold rain, we exchanged long hugs and words of love. Terry and I ended the first part of our bike trip with Erik, and with him, we began its second part.

It felt just right.

Layered in our rain gear, Terry and I rode into the rain as Erik smiled and waved good bye.

"Bye! *Vi elsker deg!*" I called to Erik in Norwegian as we pedaled away. We love you!

"*Jeg elsker dere!* " I love you! he called back.

Lotsa love – that's a powerful start for a trip.

🚲

October 9, 2012 11 a.m.

Pedaling!!

Not much had changed since the summer--we still lacked efficiency. One of Terry's bike flags was missing, so we backtracked looking for it.

Within fifteen minutes of leaving Concordia Language Villages, the rain turned to sleet, and soon the sleet turned to snow. We were back on Terry's crummy, shoulderless highway until turning onto the Paul Bunyan State Trail, a 110-mile bike trail stretching from Bemidji to Brainerd.

Snowfall doesn't make for optimal cycling conditions, but there was no doubt it was an exciting way to restart our trip. Warmer weather and rain were forecast, so Terry and I let the snowflakes fall where they may. They fell on the woods along Lake Bemidji's shore and on a deer bounding across the trail. They fell on the muted autumn leaves that barely clung to trees, and on the leafy trail. Gone were the vibrant fall colors, leaving only dull yellow, orange, and rust, now being hidden by snowflakes.

Terry's second flag fell off too. Terry wanted high visibility for his low recumbent, with two flags and a bright red light at the back of his bike. Both flags fell off within our first hour of cycling, but the red light proved effective. It was so bright I had to stay fifty feet behind to keep from being blinded by its glare.

Not only were the bike flags a problem, so were his rear two panniers and computer cadence. Because the recumbent was low to the ground, so were the bags. They were new, and they scraped the ground when Terry turned corners. I bet they wouldn't survive the trip. More optimistic, Terry insisted they would, but I figured he was just in denial.

We left the bike path and rode into Bemidji, cycling over the little Mississippi. Sixty miles from its source, it was still just a baby river entering Lake Bemidji.

Diagnosis for Terry's nonfunctioning computer cadence: no magnet, lost in bike transport from Portland. With another magnet, some lunch, and a quick visit to Paul Bunyan and Babe, we were officially on our way. It was 2 p.m. with only 12 miles of cycling accomplished, reminiscent of so many summer days before.

The snow became a stinging curtain of sleet. Terry donned his face mask before leaving the bike shop, but I hadn't been that practical. With so much time already wasted, I didn't want to stop and dig mine out of my panniers.

"I'm finally feeling relaxed," Terry said. Me too—I felt that we finally started, for real.

An old railroad track converted to a paved trail, we rode the Paul Bunyan Trail through wet woods of autumn colors. Crossing country roads, we slipped back into the woods.

Evidence of July's storm lay all around us. Fallen trees lined the sides of the trail, uprooted or snapped in two. It must have been a wild scene, and I was glad we hadn't been there to find out.

With wind against my bare face, I pedaled on. It was cool outside, but I was cozy inside my many layers. My hands were protected by mittens and overmitts – the same pair of overmitts that I neglected to bring on our first trip. They'd been hidden on the floor in Erik's room, where I staged my gear. For this second round of our trip, I was grateful to have the overmitts on my hands instead of on Erik's floor.

The sleet and snow finally stopped, leaving a chill and overcast sky. We chugged on like locomotives, breathing steam into the cool air. Warm and dry on the inside with October's chill on the outside, my spirits soared.

Our initial plan was Hackensack for the night, but with our late start, we wouldn't have a daylight arrival. Terry put his iPad to work, finding the small community of Akeley nearby, but there was no lodging information. We considered pitching our tent along the trail for the night, but we gambled with Akeley. The Heartland Trail spat us out at a mini-mart.

"Are there any motels around here?" I asked the clerk.

"No, but there is someone who rents rooms in her house. Go to the house with the For Sale sign."

Terry and I were soon ensconced in a cozy apartment at the back of the house. We cranked up the heat, ate pizza, and relished hot showers while our damp clothes adorned the furniture.

The temperature was predicted to drop to 25 F., but Terry and I were snug under the covers in the warm apartment. It was a great ending to our first day back on the bikes. We only biked sixty miles, but there would be plenty of days ahead for better mileage.

Our adventures had begun again, and all was well.

🚲

A blue sky, bright sun, and a chilly 33 degrees greeted us in the morning. After twenty minutes of riding, we began to peel off layers. By late morning, it felt like summer.

The woods slowly changed from birch to oak. Leaves still hung from trees, while others collected in piles. It smelled sharp and woodsy.

Deer season was in full swing and I worried we might get shot. Deer occasionally leaped through the brush, running across the trail in front or behind us. Fortunately, it was only mid-week. The weekend, with more hunters and a greater chance of getting shot, was still a few days away.

Like the first part of our trip, I was typically still ahead of Terry on the trail, waiting for him to catch up. His wobbly recumbent starts improved, and as long as he didn't turn corners, the panniers didn't scrape. The recumbent was great for a healing broken arm, though. With the low seat and his arms at a horizontal angle, his hands rested lightly on the handlebar with no pressure from above.

His legs were another matter, though.

"I read that it takes a thousand miles to get your legs used to riding a recumbent," Terry told me. "The recumbent uses different muscles. That means that about the time we'll reach the Atlantic, I'll finally have just developed the leg muscles I need."

He sure didn't have them at that point. Even though we were on a paved trail, Terry often pooped out on the inclines, needing to walk and push the recumbent uphill. With only a few training rides on the recumbent before we started the second trip, he clearly hadn't built up those new leg muscles yet. It might be a long ride to the Atlantic.

"You're crazy!" our waitress exclaimed.

Terry and I savored warm drinks inside a Hackensack café. Outside the window, our bikes generated conversations, just like with the first part of the trip. Now that Terry had a recumbent, the curiosity factor increased.

"I went to the kitchen and told them all about you," our waitress continued in amazement. Within a few minutes, another employee came to our table.

"You're crazy!" she said, repeating our waitress's pronouncement. "I just had to come see you for myself."

Crazy. We certainly heard that a lot. We heard it before starting last summer, too, but Terry and I generally interpreted it back then as a good kind of crazy, not a crazy kind of crazy. But with October's snow flurries, we were pretty sure that when people said, "You're crazy!" they meant the kind of crazy that wasn't a compliment.

By noon it was a balmy 44 degrees in Backus. A man stopped for conversation while we ate under the city park's covered shelter.

He ended with "I'm envious of you two doing this bike trip."
Envious. Not crazy.

We pedaled by lakes, through forests, and near water towers.
During hot summer days, a water tower meant a town and shade,
and if we were lucky, an air-conditioned business with something
cold to drink. In October's chill, we had no need for shade, and we
already had more air conditioning than we wanted.

Terry dragged his recumbent over a big log that lay across the
bike trail, putting his computer cadence out of whack again. A stop
in Nisswa found Martin's Sport Shop, where we discovered they
didn't do bike repairs. So much for that plan. Employee Jim kept
us in conversation.

"This Paul Bunyan bike trail is fantastic," Terry told him.

"The man who championed turning this old rail line into a
bike trail fought with the Minnesota legislature for sixteen years
to make it happen," he told us.

I was grateful for that man's perseverance, thinking the bike
trail should have been named for him, and not for Paul Bunyan.

My plastic water bottle bit the dust that morning. Jim rummaged
in the basement, returning with two.

"Take these with my compliments," he told us.

I extended my hand to shake his in thanks, but he said, "We
don't shake hands around here, we give hugs." So, I got a free water
bottle, plus a hug.

Near Brainerd and the end of the trail, I pulled up to a cyclist
standing beside his bike. Paul, in his early thirties, had loads of
questions.

"Where are you two spending the night?"

"Brainerd."

"Would you like to have dinner with us and spend the night at
my in-law's house?"

"Sure!" Hospitality so soon!

Paul's wife Elsye cycled up and joined us. After Paul's brief account of our trip, he gave Elsye the news.

"I invited them to your parents' place for dinner and to spend the night."

That was different. Our overnights before had always come from people who gave the invitation; Paul was inviting us to people who didn't even know about us yet.

"Yeah, I think that'll be alright," Elsye said. "I'll give them a call."

Elsye pedaled away and returned with a thumbs up.

Guess who's coming to dinner?

We arrived at the wooded banks of the Mississippi, where a big house nestled between the trees. Elyse's parents, Steve and Ellen, warmly welcomed us to their home.

"Last Fourth of July, we had kayakers stay with us," Ellen recounted. "They were on their way down the Mississippi. We got to talking and ended up inviting them for the night. We kept in contact with them afterwards. They did the river in two months, kayaking about thirty miles a day."

Now Ellen and Steve could add cyclists to their random hospitality list.

Elsye and Paul's two-month-old baby, CJ, slept peacefully in my arms as Terry and I sipped wine, told stories, and watched dinner preparations.

We learned that Elsye attended *Waldsee,* CLV's German camp, in her teenage years.

"We started our trip in front of the *Bahnhof,*" I told Elsye. She nodded; she knew.

Candlelight and a feast graced the long table. Wine flowed, as did our words. How welcome Terry and I felt, surrounded by this gracious, hospitable family.

Random acts of kindness. We couldn't have asked for anything more.

"How many calories do you burn off in a day?" Steve asked in the morning.

"I don't know, but I usually gain weight when I go on bike trips," I said. "Terry loses weight, and I gain it. I gained a pound on the first part of our trip, which was better than normal. Often, I gain up to five pounds. Based on my usual weekly weight gain, and how many weeks we thought we'd be biking, I figured that I was destined to gain seventy pounds for the trip. I was happy that didn't happen."

With well wishes from our gracious hosts, we set out in 33-degree weather. While I contemplated this family's unexpected kindness and welcoming hospitality, a car pulled over ahead of Terry and me.

"I'm curious about your recumbent," the man said. "I've ridden a recumbent for many years. I love it."

Terry and Andy talked shop about recumbents and our trip. He nodded and smiled.

"I live a block away from the Mississippi, and if it was later in the day, I'd invite you to spend the night. But I know you're just starting your day."

Brainerd folks weren't lacking in hospitality.

"I met a guy who lived on his bike," he continued. "He'd been living like that for fifteen years – a hobo on a bike. He pulled a trailer with a pet carrier and he hauled around his four cats. When I met him, he had logged over 100,000 miles on his bike. This guy, he was just off the charts." Andy shook his head.

A later break found us in a mini-mart. Seeing our helmets and cycling gear, the cashier asked questions.

"I'm jealous of your trip," he concluded a minute later.

That balanced out the score. Since yesterday, the tally was two for "You're crazy" and two for "I'm jealous."

"Would you like an energy drink?" an employee asked, offering a free sample.

"Yeah, I need some energy."

The woman looked at my bike gear and asked, "Where are you going?"

"The Atlantic Ocean."

"Well, you're going to need more than this," she said dryly as she handed me a drink.

We wound through green forests and brown farm land, occasionally seeking respite from the brisk air with indoor heat and cocoa--such a contrast to our summer escapes to icy beverages and air-conditioning.

A red fox stood on the grassy median, casually watching me roll near. Only fifteen feet away, I stopped and silently watched it for five magnificent minutes.

My next animal sighting was fake. A giant walleye fish, twenty feet long and ten feet high, welcomed us to Mille Lacs Lake at Garrison. The statue's plaque informed of Paul Bunyan's three day-struggle to land the fish. Paul finally wrapped his line around Babe the Blue Ox's horns and Babe pulled the walleye out of the lake. A sign near the big fish commanded *Keep off the fish!*

Paul Bunyan's giant walleye

Cycling lakeside under a bright blue sky, trees looked fuller, fiercely clasping their canopies of green, yellow, rust, and orange. Our autumn afternoon temperature soared to 44 degrees.

Autumn sunshine along Mille Lacs, Minnesota

But sunshine ends early in mid-October, and concluding our eighty-mile day, we exited Highway 169 as the sun sank and the temperature plunged. That left us pedaling in the dark for a mile on a side road towards Milaca. Terry led while I followed thirty feet behind, not be blinded by his bright red blinking light. Later, we learned his very effective blinking red light was illegal, so he reluctantly switched it to a steady light instead.

The first motel had no availability on the ground floor, and Terry pedaled away to look further. A car drove up beside me.

"Isn't there any room for you at the motel?" a woman's voice called out. "I have plenty of room and you two would be welcome to stay at my place."

What a generous offer, but Terry was already ahead of me, heading towards the second motel. I reluctantly turned down her kind offer, marveling at Minnesota's hospitality.

We crammed our loaded bikes into the room. How things

changed since the summer. After Terry's broken arm, we traveled through near-perfect camping conditions, and I quietly fumed about using motels instead of our cozy tent.

But times changed. It was now October, and I was grateful for a warm room at the end of a chilly day outside.

The song had it right. *Baby, it's cold outside.*

ڶ

I swiped yogurt and cinnamon rolls for my panniers, despite the motel's sign that warned *Food must be eaten in the dining room.*

Terry looked like a thug in his face mask as we set out in the 32 degree morning. I was just glad it wasn't 22 degrees, as was reported in Brainerd during the night. Under the bright sunshine, a river sparkled, edged with trees of red and gold.

Miles later, a man walked by during a break in town.

"Kind of cold for this, isn't it?" he asked, looking at our bikes.

He had that right.

Another man stopped to inquire about Terry's recumbent and our adventure.

"You have my admiration," he told us. At least he didn't say we were crazy.

ڶ

Cell phones can be worthless out in the sticks. This time, we each had a walkie-talkie in addition to a phone, and Terry frequently used his to call from behind, notifying me he was taking a break. We'd each get into a cycling rhythm, and mine was faster than his. The walkie-talkies put a shorter leash on me, and I would often return to where he rested.

Within the hour of a relaxing lunch break, my walkie-talkie chirped.

"I need to take a break," Terry informed me. "I'm getting sleepy. This recumbent seat is so comfortable that I'm about to fall asleep."

Recumbent cyclists praise the comfort of a recumbent bike seat, comparing it to a lounge chair.

With a belly full of food and sun on his face, Terry was primed for a nap, not more pedaling. He dozed in his recumbent lounge chair for five minutes.

Afternoon headwinds kept us both awake. We leaned towards Minneapolis, pushing against hours of headwinds while they gradually wore us down. I placed a phone call.

"Buck! This is Parsley! We're still a few miles from your house, but we're closing in."

Twenty minutes later, our paths crossed as Buck biked to meet us and give escort to the house, where Esther welcomed us with waving sparklers.

Erik and I had worked with Buck, Esther, and their college-age children, Finn and Sunny, for CLV in Switzerland and Brazil. Laughter and stories highlighted our dinner and the evening concluded with a nearly naked sprint to their hot tub. I found it darn chilly to be cavorting in 25 degrees dressed only in a bathing suit.

That was nothing to a Minnesotan, though.

Terry missed out on Esther's delicious birthday crêpes for Finn, as his stomach was on the prowl. Too bad—more for the rest of us.

Full of good cheer and hospitality, we rolled out in the afternoon, accompanied by their friend, Timmer. And we rolled out of a bike shop with new, higher riding panniers for Terry—thank goodness. No more scraping, no more chills up my spine, no more wondering what to do when those scaping panniers fell apart.

After lunch at a burger joint, a couple of seniors approached us. "Where did you start?" he asked.

"Pacific Ocean. We're on our way to the Atlantic." I gave the short version of our trip, including the broken arm.

"Is that your man?" he asked, nodding towards Terry.

"Yeah, that's my man."

The woman leaned towards me. "May I ask you a personal question?"

So far, there had only been one question whenever people asked, "May I ask you a personal question?"

"Sure."

"How old are you?"

"I'm fifty-four and he's fifty-nine."

The man smiled, put his arm up in the air and gave the trucker salute. Toot, toot!

"Good luck," he said.

Timmer rode with us until 5 o'clock, weaving south and east through St. Paul. A fine mist surrounded us. Terry and I wore rain gear; Timmer wore a light jacket and shorts with long johns underneath, looking like a poster boy for minimalist outdoor life.

"I have a bike that has studded tires on it, for the winter," he told us as he headed home. That's a Minnesotan for you.

Almost dark, Terry and I weren't far from where our day began, still in Minneapolis/St. Paul. With the busy traffic, we sometimes chose sidewalks, despite their poor condition. A sharp corner attacked, and only five miles after Timmer left us, I had a flat.

As usual, Terry graciously replaced my tube. Just as darkness closed in, we pulled in to the Holiday Inn. It was hard to justify that kind of money so early in our trip, but it was the only lodging around. As we checked in at the big lobby, people curiously examined us, our bikes, and gear.

"You've got my vote," one man commented after hearing of our trip.

"We're chasing the good weather," I optimistically replied.

"You'd better hurry."

Terry's stomach still rebelled in the morning, prompting us to linger at the hotel until it was time to get kicked out. After zigging and zagging through the metro area, we finally met our first Mississippi River Trail. From there, navigation was easy-- follow the river.

We did, ending our dry, chilly day at Red Wing, home of Red Wing boots. It wasn't boots that were on my mind, though. My brain had been besieged all day by the *Red Wing Polka*--that's what happens when you're in a polka band.

We left town in 29 degrees, but the sunny day promised welcome warmth. Cycling by Lake Pepin, which is actually a bulge of the Mississippi, I reminisced about stories and places from the *Little House on the Prairie* books, including Lake Pepin. Author Laura Ingalls Wilder was born near Pepin, Wisconsin, and a section of the highway we cycled bears her name.

By three o'clock, a heat wave struck with 60 degrees. A first for this trip, I was down to bare hands, and the sunshine on my face and hands was exhilarating.

Golden corn kernels lent color to the highway's shoulder. Scattered in the shoulders, we could simply follow the trail of corn kernels, like Hansel and Gretel. It was the beginning of the Weeks of Scattered Corn.

A sign claimed the Mississippi is the longest river in North America. At the headwaters of the Missouri River in Montana, a sign claimed that the Missouri is the longest river in the United States. I figured the Mississippi and the Missouri should get together and duke it out.

I plugged in my Blackberry to charge at the Winona motel. The day's warmth was obvious even to my Blackberry batteries.

Cold temperatures sucked the life from the batteries, and between my roadside writing and the cold temperatures, my batteries quickly faded. Since resuming our trip, I'd been using two batteries a day. This was only a one battery day--much warmer than a three-dog night.

Completing our first week, we biked four hundred miles and averaged fifty-eight mile per day, about our summer average. A clean ending to the week, we finished Minnesota, ready to cross the Mississippi into our next state.

We began our week with Erik and Bemidji friends, enjoyed the unexpected hospitality of Paul, Elsye, Ellen, and Steve, and then reunited with Hometown friends Buck, Esther, Finn, and Sunny. We started in snow flurries on our first day, and ended the week with warmth and sunshine. We'd been warm and dry every night. The energy from so many people boosted us every day. One state down, with lots to go. What a wonderful first week.

Terry and I felt blessed and blissful.

A cyclist pulled up to us at a light in the morning.

"What are you all about?" he asked. We told him, and then we all kept talking as the light turned green and back to red again.

"I just did half a cross-country trip this summer," he told us. "I took my nine and eleven-year-old sons, and we biked 30-40 miles a day together. My mother-in-law drove the support car, and my sons rode in the car for the rest of the day while I did more biking. I usually did about a hundred miles a day."

Terry and I enjoyed another escort as we followed him towards the river and Winona State University, where he was a physics professor.

"Have a great trip, you two!" He peeled away.

That's the way to start a morning, as well as to leave a state. From start to finish, our week in Minnesota filled us with good people and good memories.

The little river grew after we crossed it back in Bemidji. Biking across the substantially wider Mississippi and into our next state, we happily read:

Welcome to Wisconsin.

Terry crossing the Mississippi River into Wisconsin

CHAPTER 14

Rails-to-Trails — Wisconsin

Wisconsin welcomed us with a blast of color-- a field of vibrant pumpkins.

It rain, it stopped, it rain, it stopped. Clothes came on, they came off. The temperature in the 50s challenged us not to overheat inside our rain gear, but that same temperature, paired with wind chill, could push towards hypothermia if we stayed soaked with rain.

It was that kind of day, and we wished for a crystal ball. Meanwhile, the sun came out.

Welcome to Wisconsin. "Free beer tomorrow"

We traded efficiency for ambiance and left the road, cycling south on the Great River State Trail. The limestone bike trail wound its way through woods, where leaves clung to trees with the last grip of autumn. The sun shone, birds cawed, and the earthy smell of autumn rolled in waves along the trail. Much better than a highway and exhaust fumes.

The path became a wooden trail supported on stilts, crossing swamps that oozed intrigue. Paralleling our course, a train slowly approached, crossing a nearby wooden bridge. Terry and I had this mysterious place to ourselves--it felt surreal.

The Mississippi was a fine companion, but we turned the corner at La Crosse to travel east on the La Crosse River Trail. *10 states—1 River* was the Mississippi motto. It still had eight states to go, and so did we, more or less. We would just do it in different directions.

A bright red cardinal flew by. Our daily bike progress may have been slow, but the sighting of our first cardinal proved we were advancing, gradually moving from one region to another.

Limestone and afternoon winds sucked Terry's energy, reducing his speed to only five miles per hour. He wanted off the crushed limestone. Again, we merged with highway traffic, and the trail of corn kernels.

We pushed against headwinds for the last ten miles of the day, wearily arriving at the end of the Sparta Bike Trail and the little town of Sparta, which announced itself as *The Bicycling Capital of America.*

"You get what you pay for," Terry observed in the morning. We didn't pay much at our motel, and we didn't get much either. The bathwater ran all night and we had to close the bathroom door so we wouldn't hear it. That was easier said than done, since the bottom of the door scraped on the floor and required a massive shove to move it. But our room was warm, dry, and spacious.

I had the cheap motel Breakfast of Champions –Fruit Loops. The colorful Fruit Loops were one of my guilty pleasures.

My back tire hissed as I pumped it. Luckily, a bike shop was nearby.

"You've got a big cut in your tire," the bike shop employee confirmed. "Our shop's tires aren't as good as yours, so you can either buy a less quality tire, or I can patch your current tire. That would probably get you to Madison."

Madison was still 150 miles away, and I didn't want to walk there. I opted for patching my tire, and hoped for the best.

We hit the Elroy-Sparta bike trail, an inductee into the Rails-to-Trails Hall of Fame. I didn't make up that last part. The Rails-to-Trails Conservancy is responsible for converting thousands of miles of old rail tracks to multi-use trails, and its Hall of Fame highlights some of the most outstanding trails. The Elroy-Sparta trail earned its spot in the Hall of Fame as the country's first rails-to-trails conversion in 1967, featuring three tunnels blasted through the rock.

There's no doubt about it—Terry and I stood on the shoulders of visionaries. Thousands of people worked to advocate for and create the trails we were enjoying. I'm grateful for those whose dreams persisted, despite the expense and challenge of doing something so immense.

I'm also thankful for bike shops, mechanics, equipment, and the kindness of strangers. It takes a village in order to live a life on the road—at least the way Terry and I were living it. To some people, we looked independent, but we knew better. Our lives were actually quite dependent on others, either directly or indirectly, to keep us pointed towards our goal.

I've spent my life standing on the shoulders of others, in my upbringing, education, work in healthcare, work at camps, and the pursuit of my daily life.

I'm deeply grateful.

🚲

The temperature plummeted as Terry and I approached the first tunnel of the Eloy-Sparta trail. With layers and lights, we initially obeyed the sign's instructions to walk our bikes in the three-quarter mile tunnel, but we were cold and the ceiling dripped. Soon we mounted our bikes, slowly pedaling down the center. Pitch black inside, our front lights narrowly shone on the bumpy surface, while menacing ditches tried to lure us to the sides.

How nerve wracking—but not nerve wracking enough to start walking again.

🚲

While we prepared for the second tunnel, a couple near our age cycled toward us to chat. Before leaving, the woman asked, "May I ask you a question?"

You know the rest.

🚲

At the final tunnel, two cyclists in their late sixties expressed interest in our trip. Terry and I told stories, including about the generosity that we so frequently experienced.

"People respond to you," one of the men said.

I don't know if it was actually Terry and me that people responded to, or just all the junk on our bikes. It was an interesting statement, however. People did respond to us, and that was one of the most energizing aspects of our trip. The curiosity, kindness, and enthusiasm of strangers enriched our journey tremendously.

From Elroy, we hit the 400 Trail, named for the train line that carried 400 passengers over 400 miles in 400 minutes between Chicago and Minneapolis.

We passed a DNR campground, instinctively raising a red flag. My nursing background automatically interpreted it as *Do Not Resuscitate Campground*, conjuring up questionable camping scenarios.

Despite the intrigue of the DNR campground, after nonstop rain for the past three hours, we opted for Reedsburg's dry motel instead.

🚲

Layered for the chilly, overcast day, I stood guard outside while Terry shopped for groceries.

"Brrr, it's cold," a woman observed. Nice to hear it from a local; it wasn't just me being a wimp.

And it wasn't just humans feeling cold. My Blackberry was frozen, too. It had been stuck since the previous afternoon, and despite multiple attempts to unstick it, I couldn't write anything, and I couldn't toggle between screens. My only way to see a different screen was to remove the battery, reinsert it, let the Blackberry boot, scroll, select one item, and open it. And then repeat.

Friends expressed amazement that I wrote my long e-mails

from my Blackberry. It didn't amaze me--that was just how I did it. It was easy to pull the little Blackberry from my pocket and write while I waited for Terry or when I had a few spare minutes. After Terry's broken arm, a co-worker nudged me into modern life, recommending I get a laptop to ease writing and looking at lengthy text. I purchased one right before we left—skinny, lightweight, and a good fit in my pannier. The computer folks were successful in transferring only nineteen out of 600 contacts from my Blackberry to the laptop. My remaining contacts were now stuck on the frozen Blackberry. I feared that would go belly up, too.

I had to look at things in perspective—at least we were still doing the bike trip. A frozen Blackberry was a little problem compared with what we had already experienced with Terry's broken arm. I could still make voice recordings, and I could use the laptop inside. With a rest day planned in Madison, I hoped to resolve the Blackberry issue and have time to write.

A vehicle came from behind while I slogged my way uphill in the pouring rain.

"Do you need a ride somewhere? Where are you going?" the driver asked.

"I'm going to the Atlantic Ocean. Could you give me a ride there?"

He laughed and drove off.

We turned off busy Highway 14 to the lesser used alphabet roads. From County Road H we turned onto County Road HH, which was near County Road T. What the heck? The roads weren't in alphabetical order and the letters didn't seem to spell anything. A quick glance at the map revealed County Road H in multiple places throughout Wisconsin.

The naming system didn't have much going for it, but the scenery was great, even in the rain. Plenty of trees, cows, and barns graced the open farm land. Other than an occasional blast of manure, the air was fresh, and the traffic was light.

The light breeze turned to wind as the rain continued, and Terry was worn out. Much of the afternoon found him laboriously pushing his recumbent uphill rather than cycling. Meanwhile, I waited. If I wasn't lucky enough to find shelter, I just stood in the rain. My mood, sour to begin the day, grew bitter. I phoned Jo, a CLV friend of Erik and Eddy's, with whom we'd planned to spend two nights, and relayed the news Terry and I wouldn't be getting to Madison that night. I felt crummy. We didn't know Jo personally, and she was gracious to host us. I hated to flake out at the last minute, but that was the reality.

At 6 p.m. we biked under darkening gray skies and drizzle, in the middle of nowhere on an alphabet road. I wondered if we'd be asking to pitch our tent in the yard of someone's house again.

With much relief, Terry and I eventually arrived at a lodge. An hour earlier, we were lost among the confusing alphabet roads, but now we relaxed inside – warm, dry, and secure for the night. How our situation changed in just one hour.

It was a good reminder not to give up too soon.

Happy birthday to me. I was fifty-five and feeling alive. Strong and healthy, too. And darn lucky to be on this bike adventure.

I celebrated with Fruit Loops.

Terry showed more oomph in the morning, but not much. He cycled slowly, but managed to bike instead of walk.

We stopped at a mini-mart, where a Coca Cola guy replenished his stock.

"It's shitty weather," he told us. In the frigid rain, Terry and I wore our many layers of gear. The Coca Cola guy was dressed in shorts. Yeah, it certainly did seem like shitty weather to be wearing shorts.

Dressed for the weather, Terry and his recumbent

Next stop, the town of Verona, home to Ellis Manufacturing and Jo's family business. Ditching our bikes, we headed out with Jo and her family for a squeaky birthday lunch.

"Cheese curds are on every menu in Wisconsin," Jo declared while we squeaked our way through a basket of the curds.

Terry and I pedaled off with Jo's condo key. Seven blocks from her condo, Madison's capitol building looks strikingly like the U.S. capitol. The city is the namesake of fourth president James Madison, who died just before the town was founded.

My birthday ended in the company of Jo's two cats and clean laundry. Being fifty-five was off to a darn good start.

🚲

After spending most of the morning in the AT&T store, I eventually walked out with an Apple iPhone – not a simple decision or transition. The employee transferred data from the Blackberry to the iPhone with partial success. I rued relinquishing the Blackberry's easy typing keyboard, even if my letters did sometimes fly around in the wind.

I did like my new phone cover, however: waterproof. That way, I could stand out in the rain and type, which seemed entirely plausible.

Relieved that my patched tire made it to Madison, I rolled out of a bike shop with a new one.

All in all, another good Slacker Day.

Thankful for Jo's welcoming hospitality, Terry and I aimed towards Milwaukee on a quiet Sunday morning. The day blazed with color from autumn leaves and a bright blue sky and lake.

I was starting to get the hang of iPhone typing, but was nervous about its "Delete" and "Save the Draft" options. Those two choices were right next to each other. What if I accidentally hit "Delete" when I meant to hit "Save"? That would be bad news, as once a draft was deleted, there was no way of retrieving it.

The Glacial Drumlin State Trail led us on converted rail tracks through an ancient glacial valley and swamp. Autumn leaves and colors crunched beneath our tires while birds serenaded in surround-sound.

Autumn at its best on a Wisconsin bike trail

Beautiful woods transitioned to farm land, with a corn field on one side and a grassy plain on the other. Exhilaration fueled my pedaling; I loved seeing the United States this way.

My walkie talkie chirped.

"I'm gonna take a nap," Terry said. "I'm tired and getting too relaxed in this sunshine."

I cycled back to where he lay on the grass taking his fifteen-minute power nap. In May, he napped on the grassy campus of Whitman College in Washington, but the temperature was about 50 degrees higher. Melting or freezing, naps were part of Terry's adventure.

Terry's tire hissed, and three nails suspiciously protruded from a wooden bridge. While Terry worked on the rear flat, a cyclist rolled up.

Terry repairing a flat along the Glacial
Drumlin State Trail in Wisconsin

"Do you need any help?" he asked. "I don't have technical expertise, but maybe I can give you a hand."

Norm did give a hand, with one problem after another: the rear flat tire, derailleur trouble, and then the front flat tire. Those nails at the bridge had done a two-fer. The front tire was a late discovery, and Terry merely pumped it up—a band-aid until getting off the trail. By now it was dark.

"Don't feel you need to wait for us, Norm," Terry told him repeatedly. We felt badly that Norm landed in our mess, unable to easily extricate himself.

"That's okay. I want to know you are okay. I'm here for your moral support." As a retired middle school teacher, it was evident he was accustomed to helping.

Two miles later, we arrived at the little town of Sullivan. Norm had already told us there was no lodging in the area.

"You are welcome to get a ride from me. My car's parked at

Sullivan. It's not big enough for everything at once, but I could make a couple of trips and get you somewhere." More kindness; our bike angels were working overtime.

They were really working overtime—in Sullivan, we discovered that a bed and breakfast had just opened above the bar.

"I do have a room available." Linda, the bar manager, competed to be heard above loud, disjointed music. "It has a shared bath and is $140, but there won't be a breakfast."

Sticker shock. That was about twice the amount we paid for our motels. But our options were limited, and the manager knew it. Terry and I looked at each other, shrugged, and nodded.

"Okay, we'll take it."

We thanked Norm and bid him farewell. How kind of him to stay with us and offer a hand, as well as car rides. He said he was there for our moral support, and he definitely gave us that.

Linda led us to an apartment above the bar and opened the door. A big surly man in his sixties stood in the kitchen. Linda had told us we'd be sharing a bathroom with someone, and he looked like he was the someone. He did not look like a happy someone, either.

"We're broken-down cyclists," I greeted him.

He eyed me and grunted. Without a word, he walked towards us, out the door, and down the stairs. Linda led us to a bedroom where we dumped our bags and descended for a second load. When we returned upstairs, Linda had some news.

"He'll be spending the night somewhere else, so you'll have the bathroom to yourselves."

Good. I wasn't concerned about the bathroom, but the guy didn't strike me as the warm and friendly type. It turned out that he was the owner. Linda had just awakened him to ask if we could spend the night.

"His wife is out of town and she's the one who provides the breakfast. That's why there's no breakfast for you tomorrow. But you can have a free dinner downstairs."

Luckily for us, it was a Sunday night, and the loud, awful music would be shutting down at nine o'clock, an hour and a half into our deafening future. We just needed to survive until then. Terry and I plugged our ears and went downstairs for our free dinner. That wasn't one dinner for each of us, it was one free dinner total. We ordered steak. We knew what to do with a free dinner.

While we were eating, Linda came over.

"Your price will be $129, not $140", she said.

I felt better about that, since I'd seen a pamphlet that advertised the B&B price at $129 a night. I hadn't felt like confronting Linda about the discrepancy, in case she decided to kick us out and invite the surly owner back.

Linda took us into the kitchen, showing where we could get hot water in the morning.

"If you steal something, we'll have it recorded on the video camera. I work in retail and I don't trust anyone."

That was good to know, since I had been planning on stealing a lot. Not.

While we ate, two guys wailed and pseudo-sang. The harmonica guy wore a red bandana, looked at the floor, and appeared completely wasted. The one who sang and played guitar looked at his audience, all five of us. Terry and I sat as far from the music as possible.

Our waitress informed us we could have two desserts, which helped take some of the sting out of the music, getting ripped off, and not being trusted.

Upstairs, I had trouble getting into the bed. It was high, and I am not. I couldn't even take a flying leap. I had to claw my way up by grabbing the bedspread near the center of the bed and pull myself up. I felt like I was mountain climbing just to get up onto the bed.

I made it into bed, thankful for so much.

After replacing his front tube in the morning, Terry and I hit the trail in the surprisingly warm October sunshine. It felt like summer, and I was practically naked.

Already three days behind our ideal schedule, we fell further behind, and so far, none of it was due to weather. There was no sense in getting worked up; there was nothing I could do about it. Roll with the punches, and keep going.

Terry's front tire had an impressive cut from the nail, but Dousman's bike shop had neither tube nor small tire for the recumbent. A detour to a major bike shop in Milwaukee was in our future.

Rain fell for hours. Cycling under a dry Milwaukee freeway overpass, I instinctively thought it would be a good place to pitch the tent if necessary. That's how my brain worked.

"Where are you going?" A thirty-something cyclist caught up, also decked out in rain gear, reflectors, and rear panniers. Jaimie stuck with us.

"I'm a bike commuter. I ride about twenty-two miles per day. I don't use my car much. It's old and I don't want to wear it out. I like to see if I can get by on less than six gallons of gas per year."

"Six gallons"?

"Yeah, I bike year-round. I use carbide tires in the winter. They're great at gripping ice, but they're not great on pavement. I wish that it was snowing instead of raining today."

Not me—I was okay with the rain.

"Do you know where there's a big bike shop around here?" Terry asked. "I need a tube and a new front tire for my recumbent."

"There's a bike shop close to my place. I'll just take you to it."

Perfect--another personal escort through a congested town.

"It's gonna smell bad up here," he cautioned as we cycled through an industrial area. "It's a tannery and it stinks."

Good to be warned. I tried not to breathe, unsuccessfully, and discovered nothing smelled bad. Maybe the wind was blowing tannery stink in someone else's direction.

"We're planning to catch the 6 a.m. ferry tomorrow. Are there any motels around there?" Terry asked.

"I live near the ferry, and I don't think so. I'd let you stay at my place, but it's very small." After a pause, he added "I'm also somewhat of a hoarder."

Somewhat of a hoarder? Is that like being a little bit pregnant?

At the bike shop, I inquired about local lodging while someone assisted Terry. Nothing was close, and the motels were about five miles from the ferry. Normally that wouldn't be an issue, but the ferry left before daylight.

We offered to treat Jaimie to dinner at a nearby café.

"No, thank you. I don't eat out, and I don't trust food from restaurants." He left with plans to return.

At the café, Wren and Evan looked young and hip. We picked their brains about lodging, and they picked ours about our trip. Evan's laptop search yielded nothing.

"I'll make some phone calls and see what I can do." He sounded optimistic.

Jaimie returned. "It definitely won't work for you to stay at my place. My ex-girlfriend is back. She's bi-polar, lost her purse, and there's a lot of drama right now." Jaimie's situation sounded more interesting with every new nugget of information.

It felt like Mission Control at the café. The five of us gathered around two tables with maps, phones, and a computer. Three strangers put their time and energy into helping two unknown bicyclists find lodging for the night. Their friendliness and support gave me a giant, warm fuzzy.

"I've got a place for you," Evan beamed. "My friend Bill is a cyclist and has offered to let you stay in his basement. He's got about 15 bikes in his garage. He lives close to the ferry and owns a record store not far from here. He said for you to come to his store now."

Wow.

Their enthusiasm and willingness to help exemplified the kindness Terry and I experienced so frequently on our trip. And we were on our way from one generous situation to another. With heartfelt thanks, we bid farewell to Jaimie, Wren, and Evan, and headed out into the dark and pouring rain.

We dripped our way into Rushmor Records, a small store with a treasure trove of old vinyl. Bill easily identified us as his wayfaring strangers.

"I'm happy to pay it forward," he explained. "Cyclists and record people— they're like clubs. I know I could show up at a record store, get to talking with the owner or employees, and be offered all sorts of welcoming hospitality, too."

Damp and chilly from ten more minutes of street splash and rain, Terry and I eagerly arrived at Bill and Kate's. Walking between their garage and basement, I counted 19 bikes, excluding ours. Kate and I swapped nurse talk; she worked for Planned Parenthood and with victims of sexual violence.

"You've got to take a little bit of Wisconsin with you on the rest of your bike trip," she explained, giving us a bag of cheese curds while the dryer did its magic on our clothes.

Once again Terry and I were grateful. It was such a community effort to get us to this point for the night. Thanks to the generosity of Jaimie, Wren, Evan, Bill, and Kate, Terry and I were safe, comfortable, and felt welcomed into random hospitality. Again. I felt cloaked in generosity.

"The welfare of travelers is dependent upon the kindness of strangers."

Those words permanently resided in my brain, and I found them to be true, time and time again.

Up at four o'clock, Terry and I repacked everything into our somewhat drier panniers, wrote a thank you note to Bill and Kate, and departed. Ten foggy minutes later we arrived at the ferry terminal, and soon sailed into darkness.

Sometime later out in the fog, we floated into Michigan.

CHAPTER 15

Electrifying–Michigan

Hello, Eastern Time Zone, the last time zone of our trip. We were practically there.

Our watches leaped forward an hour, giving us one less hour to bike before dark.

Muskegon, Michigan, was a decision point. If the long-range weather forecast was favorable, our plan was to bike east to my cousin Jody and David's home in southern Ontario, Canada. If snow was predicted, we'd head south, hoping to escape the weather. Happily, the ten-day forecast held no snow predictions, so we aimed for Jody and David's. By choosing that route, we could also meet and stay with a co-worker's mother in Almont.

Stopping at a bike shop for some hooks, our bikes ignited conversation.

"One of our employees started an east coast bike tour this summer," one man said. "He went with a friend, and once they came to North Carolina, they decided to ditch the bikes and hitchhike to Florida. He said that when they had their bikes, people were gracious and generous to them, but once they were without their bikes and were hitchhiking, people ignored them on the roads."

The moral of that story: always have your bikes with you.

The corn saga continued. Big, yellow kernels lay orphaned along the county road's shoulder, blazing a trail towards a mysterious somewhere.

By late afternoon, the rain came and went, came and went. Lightning flashed above us in the dark clouds, accompanied by booming thunder and pouring rain. I spied a farmhouse with a big veranda, and busted my arse to get under its eaves. Terry stood with his bike under a tree by the road.

"Terry!" I yelled. "Come up to the house!"

He didn't budge. I yelled while the lightning and thunder went wild. A woman, older than me, came out from the house and joined me.

"Come up here!" she yelled at him.

Terry responded to her command.

"I'm glad you came up," she said to him. "I didn't want someone to die out under my tree."

We three stood on the porch, watching and listening. I felt awkward imposing, but the storm gave us no choice. After introductions, Terry and I told about our trip.

The storm continued, and after ten minutes of porch-talk, a car arrived and Ardie's husband, Mike, joined us on the porch.

"Our house is up on the highest part of this plateau," Mike told us.

"This area gets a lot of lightning," Ardie added, as another bolt emphasized her words.

"Are there any motels nearby?" Terry asked.

"No," Ardie responded. "There might be some cabins four miles down the road, but I don't know if they are open."

By the time the storm passed, it would be dark. Terry and I were still many miles from lodging. One option was to bike ten miles south to Grand Rapids, but that was south, and we wanted to go east.

"I could drive you to Grand Rapids to a motel," Mike offered.

"You could keep your bikes at our house tonight, and then I could come and pick you up in the morning," That was a nice offer, but I didn't want to inconvenience him, especially twice.

"I could also shuttle you and your bikes to Greenville," he added. Greenville was eighteen miles to the east, where Terry and I originally planned to spend the night. That was another nice offer, but that meant that we'd ride a car for eighteen miles, and I didn't like that idea either. Terry and I accepted rides twice during the first part of our trip, but that was for two miles in a snow/rain storm with a flat tire in Montanta, and for five miles during the heavy wind storm in Wyoming. I would thankfully accept a ride in extreme circumstances, but not just as a matter of convenience.

"Could we pitch our tent on your veranda and spend the night here?" I asked.

They hesitated but said yes. "We'll be locking the door at night," Mike said, "but you can pee off the porch." Peeing off the porch was fine with me.

"Mari, we need to talk about this." Terry didn't look happy. Ardie and Mike went inside the house so Terry and I could duke it out. "Let's just go to a motel, get inside for the night, and be near some food."

I wasn't willing to let go so easily. "We're already here, we'll be dry. We've got food for tonight, and you can get breakfast food down the road."

Neither one was happy with the other's point of view, but Terry eventually acquiesced. I owed him one.

I knocked and Mike answered. "We've decided to accept your offer to let us pitch our tent on your porch. Thank you very much."

"Okay." Pause. "Well, you might as well join us for dinner, too."

It didn't sound like a hearty invitation--more like one given from obligation. Even so, we gratefully accepted. It was win-win for Terry and me; Terry would eat something other than his pannier food, and it lessoned my guilty conscience.

We invaded the veranda with bikes, a tent tied with rope to railings and heavy panniers, and an explosion of wet rain gear.

Mike and Ardie's porch, our safe haven in the lightning storm

As Ardie prepared dinner, we spread maps and asked our hosts about possible routes. Eastwards, we needed to bike eighty miles to find lodging, but a southern detour to Portland promised a shorter day. Besides, Portland had a nice ring to it.

Dinner conversation turned to volunteer work, and Terry talked about a short volunteer stint we did in Lesotho, Africa, a couple years earlier through our church. Before dinner concluded, another invitation appeared.

"You'd be welcome to use the shower if you'd like," Mike offered. Well, yes, we would like.

While Terry showered, Ardie showed me her dining room adorned in quilts, some completed and others in the process. Winning national and international quilt contests, Ardie's designs jumped out from colorful fabric.

"I belong to a quilter's guild that makes quilts for neonatal babies and children in need."

We looked at photos of her other quilts. Ardie's talent and creativity left me in awe.

Terry came out clean, and then it was my turn. After showering,

I joined everyone in the living room, where Mike and Ardie told us about their farmhouse, built during the mid-1800s.

"When we were remodeling, we found newspapers from the Civil War under some of the flooring," Ardie explained. Cool!

Terry stood up after a while. "I'm going to call it a night," he said. "Thank you for dinner and the shower. Good night—see you in the morning."

"We have a spare bedroom and bed. You might as well sleep inside if you'd like," Mike offered.

Terry and I looked at each other and at Mike and Ardie. That was unexpected. Sleeping inside did sound cozier than sleeping outside, and we happily accepted their offer.

What an unexpected ending to our day. We'd met Ardie and Mike four hours ago, and apparently that was sufficient time to convince them we weren't serial killers or going to bike away with their belongings. Once more, we felt lucky. So close to the lightning storm earlier, we were now safely ensconced inside a house. Clearly, Ardie and Mike were reluctant hosts initially; Terry and I were like ticks that clung and wouldn't go away. I was happy to receive permission to camp on their veranda, and then the evening gradually progressed from one welcome surprise to another.

Terry and I drifted to sleep, warm and snug under Ardie's quilts, and grateful for her and Mike's hospitality to two refugees from a lightning storm.

"We had a wonderful sleep under your beautiful quilts, Ardie," I said at breakfast "Thank you for the cozy night, and for all the hospitality you've given us. From dinner to showers to inviting us to sleep inside, you've been very kind to two strangers who unexpectedly landed on your doorstep."

"I'm just glad that Terry didn't die out under my tree." Ardie repeated her sentiment from the day before.

"It would have been awkward for us to eat dinner inside last night and have you outside in the cold, eating whatever you were going to eat," Mike declared. We all laughed.

"It ended up being a pleasure to have you." Mike smiled and Ardie nodded.

That was a relief to hear, since I bet it didn't start out being a pleasure to have us.

With heartfelt thanks for their kindness and willingness to take us in, Terry and I pedaled into thick fog. Mike and Ardie's hospitality provoked a great deal of thought. The whole thing transitioned one step at a time, with long pauses between the steps. Run to someone's porch in a lightning storm. Pause. Ask to pitch a tent on their porch. Pause. Get invited inside for dinner. Pause. Get invited to shower. Pause. Get invited in to sleep for the night. It was clear that Mike and Ardie were uncomfortable with us at the beginning, but it was equally clear they were comfortable by the end. The whole process gave me more to chew on.

People live in their world of norms. "What is normal for the spider is chaos for the fly" Morticia Addams notes from the Addams family, via Charles Addams. What is normal for one person may be horrifying to another. We get accustomed to our own ways of thinking and behaving, and assume that everyone should feel the same way.

One of the rewards of bike touring is meeting people outside my regular sphere. If I only interacted with people who thought like me, who would awaken me to new ways of thinking? I can learn new perspectives from reading or listening to media, but it pales in comparison with the face-to-face interactions that are inherent on a bike journey.

Acceptance of new ideas is often a slow process, occurring in small amounts. As one gets accustomed to one new idea, there is receptiveness for another.

Sometimes acceptance occurs in a flash and sometimes it occurs incrementally, but it always leads to new beginnings.

Gradually a clear world appeared from the fog, as did some poor shoulders and more corn kernels.

At a vibrant pumpkin patch and country market near Greenville, we loaded up on goodies and feasted outside near the check-out counter. Terry and I made a second pass through the market for more apple cider.

"You're back," a clerk noted. We were hard to miss in our fluorescent-green safety vests. Clothing subtlety was not our strong suit.

"That cider is great. We're on a cross-country bike trip and that's the best drink we've had in a long time. We're loading up."

"A cross-country bike trip? That's what all that stuff is on your bikes?"

"Yeah." That led to my favorite conversation, which led to the clerk calling to another employee who was standing nearby.

"Did you hear that, they're biking cross-country!"

It was a ripple effect. One clerk enthusiastically told another, and then both women were telling other employees. Within a few minutes, Terry and I felt like celebrities as a handful of people gave us kudos, compliments, and words of support.

We left the market with nourishment for both our bodies and our spirits – and we left with some news.

"There's a hurricane coming next week," one woman told us, "but this area of Michigan shouldn't be affected. Its name is Hurricane Sandy."

A hurricane. Terry and I figured we'd probably encounter some snow on this leg of our trip, but a hurricane wasn't on our radar. That gave us something new to consider.

The trail of corn kernels led us through the afternoon, bringing us to a town and a sign: *Welcome to Portland, City of Two Rivers.* Hey, that was like our Portland, too.

We arrived well before twilight, completing a smooth, sixty-seven mile day. That was just what Terry wanted – to stop early, with plenty of time to relax in the evening. Our cycling styles during the summer had been yin and yang; if conditions were good, I was happy to keep cycling into the evening, as long as there was enough light. Terry wanted to spend his evenings relaxing, and was often unhappy with my desire to get further down the road.

No yin and yang wrestling today. After two nights of imposing ourselves at the last minute on unsuspecting hosts, we slipped into the easy anonymity of a motel: no dramatic entrance, no outlandish request to pitch a tent on a porch, no surprise or hesitation to take us in. With a vacancy sign on their part, and a credit card on ours, Terry had a taste of how he liked our cycling days to end: early, and with prolonged relaxation to follow.

In the morning, we headed north from Portland on the Divine Highway, which was flagrantly misnamed. A two-lane highway with no shoulders, the meter-wide swath of road furthest to the right was full of cracks, bumps, and debris, making it difficult to cycle straight. The best pavement was close to the center of the highway. Terry and I would take over our entire lane when we could and move to the side when we couldn't. Whatever the highway was like back when it was named, it was certainly no longer divine.

We did find our divine in the small town of Westphalia, though. Terry and I stopped at a little market to replenish snacks. The two clerks, who were sisters, spied our loaded bikes through the window, leading to an animated conversation.

"It's such a fantastic adventure," one of the sisters said. "It's inspiring to hear your stories." She handed us a package of teriyaki beef jerky. "Our family makes this jerky. It's well known in this region. Please take this as a gift. This will give you some energy for your ride."

How kind. She was right—that teriyaki jerky would give us energy, but she probably didn't realize that the biggest power lay in its emotional energy, not its caloric energy. It represented generosity and encouragement. With thanks to the women, Terry and I rode away while their supportive words and gift of jerky boosted us down the road.

We had summer cycling on a late October day. With the temperature in the 70's, my skin craved the breeze and sunshine, clamoring to be exposed. I rolled up my cotton pants and bared my arms to the sun, relishing the refreshing breeze against my skin. I savored our beautiful day while I could.

We passed a house in the country with a row of blue-gray pumpkins on its lawn. A sign read *Blue pumpkins for pies, $3 each*, with a Folgers coffee can next to the pumpkins. That's how business was done in rural Michigan. Easy and trustful.

Other folks tended their leaves and rode lawn mowers. One man was even shirtless. Michigan was making the most of a warm, inviting afternoon.

Four motorcyclists approached us from the other direction, and we all did the low five motorcycle hand wave. That was a triumphant wave. It felt good to be included in the motorcycle hand wave club again. I missed it while driving across the U.S. in the van.

Wind chimes went crazy as the afternoon shifted. We rode east and the winds blew north, sometimes with alarming results. An oncoming car and a particularly big gust of wind appeared simultaneously. The gust shoved me to the center lane in one big swoop. Two fearful faces eyeballed each other, both aghast as the oncoming car and veering bike nearly met. The car sped past as my heart hammered. That was a close call.

We rolled into Durand well before dark, exhausted from fighting the new wind. That was two days in a row of arriving somewhere without experiencing darkness, a flat tire, rain storm, or a lightning storm. How deliciously bland to arrive during daylight without a crisis.

Terry's recumbent legs were finally kicking in. Cycling faster on the flats and hills, he could pedaled up inclines without having to walk. Told it would take a thousand miles to develop his recumbent muscles, he was now over eight hundred. His faster and stronger riding encouraged us both.

Goodbye to summer weather. A big temperature drop was predicted for the night.

We awoke to clouds and 46 degrees. Autumn returned while we slept.

Hurricane Sandy hogged the news, having first slammed through Jamaica and Cuba, spreading death and destruction before heading north off Florida's coast. It was predicted to pummel its way up the east coast into New Jersey and New York, right where we were headed. Our destination was a New Jersey beach, but we weren't expecting to arrive for another three weeks. Hurricane Sandy's arrival was anticipated for a week earlier, shortly before Halloween. It already earned a new moniker: Frankenstorm.

Our day filled with hills and dropping temperatures. Terry continued to cycle uphill, wearing his alarming looking face mask. He looked like a force to be reckoned with, on his motorcycle-looking recumbent.

Cycling uphill, my bike stopped short and I barely managed not to fall over. I tried to pedal; no go. My back tire was stuck. A large stick, two feet long and almost an inch thick, was jammed in the back. I pulled it; still no tire movement. My rear fender was bent with my tire jammed against it—all were stuck.

Terry began roadside surgery. Off went gear and tire. The fender was kaput, but we had to remove my bike rack and kickstand first. We busted the fender in two places in order to remove it.

It was definitely a two-person job. Once again, I was grateful for Terry's assistance. While I can ride my bike, I am certainly not adept at fixing it.

Thirty minutes later, the screws and tire were in, and brakes were adjusted. My kickstand plus three pieces of fender nestled under the bungees behind me. Who needs a kickstand and a fender anyway? Lots of cyclists live without them.

"It's a good thing you didn't take a fall," Terry noted. "If you would have been going fast, you'd have probably been thrown off your bike."

Luckily, I'd been going up a steep hill--no speed in that.

"Welcome! You must be Mari and Terry! I'm Barb. Do come in!" Barb welcomed us warmly as we stood outside her country home a short time later.

Barb was a riot, just like her son, Kevin, my co-worker at Home Infusion. Terry and I felt so welcome, so fast. We ate in the living room, in the presence of family photos and a big hutch. A little Kevin smiled out at us from a photo on an end table, and dozens of eyes peered down from the hutch. The eyes belonged to Barbie and Ken dolls – five shelves of them. More Barbies and Kens watched from their unopened boxes on the floor.

"Many people call me Barbie. My husband's name was Ken, and people started giving me Barbie and Ken dolls. I ended up with so many that I made a collection."

Barbies in ball gowns and swim suits, Kens in beach attire and a top hat—dozens of Barbies and Kens eyeballed us from the hutch while we ate. If a person was inclined to get creeped out by Barbie and Ken dolls, that would have been the place. While growing up, I never liked my Barbie doll, but I didn't mind an entire hutch of them that belonged to someone else. After all, for a human couple named Barbie and Ken, it only made sense that they had a posse of Barbie and Ken dolls in their living room.

The dolls listened in as we made a phone call to my workplace back in Portland. I asked for the Intake Pharmacist at Home Infusion.

"Hello," I said without identifying myself. "I'm feeling a little dehydrated. Could you please send some bags of normal saline to Almont, Michigan?"

"I'm sorry, ma'am, but we don't ship that far," Kevin laughed.

Terry and I started and ended our week as guests in people's homes, with some guesting in between. A week earlier, we were guests at Jo's in Madison; two nights later we were guests at Bill and Kate's in Milwaukee; the next night at Mike and Ardie's; and now we were guests at Barb's. Back in Portland, our church advocates radical hospitality, and Terry and I were frequent recipients of radical hospitality that week. We received refuge from a rain storm and then a lightning storm, received a gift of homemade jerky, and were graciously welcomed into a co-worker's family home. Radical hospitality was that week's theme, in both physical and psychological ways.

We gratefully received it.

Barb pointed to a field.

"Geese are landing there for the nights now. They arrive in the evening and take off in the morning."

That sounded like Terry and me. I wondered if the geese had tired wings at the end of their day, like we often had tired legs.

Goodbye to Barb. She was so welcoming, friendly, quirky, and we felt right at home with her. It was easy to see from where Kevin acquired his friendliness and sense of humor. What a gift to connect with his family as part of our adventure. Some of the best parts of our bike trip were the human relationships, old and new.

Eating Kate's Wisconsin cheese curds, we had been curding our way across Michigan, although my iPhone's Spell Check automatically changed "curding" to "cursing." It was time for some serious eating before hitting the Canadian border, since cheese curds might be considered too dangerous for a border crossing.

Roadkill was on the ground and politicians were on the billboards. Cynics might have claimed they were one and the same. With election day less than two weeks away, politicians and political views bombarded us from signs along the roads.

Who needs a kickstand and a fender? I contemplated that question the day before and came up with an answer: me. Well, I didn't need them, but I *wanted* them. I was without my kickstand for only 24 hours, but it was darn inconvenient. I either needed to prop my heavy bike against something, or lay it on the ground. Laying it on the ground was the easy part; getting it back up with all its heavy panniers and gear was a piece of work.

We rolled into a Port Huron bike shop to accessorize my bike. With all the potential rain in our future, a fender made sense. Fenders, however, came in pairs.

"Do you want the other fender?" the bike guy asked me.

No, I did not want to carry a spare fender with me. I already had an excessive amount of crap, and I certainly did not need an extra fender on top of everything else.

With a working kickstand and a new rear fender, it was time to leave the country. With mounting excitement at reaching a new border, and an international one at that, Terry and I followed the sign for *Bridge to Canada*. Because the bridge does not allow bicycles, a Michigan Department of Transportation employee motioned us to a picnic table to wait. Several minutes later, a woman appeared.

"My name is Vicki and I'll be taking you over the bridge in my truck. Put your bikes in there." Vicki motioned to a MDOT pickup.

Bike went in the back, and the rest of our stuff, plus us, went into the double cab.

"Do you two have your passports?" Vicki asked us.

Yep, we hadn't lost them yet.

"It's been about six weeks since any cyclists came over this bridge. You're cycling late in the year."

Yeah, we knew that. We told her our excuse.

The Blue Water Bridge is a toll bridge, charging vehicles three bucks to cross. The charge for delivering our bikes and gear in a MDOT truck over the bridge? Nothing, nada, zero. Thank you, Michigan tax payers.

Vicki stopped at the customs booth. "I have two cyclists who are biking across North America."

The customs agent peered into the truck at us.

"Do you have any weapons or knives?" he asked.

"Just Swiss Army knives," Terry answered.

The customs agent looked bored with that answer, and that was the end of our interrogation.

With our thanks and good byes, Vicki drove off, leaving us with bikes and gear piled before a stone building, whose entrance sign read:

Canada Customs Immigration.

CHAPTER 16

Stormy—Ontario

I approached a customs agent.

"Is it okay to get a photo of the customs sign with our bikes?"

I knew that photos aren't allowed at some international borders; when I took a picture at customs in Lesotho, an agent became agitated and personally deleted photos from my camera. I didn't need to start an imbroglio with Canada.

"I don't know," he said. "Go inside and ask someone in there."

I went inside to a customs agent at a counter.

"Would it be okay to get a photo of the Customs sign?" I asked.

"I guess," he shrugged. "I didn't even know we had a sign." Canada seemed relaxed about the whole photo thing.

I went back outside. As I was getting ready to take a photo of Terry, his bike, and the Canada Customs Immigration sign, a different customs agent came over.

"You aren't allowed to take photos here," he sternly told me.

"I asked someone inside, who said it was okay."

He raised his eyebrows, saying nothing.

"Could you please take a photo of the two of us and our bikes here?" I asked him.

"That would be going too far," he replied.

Sarnia, Ontario, Canada. Yeah, baby.

Terry and I already knew the roads near Jody and David's were shoulderless, and that the main highway from Sarnia to London was too busy for our comfort. A rural road south of the highway took us to Wyoming. We had just arrived at Ontario, and now we were in Wyoming. More craziness. We settled in at a motel.

"Storms are converging and it's expected to get pretty windy and wet in the next 24 hours," the owner said.

That made me nervous. In twenty-four hours, we expected to be at Jody and David's, but what if the storms came before then? What if they turned out to be wild things?

With six hundred miles to the Atlantic, we were closing in—but a storm was brewing.

The butterflies in my stomach fluttered wildly, making it hard to sleep.

We watched the TV's morning news. Downgraded to a tropical storm, Sandy still expected to wallop and kill.

"Sandy is expected to make landfall tomorrow in New Jersey and Delaware," a meteorologist grimly informed us. A cold front from the north was anticipated to push Sandy westwards, putting Washington D.C., Philadelphia, and New York City right in line for Sandy's violent onslaught.

Inland and near Sarnia where we entered Canada, rain and 20 miles per hour winds were anticipated. That kind of wind is nothing compared to a hurricane, but while riding a bike, it's something to consider. Headwinds could push against us, crosswinds could blow us around the road. We could only hope for tailwinds.

I peered from the window. Still dark, I watched tree branches claw at the wind. We hoped to make Jody and David's by nightfall. That statement seemed defeatist. I changed my outlook to "We *will* be at Jody and David's for the night," even if it meant nabbing a ride in a vehicle in order to get there. If a big storm was coming in twenty-four hours, we needed to be at Jody and David's, one way or the other. Terry and I packed up and waited for daylight.

We just wanted to be on our way and get 'er done. I felt tense. Plans for a smooth ride often fail: flat tires, sticks attacking fenders, injuries. If we encountered trouble and a delay, we could be in for a dicey situation out in a storm. Terry and I left in the dark.

A path of corn kernels led the way, and the cold wind bit menacingly.

We stopped at a little store out in the sticks, and a man walked over to our bikes.

"Where are you going today? You do know there are storms on their way, don't you?"

"Yeah, we know. We're heading to St. Mary's, where we'll stay with my cousin. We hope to get there this afternoon before the two storms converge."

"Two storms? There are three of them. One is coming from eastern Ontario, one is a hurricane that's coming up the east coast of the U.S., and one is a storm that is coming from the west, from Calgary. They are all expected to converge here in southern Ontario tonight. It's expected to be quite a storm." He eyed us nervously.

Three storms. We didn't realize there was a third one. Now I was even more tense. It was a good reason to get back on the bikes and start pedaling again.

A half hour later, the wind picked up, busting at us from the north as we cycled east. Gusts pummeled us on the road, but at least the rain held off. We were cold, blown, but dry, which was better than being cold, blown, and wet.

I phoned Jody.

"We expect to get there before dinner. But if something happens and delays us, could you or David pick us up?"

"Sure, just keep us posted. You'll be getting here just in time."

We sure hoped so.

We sought lunchtime refuge in a mini-mart, our first chance to escape into a public building in the last two hours. We were more than ready for a break from the cold wind. Besides the chance to thaw, I liked wandering the aisles of French. The bilingual labels and signs were a French lesson in itself. O Canada, you are so much fun.

Soon I saw a corn swoosher--not its technical name. A farm vehicle with a big, cylindrical arm swooshed yellow corn kernels into a long truck. Attached, the two vehicles appeared to be mating. Ahh... a source of my mysterious corn kernels.

The winds persisted, and a gust blew me right off the pavement. Fortunately, it blew me into the rocky shoulder on the right, and not into traffic. By mid-afternoon, the rain let loose, but there wasn't much more clothing to put on. We already wore most of it, trying to keep the cold wind from boring through.

Tension pulsed through every pedal revolution. Could we reach Jody and David's before the wind, rain, and cold took a dangerous turn?

Storms were on their way, and Terry and I were understandably concerned for our safety. But what about the safety of others? My immediate thoughts weren't on others, just Terry and me. As usual, my focus wasn't on the bigger picture.

These storms impacted us, but they had a far greater impact on thousands of other people. It's easy to go through life being near-sighted, only noticing what's near and pertinent to you. It takes more effort to be intentionally aware of the broader world.

The mere fact that we were on a cross-country bike trip illustrated a myopic slice of life. We had the time, health, and money to do a lengthy, self-serving trip, while much of the world struggled on a daily basis just to survive. We struggled on a daily basis, too, but ours was a self-inflicted struggle, unlike conditions for so many others.

I wasn't concentrating on the bigger picture, but fortunately, many others were. Thank goodness for them—people who cast their nets wide to help, not only for these storms, but for the other storms of life, both physical and mental, that assault people on a daily basis around the world. Thank goodness for people whose planning and actions save or assist thousands of lives. And thank goodness for heroes whose selfless deeds save or assist the lives of a few.

As usual, there's much for me to learn, and many people to appreciate.

⬥

Hours later, and dripping with water and relief, Terry and I finally rolled into Jody and David's driveway. We'd made it.

Safe from the increasingly malevolent weather, Terry and I could finally relax. We ate, drank, and warmed up, shedding worries as we laughed and talked inside Jody and David's comfy house. Anxiety vanished. After all, I was in a brick house. I knew from the Three Little Pigs that a house made from bricks was a strong one.

The big, bad wolf was coming, but I wasn't scared.

⬥

Slacker Day.

The two approaching Canadian storms escalated while we slept, and Sandy veered towards New Jersey. All three whipped up a froth. It was easy to check storm reports throughout the day, as TV and computer updates were practically nonstop. Rain and wind increased as the day progressed, pounding the world outside. Tree branches waved wildly. In contrast to the mayhem outside, life inside was tranquil. I contentedly spent my time writing, chatting, playing the piano, and being lazy.

Before the storms entered the picture, our plan was to spend two nights with Jody and David, allowing one full day together. But with the wild weather, Terry and I decided to hunker down until it was safe to be out again, whenever that was. We had our port in the storm, plus it was a port filled with laughter, love, and Jody's delicious food. How terrific was that?

By the time we went to bed, Superstorm Sandy slammed ashore, bringing an especially high tidal surge. In New York City, water overflowed the seawall, flooding streets, part of the subway system, and a tunnel linking Manhattan and Brooklyn. Trees and power lines toppled throughout the eastern states and Canadian provinces, eliminating power for millions of people along the eastern seaboard.

Outside Jody and David's house, the local storm pummeled and poured. We were safe, but we knew that wasn't the case for others. Sandy was expected to continue battering New Jersey and New York throughout the night. Millions of people lived in the wide swath of the three storms, which promised to become more lethal in the hours to come.

We reluctantly turned off the news and went to bed.

🚲

Hurricane Hang Out Day.

Up early, I watched trees thrash in the wind. Snatched from the house, a deck awning lay on the ground, with crumpled metal poles.

We watched news of the Atlantic coast's devastation. The winds demolished houses and buildings, people were crushed by falling objects or drowned in the flooding, and countless were injured, homeless, and devastated.

A hundred miles away, Toronto experienced a massive power outage from the convergence of the three storms. The storm toppled trees, wrecked cars, and claimed more lives. The Canadian Hurricane Center reported that Sandy's impact extended over six hundred miles from the superstorm. Winds, including those backside, were still on the move and traveling north, towards us.

Much of the eastern coast and the inland areas were in chaos, and we sat transfixed by the appalling images on TV.

And what of local conditions? In the afternoon, Jody and David's son, JD, stopped by.

"The roads are clear between here and Niagara Falls," he told us.

That was just what we wanted to hear, and just where we were headed. Terry and I wondered if our bike route might have power outages or not be passable with fallen trees or power lines, but JD drove much of that route that day. With his knowledge of the roads, he planned a route for us and scanned some local maps.

"If there are problems and you get stuck somewhere with no place to stay, give a call," Jody offered. "David or I can come pick you up." Her promise was a welcome safety blanket.

Weather conditions changed from one night to the next, becoming almost balmy compared with the wild night before. With JD's report of clear roads, it appeared that conditions were safe for us to resume biking in the morning. With three weeks and twelve hundred miles of cycling behind us for this second leg of our trip, it was time to venture into the post-Sandy world and continue towards the Atlantic.

We just hoped it wasn't a dumb thing to do.

Halloween! What were we? The tricks or the treats?

In a light rain but no wind, we headed out. With plans to join us at Niagara Falls, we'd be seeing Jody and David again soon.

Superstorm Sandy moved inland with winds and rain but had lost its initial ferocity. The post-storm world was still a dangerous place, though. Behind us in Sarnia, where we crossed the U.S./Canadian border three days earlier, a power worker was electrocuted while restoring power lines.

JD was right--the roads were in good shape. Nicely paved with minimal traffic, they were remarkably free from debris. The cycling was easy and I suspected a subtle tailwind. Although the two Ontario storms already passed, Sandy was still moving northwards, and Terry and I were cycling straight towards its projected path.

What wasn't clear was what the wind strengths would be, nor what Terry and I should be doing in relation to them.

At a produce market, Terry and I sat in our wet clothes under the building's eaves, watching the rain fall while we ate market goodies. Filled with a lemon bars, pumpkin muffins, and a quart of apple cider, my pannier became a diabetic's nightmare.

A few wet miles later, we arrived at Mt. Hope, our Halloween motel for the night, and the end of our 76-mile day. Halloween came without fanfare—that was the trick. At least I had a little pumpkin, otherwise my favorite holiday would have been completely snubbed.

A sign welcomed us to the City of Niagara Falls. Rolling along downriver from the falls, we were like children waiting for Christmas--all that excitement as we anticipated seeing Niagara Falls at every turn. We passed by old, grand houses along the river, and cycled under the Rainbow Bridge, which connects Niagara Falls, Ontario, Canada, to Niagara Falls, New York, USA. Two towns with the same name live across from each other in different countries.

Finally, American Falls came into view. What a spectacular sight to watch the thousand-foot-wide swath of whitewater fall, crashing against the rocks below. The magnificent half-mile-wide Horseshoe Falls thundered beyond it. Standing on the sidewalk next to its drop off, we watched the falls disappear practically right beneath our feet.

What an incredible feeling to reach Niagara Falls from the Pacific Ocean by our bikes.

Niagara Falls, Ontario, Canada

We turned our sights to the more mundane matter of lodging, where our bikes complicated the check-in process. Suspicious of them, the desk clerk called a housekeeper. Terry's recumbent was too long to fit in the elevator, so he stayed behind while the housekeeper accompanied me and my bike up to the room. Entering the room first, she spread an old sheet on the floor. Like housebreaking a puppy, my bike was supposed to make its mess on the old sheet.

Meanwhile, Terry parked his recumbent somewhere on the first floor, receiving a similar treatment with an old sheet. Our bikes would be housebroken in no time.

Up in our room, our wet gear and clothing dripped. Good thing for the giant diaper on the floor.

Evening found us leisurely meandering along the boardwalk above the river. With two more days at Niagara Falls, we could be lazy.

Slacker Day.

Terry and I needed to make another critical decision for the trip, due to Hurricane Sandy's devastating sweep of the East Coast. Cycling to Philadelphia had been one of our potential plans, to pick up our friend Clifton on his bike, and cycle as a trio for the final day of our trip. Terry and I would end our cross-country bike trip at Clifton's favorite New Jersey beach, with Clifton's mom and brother meeting us there for a big celebration. That was a marvelous idea.

However, our marvelous idea wasn't so marvelous anymore. New Jersey was battered. TV reports showed demolished buildings, boats, and other structures. New Jersey had enough problems of its own without having touring cyclists show up seeking housing.

Boston lay due east from Niagara Falls, and it was on the Atlantic. Thirty-two years earlier when I first hatched my cross-country bike idea, I envisioned ending the trip in Boston. Now, post-Superstorm Sandy, Boston again emerged as a candidate.

I phoned Clifton.

"Parsley!"

Clifton, his mom, and his brother were all okay, having safely made it through the storm. After swapping news of everyone's welfare, Clifton gave some other news.

"I recently received a fellowship through Teach for America to go to Mexico for some home building. I'm scheduled to leave for Mexico on November 11, and I'll be working with people from nine countries and three organizations to help build a home for a Mexican family."

The opportunity sounded fantastic.

"It's ironic," he continued. "The organization is paying me to fly across the country to help build a house for one family, and yet there are many families, literally in my back yard, who have lost homes from Sandy and need help, too. What if we changed the Mexico trip, brought that Mexican family here, had the Rudds here, and we all spoke in Spanish and helped rebuild homes in New Jersey?"

That sounded terrific but unlikely, especially since I didn't speak Spanish.

The timing disappointed me--I wanted to see Clifton. Perhaps Terry and I could get to Philadelphia in time. That schedule was workable, a week away, but what if we ran into problems and didn't arrive until after Clifton already left? That area no longer had a welcoming beach, anyway.

Boston looked like the best option. Boston had a harbor, and possibly a beach. Or, maybe we'd just keep going to Cape Cod and end a little further out in the Atlantic. Cape Cod would require another two days of cycling beyond Boston, and we didn't know what services were open in November. Terry and I had been laughed off our bicycle seats for assuming that Maine had easy beach access and lodging in November; maybe Cape Cod fell in that category, too.

I'd seen Facebook that morning. Someone saw the photo of me by the City of Niagara Falls sign, and thought the sign read *Viagra* instead of *Niagara*.

I went to bed having thought about Viagra Falls all day long.

Another Slacker Day.

We piled into Jody and David's car for a day of exploring. Cold and blustery outside, life was easy from the plush seats inside the car.

Evening found us on the Ferris wheel, with a bird's eye view of the illuminated falls. Back on the ground, the night filled with colorful lights on the falls, while fireworks exploded in the sky above us.

Niagara Falls was tremendous and mesmerizing. I found it hard to turn and walk away.

How wonderful to be with Jody and David twice within four months, but this was the long good bye. With a round of big hugs, Terry and I pedaled out under an overcast sky.

A ten-minute ride from the magnificent falls brought us to the Rainbow Bridge, linking Canada and the United States. We rolled up to the U.S. customs booth for interrogation.

"What's the purpose of your trip?" he asked, looking at our bikes and passports.

"We're doing a cross-country bike trip."

After learning where we started and why we veered into Canada, he eyeballed Terry's recumbent. Our passports seemed of less interest to him than Terry's bike.

"That's a great bike you have there. How do you like it?"

He and Terry spoke recumbent talk for a few minutes while Terry gave him a primer on recumbent bicycles. After many questions from the customs agent, which were mainly about recumbents and not about us entering the United States, he handed back our passports.

"Good adventures to you and have a safe trip."

Minutes later, a sign greeted us:

Welcome to New York – the Empire State.

CHAPTER 17

Winter–New York

We had a plan, compliments of a New York cyclist named Harvey Botzman. After changing our final destination from storm-struck New Jersey, Terry e-mailed several New York cycling organizations for route recommendations. One of them contacted Harvey, who then contacted us. As an author about cycling the Erie Canal and the Great Lakes, Harvey knew his way around northern New York. Armed with his friendly e-mail support, Terry and I left Niagara Falls for the Erie Canalway Trail, plus a lunch date with Harvey for the following day.

We practically had the roads to ourselves, with fresh snow draping roofs and mailboxes. Terry looked like a thug in the Sunday morning chill. I would have donned my face mask, too, but as usual, it was buried and I lacked motivation to unearth it.

At Lockport, we intersected the Erie Canal. Snowflakes gently swirled as Terry and I pedaled onto the canal's dike. A car with snow piled high on its roof passed below us on the road – a harbinger of things to come.

Erie Canal at Lockport, New York

Completed in 1825, the canal was constructed to provide a 360-mile water route between Albany and Buffalo, at the edge of Lake Erie. Mules and horses plodded on the towpath, pulling barges along the waterway, until railways made the canal virtually obsolete. The canal's towpath was later converted to a bike trail. Now there are more bikes than boats.

Terry and I cut through orchards and farmland on the trail's finely crushed gravel. Branches lay scattered on the ground, an aftermath of the storms. Houses and farms sprang up in increasing numbers. Houses meant people, and if we ran into problems, we could potentially get help. That thought was frequently present as we cycled in and out of isolated areas.

Terry checks a map along the Erie Canal

Following the water route also meant more wildlife. Fifty ducks suddenly rose from the water, splashing, quacking, and flapping in a noisy cacophony.

I played leapfrog with a heron. Its skinny body, long neck, and six-foot wing span reminded me of Jurassic Park flying dinosaurs. I'd rarely seen birds in flight with that kind of wing span, and to be so close thrilled me. The heron would land ahead of me, stay there until I passed it, fly ahead of me and land, and wait until I passed again. I was sad to see our game end.

Terry and I were a century too late for the best barrels along the Erie Canal. The little town of Knowlesville had the reputation for the best coopers, or barrel makers. Once the canal was complete, New York state's agricultural industry boomed for export, and New York apples were packed in locally made barrels for destinations as far away as Africa.

"This trail is killing me," Terry said at a break. "I'm only going seven miles an hour unless I push it, and then I'm going nine. I don't want to stay on this trail tomorrow. I want to get back to the pavement where it's easier to pedal."

Bah.

"I really like this trail," I countered. "How about if we do a mix? Trail some of the time and paved road some of the time."

"Okay. I just don't want to spend the whole day on the trail tomorrow."

Whew.

Déjà vu of the Mickelson Bike Trail in South Dakota, where I was a bad sport about leaving the trail. Realizing that staying grumpy did me no good in the long run, I had vowed not to let grumpiness get the better of me again. So, I made good on my vow. We had been on the Erie trail for a good chunk of the day and I enjoyed it while I could. So be it. I rolled onto a paved road at the next opportunity.

Navigation is a significant part of a bike journey, and that includes navigating disappointment as well as miles. "Choose your battles" they say—and I became better at choosing mine. Life at home isn't the same as life on a bike. At home, Terry and I could often skirt conflict because we knew each other's priorities, and slipped into routines we created to navigate the (usually small) minefields present in the nearly three decades of our marriage.

Fortunately, experience is a good teacher, and lessons learned in one region of the country transferred well to other regions. I learned more about making accommodations, realizing that there is another day, another season, to try something again. The trip's biggest disappointment had been Terry's broken arm in Minnesota and the premature ending of our bike trip—but here we were, back on the bikes a few months later.

Just because something doesn't happen when I want doesn't mean it will never happen; it just isn't happening at that time.

There are still plenty of second chances out there--for me and for others.

Temperatures were 10 degrees below normal for November, according to the morning news. A light dusting of snow covered ground and cars, and a nor'easter was on its way. With the ground already saturated from Superstorm Sandy's torrential rains, experts predicted hundreds more trees to topple in New York and New Jersey, causing further disruption of power lines. I was just happy the prediction was for rain and not for snow. As long as Terry and I could stay away from snow, I felt optimistic.

My optimism blindly ignored the lightly falling snow and 24-degree temperature.

A woman approached us at a mini-mart, eyeing our loaded bikes and layers of clothing.

"I live around here. Do you two need a place to stay?"

"No, thank you, we're just taking a break. We're hoping to avoid snow," I said, rather unconvincingly as we looked out on the falling mix of snow and rain.

"Well, I'd be happy to have you stay with me if you'd like."

What a generous offer, and if it had been six hours later in the day, we probably would have accepted it. A couple minutes later, a man walked up to talk.

"We're almost to the end of our trip," Terry told him after a few minutes of conversation.

The man looked out at the falling snow and rain, eyed us, and said in a somber tone: "You two still have a long ways to go."

I hadn't been missing the Erie Canal until I saw it below us as we biked on an overpass. I looked down at the tree lined, still-water canal, wishing I were biking along the scenic water way instead of the highway. I couldn't really complain about the road, though, since it had a shoulder, was paved, and had minimal traffic. Still, I coveted the Erie Canal.

"How Swede it is," Terry observed as we pedaled through the town of Sweden. He might have been talking about biking on the pavement, too.

After four weeks of pedaling, my legs were finally getting strong again. I could go uphill at a pretty good clip, much faster than even two weeks before. That was good timing, as we drew near to the

Appalachians. Their elevation couldn't compare with the Rockies, but they were still higher than any hills we'd encountered since starting the second leg of our trip.

At Rochester, we escaped the congested roads to return to the Erie Canal Trailway. The paved trail took us through woods and brush. A cyclist came from the other direction, waved as he approached, and stopped.

"What's your trip?" the middle-aged cyclist asked us. We told him.

"I'm on my way to work. It's a five-mile commute, and I haven't missed a day of bicycle commuting in six years." That was impressive.

"We're on our way to have lunch with the man who gave us information about cycling through New York," Terry said.

"Who are you meeting?" the cyclist asked.

"Harvey Botzman."

"Oh, Harvey! Yeah, he's a great guy. Tell him hi from Bruce."

Ha. It was like playing *Connect the Dots*. I liked this connected and friendly bicycling community we were privileged to share.

We found Harvey at our scheduled meeting spot along the trail – a short, middle-aged man layered in clothing for rain and snow, just like we were.

After an initial chat, Harvey directed us to follow him. He took off, and we had to hoof it to keep up with him. He led us through a maze of bike trails, taking us along the canal, veering through a park, over the bridge and through the woods. It was not to Grandmother's house we went, though—we ended up at a restaurant where I was happy to shed my damp layers and sit in a warm, comfy room.

"Here are some bike maps for this area and here is my guide book." Harvey spread maps and a paperback book on our large table and proceeded to recommend a route through New York. He was well prepared, with written recommendations that included a mix of the canal bike trail and paved roads, and a mix of back roads and busier roads. His suggestions would get us to the eastern border of New York and into Massachusetts.

"I'll work on getting you through Massachusetts, too," he told us. Harvey was a retired teacher, and it was clear that he was accustomed to giving explanations. Good ones, too.

One long lunch later, we three hit the bikes with Harvey as our escort. Harvey easily led us through the maze of Rochester, along the Erie Canal, and past a couple of canal locks.

"Parts of the canal are drained every winter and refilled in the spring," he explained as we looked at one of the locks. "My bike was made in Eugene, just two hundred miles down the road," he added after a pause.

"Oh really? Where is Eugene?" I wasn't aware of a Eugene in New York.

"Two hundred miles down the road from you."

"Oh, yeah, I know that Eugene."

Harvey's bike was a Bike Friday, a folding bike built in Eugene, Oregon.

"This bike is great," Harvey went on. "I just put it in a box or a bag and take it on planes, trains, or long-distance buses. I can easily take it with me, and it's so good for traveling."

I knew about Eugene's Bike Fridays, but this was the first time I heard talk about taking them on planes or buses. That sounded like a great way to explore.

We cycled from the town of Pittsford into the village of Pittsford, where Harvey bid us goodbye. Our lovely asphalt trail ended and spat Terry and me out onto busy Highway 31. Harvey was smart to turn towards home while bike life was still good.

With thanks and waves, we cycled in opposite directions. Terry and I merged with rush hour traffic on a crowded highway. With night quickly approaching, we stopped at the first motel we encountered. We didn't make the mileage that we wanted for the day, but it was prudent to stop before we rode into trouble with the dark and congestion.

Good thing we had warm clothes. The nearby restaurant's heat was kaput, so we ate dinner wearing our many layers of clothes. Spending an hour outside on our bikes didn't look much different than spending an hour inside the chilly restaurant.

It was the end of our fourth week, with over 1400 miles behind us.

Election Day morning, 2012.

The night before, I jammed my bike in the narrow space between the bed and the wall. I didn't feel like braving the cold temperature outside to lube my squeaky chain, so I stood on the bed, hoisted my bike from its narrow space, flipped it upside down while standing on the bed, and lowered it back to perform my maintenance. Undoubtedly, the motel would have preferred me to do it outside --but I didn't leave a trace.

The tranquility and beauty of the rural Erie Canal beckoned nearby, but Terry wanted pavement, so we had the noise and congestion of Highway 5 instead. I vowed to come back to the Erie Canal and bike its entirety someday.

Since it was election day, I wondered if we would cycle past polling places. As Oregonians, we had the convenience of voting by mail, and had sent in our ballots a couple weeks earlier. I knew New York still voted in person and I hoped to see the voting process in action from our bikes.

I was thrilled to see *Vote Here* calling to us from a big red, white, and blue sign outside a building in Palmyra. It sparked memories of my early voting days, of going inside a mysterious little voting booth, closing the curtain, and pulling a metal handle. If this had been a movie scene, people would have been coming or going from the building, but in the ten seconds that we cycled near, I saw no one.

Terry and I stopped to warm ourselves at a McDonalds in nearby Newark (that's Newark, New York, not Newark, New Jersey). As we prepared to leave, a man rolled down his car window and began asking the usual questions. After a couple of minutes, he asked one more.

"May I be nosy and ask how old you are?" he asked.

"Fifty-five."

"Yeah, you look young. You look healthy. It looks like being outside agrees with you. You look good."

Well, thanks.

A few minutes later, I stopped in a residential area to change from gloves to mittens. A man raking leaves stopped, walked across his lawn, and asked questions about the bike and trip.

"Good luck, baby!" he said as I readied myself to pedal away.

Baby. The town of Newark really knew how to boost my ego.

Lunch time found us watching election coverage in a café in the small town of Port Bryon. The news showed long lines in Florida, where people stood outside waiting under the hot sun. One woman passed out from the heat. What a ridiculous way to vote. Inefficiency drives me crazy, and this seemed like an extremely inefficient way to vote. If people have to stand in line for hours simply to cast their vote, only to pass out from the heat while waiting, something has to change. Oregon was the first state to transition to vote-by-mail for all of its elections, and has been giving its citizens the right to vote from their kitchen tables, or anywhere else in the world, for years. Nobody in Oregon was passing out from having to stand in lines for hours just to cast a vote.

All fired up about inefficient and unjust ways to vote, I climbed back on my bike saddle. I was irritated at Florida—and my irritation made me pedal faster. Since Terry wasn't irritated at Florida, we ended up with more distance than usual between us. I had to stop, wait for Terry to catch up, and settle down.

Terry was game for Erie Canalway Trail again, so we left the traffic to bike through woods. Most of the trees were bare except for a few leaves which stubbornly clung to the topmost branches. Weeks earlier, the golds, reds, oranges, and yellows still hung from trees, but now leaves were brown and withered, scattered on the ground. An afternoon chill enveloped us and whispered that winter was on its way.

We arrived at Baldwinsville before dark. Due to falling back an hour to Standard Time, our daylight now ended an hour earlier, making it an extra challenge to get off the road before dark. Because campgrounds were closed, we looked for motels, which generally operated in towns. Towns had traffic, and east coast towns had even more traffic. Because of the time change, daylight now ended during rush hour, putting darkness, towns, rush hour, and the need for lodging all in one congested package.

But by ending our cycling day an hour early, Terry and I had an extra hour to watch the presidential election coverage. We ordered a pizza and settled in to watch the news. The Erie Canal area was saturated with campaign signs supporting Mitch Romney. Although the TV reported that New York was a blue state, it was clear that along the Erie Canal, Republicans ruled.

Living on the west coast, we were used to the east coast sometimes announcing their results before the west coast polls even closed. Often, pundits used the east coast results to project a national win. By the time eastern, central, and mountain time zones began reporting, sometimes westerners questioned if their late-in-the-day voting even made a difference.

This time, though, Terry and I had front row seats in the eastern time zone. It was exciting to be at the start of the news wave, rather than near the end of it.

We heard presidential predictions and we heard weather predictions. The temperature was predicted to fall to 21 degrees. Not only was it chilly outside, but it was also chilly inside our bathroom. The bathroom was so unexpectedly cold that Terry used it as a refrigerator for his milk and yogurt. Our bedroom was warm, however. We flopped on the bed, anxiously watching the news.

By bedtime, Barack Obama had been re-elected for another term as President of the United States.

While the rest of the world was in a frenzy the next morning about the consequences of the election, it was back to business as usual for Terry and me. Our goal was unchanged by the presidential outcome: get on our bikes and aim for the Atlantic. With frost on the ground, icy puddles in the streets, and gray skies overhead, we set out knowing that a cold nor'easter was predicted to dump before midnight. Hopefully, we would be inside well before that.

A sign at a small town indicated it was incorporated in 1774. It's easy to impress Pacific Northwest people with old stuff. Oregon didn't even become a state until 1859.

At a mini-mart in Verona, Terry and I watched TV while we ate lunch. According to the TV, it was National Eating Healthy Day, but it was already too late for that. I jammed hot, greasy calzone into my mouth and topped it off with a handful of chocolate.

Terry and I had been in Egypt the day before, and in the afternoon, we cycled through Rome. Such a worldly view from our bikes. Cycling along the edge of Rome's correctional facility, surrounded by razor wire, I was thankful to be outside on my bike, and not inside. As a clinical instructor for a nursing school in Portland, I had nursing students whose clinical site was the Oregon State Penitentiary infirmary. My brief forays there to visit my students had been a sobering experience. I doubly appreciated the freedom and adventure that I was living while on my bicycle.

🚲

Utica's morning TV reported that the nor'easter dumped snow during the night. New York City received four inches, the largest snowfall on record for that early in the year. New Jersey lost power in places where it had just been restored the day before. The nor'easter was headed our way, with predictions for wind and cold during the day and heavy rains during the night. Any cycling Terry and I could get done before another storm came would be to our advantage.

🚲

As usual, people stopped to talk. The general parting sentiments were *Be careful, Be safe,* and *God bless.* Days had passed since we heard anyone say *You're crazy!* Now that we were in New York, making it to the Atlantic didn't sound so crazy after all.

Puddles turned to ice, and ditches along the road were white with frost, but compared to the previous morning's 25 degrees, our 35 degrees felt like a heat wave. In addition to our mild heat wave, we warmed up with a half hour climb up a long hill, bringing us to a plateau. Below us lay miles of rolling farmland where gigantic, white wind turbines spun in the wind.

The plateau was just a warm-up for the hills to come. Terry and I went up and down, up and down. The flat lands were behind us and we were gearing up for the Berkshire Hills of Massachusetts, part of the 1500-mile Appalachian Mountain chain extending from Newfoundland to Georgia. Being old, the Appalachians have had plenty of time to wear down, with the highest peak in Massachusetts reaching a mere 3500 feet. The tallest and most challenging mountains of our trip, the Rockies, were far behind us.

Two truckloads of corn kernels drove by as gusts of wind blew kernels off the truck. With the windy day, a trail of yellow corn kernels along our shoulders was guaranteed. But the winds arrived with a vengeance, boring through my mittens and driving the cold right into us. I pedaled hard through the frozen shadows to return to open fields and sunshine.

The wind shifted to become a tailwind, pushing us through the town of Canajoharie. With the sun at our backs, we bicycled straight into our shadows. I could see the ventilation holes of my helmet's shadow, confirming that I did, indeed, have holes in my head.

The sun dipped below the horizon, the temperature dropped, gray clouds filled the sky, and the day grew dark, all before 3:30. I clicked on my front and back lights, the earliest I'd used them on rainless days. Terry and I called it an early day near Amsterdam, checking in to a cheap motel surrounded by shuttered businesses. We ordered Italian food with free delivery, our second night in a row of having our dinner delivered to us at a motel.

I could get used to that.

The nor'easter dumped snow in other areas, but in Amsterdam, our morning roads were merely frosty. Fortunately, the pavement was lumpy and our bikes didn't slide. We followed the Erie Canal, which made me halfway happy. If I couldn't be biking on it, at least I could be looking at it. I vowed to return and be more faithful to it the next time.

Turn in a gun, get a gift card, proclaimed a billboard in Albany. Albany offered bike shops, too, in addition to gift cards for guns. The day before, Terry's chain fell off eleven times. That meant stopping, getting off his bike, and manually replacing the chain, a time consuming and annoying process. We arrived at a bike shop at 12:30, figuring this would be an easy fix and that we still had plenty of time to bike to the eastern border of New York state.

Not such an easy fix. Terry's bike chain had stretched enough that he needed a new chain. With his long recumbent, he actually needed three chains, and of a different kind than the bike shop stocked. After calls to other bike shops, we found one with the three desired chains, but it was five miles away. Terry took a taxi while I stayed at the bike shop and wrote, and my bike got a little spa treatment with a brake adjustment.

Four hours later, we were finally ready to leave. With instructions from the bike guys how to cross the Hudson River and get to a motel, we finally left the bike shop at 4:15 p.m.

We hit Albany's rush hour traffic with its narrow, busy lanes, and I gave my newly-tweaked brakes a good workout. Multiple cars honked at us. I popped up onto sidewalks when possible, but sometimes the sharp edges of the sidewalks just invited other problems. Albany at rush hour in the twilight was a nerve-wracking experience.

I entered a pedestrian ramp with optimism, glad to be out of traffic. A sign ordered us to walk the bikes, but I was already pedaling when I saw it. I stopped, straddled my bike, and swung my right leg to dismount – but not high enough. My leg caught on my sleeping bag behind my bike seat and I fell backwards, hitting my helmeted head against the concrete wall while my bicycle crashed on top of me. A man approached and stood just behind me. Because the ramp was so narrow, he had to wait until I picked myself up and righted my bike. He passed me without saying a word.

Welcome to Albany.

By then it was dark. The pedestrian bridge did not cross the Hudson River. Something black lurked below the bridge—but not water. We were in downtown Albany somewhere, nowhere near where we wanted to be. I saw a sign for Hampton Inn a few blocks away. Spooked about being on the dark streets of Albany at night, we headed there. Hampton Inn is not cheap lodging, but it was close and safe, and that eclipsed the money issue.

Terry stayed outside with our bikes. I walked in to the fancy lobby and stood behind a woman who was checking in. She was dressed in high heels, a beautiful scarf, and had a fancy looking purse and luggage. She checked in and walked away. I stepped up to the counter, wearing my over pants, boots, rain jacket, fluorescent-green safety vest, and bike helmet. I did not look fancy.

"What's your least expensive room for two people?" I asked.

"Least expensive? I can give you a room for $129 that's normally $189," the man said.

"I'll take it." I paused. "We're cycling and had expected to get beyond Albany, but we had bike problems today. We were trying to get over the Hudson River."

"Where did you come from?"

I went into the story. An employee passed by, and the reception clerk called to him.

"Hey, they're bicycling cross-country and they're almost done!"

The passing employee gave me a thumbs up and a big smile.

"Do you have a room that has a lot of floor space?" I asked the clerk. "Our bikes and junk take up a lot of room."

He searched the computer. "Yes, I have a suite available, and I'll give you a free upgrade," he said with a smile.

Wow, nice.

It was a huge room with a sofa, big soft armchairs, a desk, and plenty of floor space in addition to a big bed. I instantly become a fan of both Hampton Inn and Bernie at the front desk.

🚲

Hampton Inn provides a darn good breakfast, and I drank my day's hydration just from their exotic fruit juices. I was even more of a Hampton Inn fan by the time I walked out of their breakfast room.

I discovered a shattered bike mirror, which must have occurred when I fell on the ramp the night before. I had come to rely on my mirror for looking for cars and Terry behind me, and the thought of heading back out into traffic without it was daunting.

We rolled our bikes into an overcast, dry, and 45-degree morning, a veritable heat wave compared with temperatures from a few days earlier. We found the correct pedestrian bridge after learning that someone gave us an incorrect street name as part of our directions from the previous day. Navigation errors were nothing new to us, but this one was not of our own doing.

The first bridge led us over eleven lanes of freeway traffic—that was the most traffic we'd seen in our entire continental journey. A second bridge brought us over the historic Hudson River. The strip of pavement reserved for pedestrians and cyclists was full of debris, and required zig zagging in order not to run over sharp objects.

Terry and I stopped at the middle of the bridge to admire the Hudson. A log flowed down the wide gray river on its way towards New York City. Upstream and out of sight, the Erie Canal stretched westward towards Buffalo. The river looked simple, pure, and modest.

Out of Albany and on the other side of the Hudson, our civilized world included the ubiquitous Dunkin' Donuts. Ever since entering New York, Terry and I saw Dunkin' Donuts practically everywhere. There are a handful of them in the Pacific Northwest, but in New York, the doughnut business was rampant. Dunkin' Donuts was New York's version of a Pacific Northwest Starbucks.

Ironically, there wasn't a Dunkin' Donuts to be found when

I needed to pee—all that exotic fruit juice from Hampton Inn needed to escape. Spying some evergreen trees between two houses, I decided it looked like an adequate spot. I didn't see lights or movement in the house and made my move. I opened the gate, slipped behind the trees and did my business, hoping that I wouldn't get shot at or arrested. A Dunkin' Donuts would have been my first choice in the daylight in a town, but a household tree was good enough. My bladder thanked me.

Heading southeast from Albany, a road sign announced mileage to Boston. Close enough to have its own mileage sign, the end of our trip was practically within reach. We celebrated with a break at Nassau, where I fueled up with pumpkin ice cream.

Up, down, up, down. Terry and I pedaled through farms, woods, and the foothills of the Appalachians in bright, November sunshine. I shed my boots for cycling shoes, only the third time since resuming our trip. My feet practically floated in the light weight footwear.

A car passed and a woman stuck out her arm from the window and pumped a fist.

"You go, girl!" she yelled as the car passed.

I did go, and with increased energy from her salute.

Terry and I both went, up a rural road flanked by dense woods and spiked with color. The hill brought us into the Appalachians, and a road sign announced:

Welcome to Massachusetts.

CHAPTER 18

Winding Down— Massachusetts One

Massachusetts didn't mess around.

Just to enter the state, we first had to conquer a long slog uphill, and once there, the Appalachians welcomed us with a serious workout through their dense, autumnal woods. Off came layers of clothing as I worked my way uphill, and on they came while I waited in chilly shadows for Terry. It was a rhythmic cycle of stripping and bundling. Massachusetts calls what we climbed a mountain, elevation 1500 feet, but back home mountains rise well over 10,000 feet, and mountain passes are three times higher than this mountain. Even so, it was a slog.

Say what you will about New York, but their roads have great shoulders. Unfortunately, good shoulders were rare on the Berkshire highways. Traffic whizzed by on the narrow road, too close and too fast.

Terry and I cycled through a forest of towering trees, past a ski area biding its time before welcoming skiers, and a wildlife sanctuary. One eye took in the scenery, while the other looked out for traffic. One little spot was still intact with my shattered bike mirror. If I positioned my mirror just right, I could see behind me. Fast cars made me nervous, especially when the only shoulders were the ones on either side of my neck, and no amount of pretty scenery would ever change that. I wanted to see what was barreling down the road towards me.

The afternoon still had a little life left in it when the Berkshires dropped us down to a lakeside inn an hour before sunset. Terry took off in quest of dinner, a ten minute ride to the mountain town of Lee. I'd had enough of spooky Highway 20. I preferred to eat food from my panniers, or maybe even starve to death, rather than get back on that road.

On Laurel Lake's shore, I watched the twilight sky and its reflection on the lake. Pink, orange, and yellow streaks painted the surface, while the air rang with honks from geese and ducks. The silhouettes of trees across the narrow arm of the lake rose like sentinels to watch over me.

We were in Massachusetts, the final state of our trip. But now that we were here, decades of anticipation for the trip vanished, replaced by a sense of wistfulness and melancholy. Our trip was almost over, and I wasn't ready for it to end. Every morning brought excitement to be on the bikes and to pursue another installment of miles; I still awoke with the feeling of being incredibly lucky to be seeing the continent in slow motion, and to be experiencing whatever unknown adventure each new day brought. Always, there was curiosity and anticipation for each day, and I went to sleep each night fatigued but satisfied with a day well-traveled.

The land that we saw, the people that we met, the adventures that we had – our experiences were rich and vivid, and I wanted more. I felt strong and healthy, and I loved spending my days pedaling and being outside. That man in New York was right: being outdoors did agree with me.

I was about to complete my 32-year-old dream of bicycling cross-country, but to my surprise, I wasn't emotionally ready for the journey to end. I had expected joy, excitement, and a huge sense of accomplishment at the end; I hadn't even thought of sadness. I only thought about getting to the goal.

I further pondered. What is the purpose of a goal, anyway? Is it to actually achieve the milestone? To improve along the way? To achieve mastery? To show superiority over other people? To show others that you could do it?

There are equally as many reasons to pursue a goal as there are people pursuing it—everyone has their own reason.

With thousands of miles, a dozen states, and two countries behind us, Terry and I were closing in on our goal. After focusing on a goal for thirty-two years, what happens when that goal is finally reached? Although our goal was about to be accomplished, I realized there was more to it than I initially thought. There was the process—the process of twelve weeks of pedal pushing, experiencing life from one ocean to another.

I liked the process. What would happen when that process no longer existed?

I wondered.

🚲

"I don't want this trip to end," I said to Terry after he returned from dinner.

"Well, I'm ready" Terry replied. "I'm glad we're coming to the end."

No surprise there. This had been my dream, not Terry's. But it really didn't matter who was or wasn't ready. Our bike trip was ending soon, ready or not.

I went to sleep wrapped in melancholy.

🚲

I awoke in the morning with that familiar, sudden hit of excitement. The old part of my brain was still fired up about completing the trip, while another part braked, trying to delay the inevitable end. A cerebral yin and yang.

We breezed downhill into Lee, turned east, and immediately

began climbing Jacob's Ladder Scenic Byway. Aptly named, we pedaled miles up that asphalt ladder, passing huge, stately, houses that radiated New England charm. Need a place to house a couple dozen people? Try one of these sprawling old houses graced with balconies, bay windows, and ornate wooden carvings. Those big homes had stories to tell, and I wished that we could have pulled over and listened.

There were other hidden stories as well.

The sign read, *Appalachian Trail*, reigniting a smoldering desire to hike its 2,181 miles between Maine and Georgia. Built by volunteers in 1928, the Appalachian Trail is the world's longest footpath, with over eight thousand people reportedly having hiked the entire length, usually in four to eight months. Ninety miles are in Massachusetts. The Appalachian Trail intrigued me for decades – perhaps once I finished going west to east on my bicycle, I'd start going north to south on my feet – or not. Traveling with heavy panniers on a bicycle is far easier than traveling with a heavy backpack on a back.

I wondered about hikers' stories on this long trail. I could merely wonder, though, seeing only cars at the trailhead, not people.

Terry and I resumed our climb of Jacob's Ladder, ascending hundreds of feet while surrounded by trees, sunshine, and chill. Once at the Ladder's top, we bundled up for the crisp descent. We hopped off the Ladder at the small town of Chester to escape the chill inside a nearly empty café. With a steaming latte in hand, I addressed two men at the bar.

"Are either of you familiar with the Boston area?" I queried.

"Yes, I'm from Boston," one man replied.

Gold mine. Terry and I bellied up to the bar, spread our maps, and engaged the men in our quest for a tire-dipping beach near Boston.

"There are good beaches in New Hampshire, just north of Boston. Boston doesn't really have any good beaches."

New Hampshire. I never thought about ending our trip in New Hampshire—I didn't even know that New Hampshire touched the ocean. It turns out that is does, for about 20 miles.

"We were also thinking about ending our trip at Cape Cod," Terry said. "We don't know if there is easy access to motels and other businesses this time of year."

"Oh, that won't be any problem. There are plenty of places open at Cape Cod, all year round."

Clinking our mugs of latte and hot chocolate, Terry and I toasted our decision to end our cross-country bike trip at Cape Cod. It was as far east as we could go, with its skinny scorpion tail hook flung out into the Atlantic. Two more days of pedaling would be needed to get to its northern tip, but we had the time. And by extending the trip to Cape Cod, our journey wouldn't be over so soon.

Cape Cod held interesting possibilities. It was a place worthy of the end, plus it was close to Nantucket Island. My paternal family history goes way back to Nantucket during the early days of settlement. My ancestor William Worth married Sarah Macy (part of the Macy department store dynasty, long before the department store existed) in 1665, the first marriage on the island. I e-mailed my family lore keepers for our Nantucket geneology and planned visiting a Nantucket graveyard or two.

Terry and I had a Worth-y plan. With thanks to the men at the bar, we cycled from Chester and pointed ourselves southeast on Highway 20, aiming towards Cape Cod's scorpion tail. To get to Cape Cod's entrance, we would pass through two more states.

Turns out we weren't in our last state, after all. Silly me.

Sunday morning's light traffic compensated for the piss-poor shoulders of the road. We pedaled down Massachusetts' rural hills, past woods, meadows, and old homes. The sun came and went, as did the chill. In our familiar ritual, we put clothes on, we took clothes off. We felt content—it was dry, intermittently warm, and all was well with our world.

"Good morning!"

Six cyclists approached us from the other direction, waving their arms in greeting. Groups of motorcyclists passed. The bikers were out to play in the seductive 58 degree temperature and beautiful scenery. In our month of cycling, it was our first sighting of a group of cyclists out for a ride. And no wonder they were out--the day was absolutely lovely.

By the time we'd cruised down into Westfield, the Berkshire Hills and the Appalachians lay behind us. Carillon bells serenaded us with *God Bless America* and other patriotic songs as we sat on a sun-drenched bench and ate. It was November 11th, Veterans Day. A big sign reminded us: *All gave some, some gave all. Thank you for serving.*

Several people dressed in shorts frolicked on the main street in the 66-degree sunshine while birds chirped as if spring arrived. Terry and I felt giddy, too. It was our first outdoor meal in over a week. Within that week, we'd gone from snow flurries to short-sleeves.

We pedaled across the wide Connecticut River and into Springfield, hometown of Dr. Seuss. Alas, no Dr. Seuss character entertained us as we cycled through town.

Honk, honk beeped a car. In the linguistics of car honks, those short, successive honks were the friendly ones, often accompanied by arm waving. Short honks translated to *That's cool and I wish I was doing it too.* I liked those, and pedaled with renewed vigor.

"I think my recumbent legs have finally kicked in," Terry declared triumphantly.

He'd been riding in front for much of the day, and it wasn't just because I was being a slug. Now that we were in Massachusetts, Terry was finally riding faster, as long as we weren't climbing hills. Sometimes I actually had to work to keep up with him. What a tremendous change. Just as our trip was about to end, Terry was finally moving into power.

Our cheap motel in Palmer didn't provide breakfast, not even Fruit Loops. Instead, I cooked up the ten-grain cereal I'd been carrying around for a month. No sense in only taking it on a joy ride. As we zeroed in on the Atlantic, it was time to focus on eating up the food. There would be no extra credit for arriving at the Atlantic with excessive food in our panniers.

The temperature nose-dived to 40 degrees, and we passed mounds of old snow in ditches and yards. Old snow on the sides was more likeable than newly packed snow on roads. That kind of snow could have sounded the death knell for our bike trip, unless we had taken to studded bike tires like some tough mid-westerners we met.

This is the way we liked our snow--piled on the grass

Meanwhile, my shattered bike mirror fell from its housing, leaving behind only a plastic pocket. On the open rural roads, I was generally content to just look ahead, but in populated areas, I wanted to see behind before veering left to pass parked cars on my right.

In Sturbridge, the town's bike shop was closed, so we sought the toy store instead. I bought a little mirror and electrical tape, taping the new mirror over the broken housing. I was pleased with myself--until I tried to use it. I had an excellent view of my left, rear panniers. With prolonged adjustment, I finally managed to get it aligned. My toy store mirror was definitely not as good as a bike mirror, but it did the job—sort of. But how much could I expect for a buck fifty?

Now that we were in Massachusetts, my vocabulary was on the rise. Repeatedly, I saw words that aren't common on the west coast: grinders and package stores. Some detective work cleared up that mystery and put them into words I understood: submarine sandwiches and liquor stores.

Whether these foreign words belonged only to Massachusetts or to other New England states, we were about to find out. Moving southwest along the Quenebaug River, we happily pedaled to a new border and sign:

Welcome to Connecticut.

CHAPTER 19

Eat Your Broccoli—
Connecticut

Quinebaug, Connecticut. Any state that welcomes you with a Q is alright with me.

Two days earlier, I had no idea we would be cycling in Connecticut. In New York, Terry and I thought we were headed due east to Boston, but now we pedaled south to slice off a tiny piece of Connecticut on our way to Cape Cod.

Terry and I parked our bikes under the *Welcome to Connecticut* sign for our ritual new-state photographs. A scruffy-looking man walked our direction. Skinny, with a beard, scraggly hair, and worn clothes, he kept his eyes averted as he approached. I hesitated before asking him if he would get a photo of Terry and me under the sign. What caused my hesitation? Was I afraid that he was going to run off with my camera?

"Could you please get a photo of us, our bikes, and the sign?"

"Sure," he replied. He took a few pictures and handed back my camera.

Silly me.

I was hungry. Connecticut's little towns were full of churches whose reader boards advertised dinners. A spaghetti dinner was coming up for one church, and a turkey dinner for another. A telephone pole boasted two flyers: one for the previous week's election night dinner, and one for an upcoming Thanksgiving dinner. It would be fun to attend a church dinner if Terry and I happened to be around at just the right time, but it looked unlikely since we were almost done with our trip.

We entered the little town of North Grosvenor Dale, where a sign in front of a white clapboard church caught my hungry attention. A drawing of a steaming bowl of soup, with the words *Community Kitchen, A Friendly Place to Eat and Meet, Free Meal 12 Noon Today, Courtesy of this Church* compelled me to look at my watch. It was noon, straight up.

Terry and I locked our bikes and went inside the open doors of the Methodist church.

The basement was crowded with about fifty people seated at long tables, and Terry and I became the focus of their attention as we stood at the entrance the room. A woman walked over to us, looking flummoxed. "I'll find some seats for you," she said.

Another woman came over, introducing herself as Pat.

"Tell us about this lunch," I said. "Who comes for it? Who provides it?"

"This Methodist church houses the lunch every Monday, and there are four churches who rotate providing the hot meal. Woodstock Congregational Church is providing today's meal."

"Can we make a donation for our lunch?" I asked.

"No, it's not set up that way."

That was unexpected.

Terry and I looked around the room. It was full of senior citizens, many of whom looked frail or appeared to have disabilities.

There was no more room at the inn, or at least not in the main room. The flummoxed woman returned and motioned for Terry and me to follow her. We passed from the crowded room through a large doorway that led directly into another large room. She pointed to a long table that was loaded with plastic bags of bread and pastries.

"You can sit there." She disappeared.

Pat stood by while we seated ourselves at the bread table.

"Help yourselves to bread, and do it fast, because everyone's going to come in here and get it. There won't be any left for you if you wait."

Neither Terry nor I moved.

"Take some right now, or it will be gone," she instructed us again. She sounded urgent.

We did as we were instructed. Dozens of baked goods wrapped in transparent plastic bags were piled on the table. Most were loaves of bread, but there were also bags of cookies, muffins, and other pastries. A whole loaf of bread didn't interest me, but some chocolate chip cookies and a muffin did. Terry rifled through the bags and picked out some bread while I took the sweets. Less than a minute later, a grabby crowd arrived, snatched up bags, and returned to their tables in the other room. Pat was right. It was like piranhas had come and stripped the table clean.

"Everyone! Can I get your attention please?" Joan, no longer looking flummoxed, called out to the main room. The noise died down and she resumed in lower decibels. "Please remove your hats, bow your heads, and assume an attitude of prayer." Hats went off. I had sunglasses on top of my head and wondered if I should remove them. I didn't, figuring that God probably didn't care. Joan gave a prayer of thanksgiving for the food.

"Will the veterans please stand up?" she asked at the prayer's end. A couple dozen men stood and the room gave them a round of applause.

Pat pulled a chair up to Terry's and my long table.

"You two go up when table number nine is called."

Various table numbers were called out. People rose from their tables and assembled in a line that slowly inched towards a long table that was laden with food. Some people were pushed in wheelchairs, some shuffled. While we waited, Terry and I sat with Pat and Whitlock. Whitlock, a silver-bearded and mustached man, slipped back into the main room and raised his finger towards his chin. He studied the room, dipping his finger at each person as he counted, muttering numbers under his breath.

There were 59 of us there for the free lunch.

"How many of you are under the age of 69?" he called out. Terry and I raised our hands, along with three other people. "How many of you are between 70 and 79? How many of you are between 80 and 89? How many are 90 or older?" The under-69'ers were way outnumbered by everybody else, and nobody confessed to being 90 or above.

"Table number nine!" Joan's voice boomed out over the conversation in the room.

Terry and I joined the line with table number nine.

"We've seen snow on the ground around here," I said to a petite old woman who fidgeted in line ahead of me. "When did it snow here?"

She thought for a moment.

"The snow's from five days ago. It snowed eight inches. Normally I don't eat much vegetables, but I ate a lot of broccoli that day, and I think that's why it snowed."

She didn't smile or laugh. I blinked. I wasn't sure how to respond to that other than with a thoughtful "Hmmm."

Volunteers stood at the food table and scooped food from big metal serving bins. A man handed the broccoli lady and me plates of tomato and beef pasta, green beans, and fruit cocktail. The broccoli lady returned to her table and I reluctantly returned to mine. I wanted to sit with her so I could hear more of her interesting train of thought.

Unbeknownst to me at the start, it was people that would gave meaning to our trip, more than the miles. While the feeling of accomplishment in reaching state borders and destinations was tremendous, it was humanity that was most expanding our world, not just the miles we pedaled.

Curiosity about our loaded bikes often sparked initial conversations, which sometimes led to deeper experiences such as meals and overnights with people who were unknown to us just before.

Our bikes were the catalysts, prompting encounters with people that we were unlikely to have met otherwise. My world was bigger and I was wiser from meeting people who were so different from me. Some people had known names, such as Larry (the Gopher Killer), or Pickles, who repeatedly told Terry and me that it was a mistake not to be carrying a gun. Other people were nameless to me, such as the broccoli lady, but their personalities, stories, and impact still resonated through the miles. Every day carried possibilities for people interactions, and there was no predicting what those interactions would be.

Positive, negative, or neutral, those people encounters often gave me something to reflect on as I pedaled the miles.

Pat and Whitlock sat down with their plates of food.

"If you come back next Monday, you'll get a different menu," Pat told Terry and me. "Next Monday is Bingo Day, and it's always quality food on Bingo Day." She put the emphasis on the word *quality*. Evidently, she didn't consider the present week's fare quality food. It's true, it wasn't five-star dining, but it was fine for a free meal. The fruit cocktail was great.

Terry and I lingered while people began to leave. As we stood, a volunteer spoke to me.

"Do you need to use a bathroom?" she asked.

"No, I used a bush right before we got here."

She raised her eyebrows at me and gave me a disapproving look. "You're lucky you didn't get arrested."

If she had known about my peeing episode back in New York in front of that house, she probably would have raised her disapproval even a notch higher.

I was glad she didn't know.

Terry and I pedaled off into a warm and sunny afternoon – the end of a string of sunny New England days, according to the weather man. The next day promised to be rainy and cool. Terry and I soaked up the 65-degree sunshine while we could.

A hitchhiker faced us as he slowly walked backwards with his thumb outstretched.

"Sorry, no room," I told him as I cycled past. Usually, I flew past hitchhikers in my car on the freeway. This was the first time I'd turned one down on my bike.

A few minutes later, the hitchhiker was behind us and so was Connecticut. A sign greeted us:

Welcome to Rhode Island, the Ocean State.

CHAPTER 20

The Island That's Not an Island— Rhode Island

Terry and I planned to bust through Providence and out the other side, so we ignored the one motel as we entered the state capital from the west. Reality thwarted our bust-through plan because, as usual, we just didn't move fast enough. On to Plan B.

"The nearest motels are in East Providence," a downtown passerby informed us. "But you'd have to go through a big construction and industrial area to get there. I wouldn't advise it after dark."

On to Plan C.

The Biltmore Hotel had $99 rooms available, according to the internet. Ninety-nine bucks for a Biltmore Hotel room? And only blocks from where we stood? Who could pass that up?

Two lanterns and a plethora of small lights lit the entrance of the fancy hotel. Three doormen, dressed in black suits and gold buttons, stood at attention on the brick sidewalk near two doors. In our customary safety vests and bike helmets, we walked our bikes to an entrance. Once the two doormen comprehended that we intended to enter their hotel with our bikes, and not just gaze at it, they leapt to open the doors for us.

"Good evening," they said in unison as we entered.

Just inside, we encountered one more door and one more doorman before we strolled and rolled into the luxurious hotel. The Providence Biltmore Hotel opened in 1922 and is listed on the National Register of Historic Places. In its old, dark, elegant lobby, Terry and I looked like aliens, clad in our fluorescent-green get-ups and rolling our ponderous contraptions. Men and women in business suits passed through the lobby, looking professional and purposeful.

But the Biltmore took our money, and they took more than ninety-nine dollars. No surprise there. Ninety-nine dollars sounded too good to be true for the Biltmore, and it was. Once again, though, we were relieved to be off the streets in a crowded city at night.

"You can take your bikes in the elevator up to your room." The clerk pointed to some elevators.

Easier said than done. Terry's recumbent was too long for a standard elevator, so an employee took us to our fifteenth floor in the service elevator. Thank goodness for that; it would have been a long haul up all those stairs dragging the recumbent.

As is frequently the case with a more expensive hotel, the more you pay, the less you get. For all of its fanciness, the Biltmore Hotel didn't have a pool or a hot tub, and it didn't provide free breakfast. You can knock those Super 8 and Motel 6 chains all you want, but with them, Terry and I often had access to a pool, a hot tub, and all the Fruit Loops I could eat, for a lot less than we paid at the Biltmore.

But the Biltmore had doormen to open my doors, and the cheap motels did not.

Relaxing in the bar, Terry and I soaked up our elegant surroundings. Our stay at a luxury hotel was premature for the trip's final celebration as we were still a few days short of arriving at Cape Cod. So be it, that was where we landed for the night. Maybe more luxury awaited us at the journey's end, as well.

Perhaps prompted by my Bailey's, I mused on our host state's name: Rhode Island.

Who was Rhode Island trying to kid?

I used to think Rhode Island was an island; after all, that's its name. It's easy to make assumptions—we do it all the time. We hear something, see something, and then we think something. We make assumptions about people we meet, looking at the superficial and seeing what we're conditioned to see. More often, we make assumptions about people we've never met, believing stereotypes about groups of people local, domestic, and worldwide. We make jokes when we have no idea about something's significance, and often rely on others' opinions when we haven't bothered to learn about something for ourselves. Frequently, ideas are already rooted in prejudice, and we take them on unknowingly.

It's harder to look deeper, to be more intentional, to ask questions. We might discover hard truths about ourselves on our journey to discover the truths of others. There's a power in honest examination, leading to new understandings that can open up our world.

I reflected on Rhode Island's contours and its deceptive name. It's not an island; it's part of the mainland.

And that's okay.

It was the last day of our fifth week. Terry and had I biked over 1600 miles since Minnesota and we were now at Rhode Island, the island that's not an island. There wasn't much further east we could go. My melancholy was gone, replaced by a gradual acceptance of the contradictory feelings I had about ending our trip.

I looked forwards, I looked backwards. I was in the middle, and it was a good place to be. The wisdom of my former oncology patient spoke to me: Anticipation. Participation. Recollection.

I had my burners going on all three.

Terry overinflated his tube while pumping it, prompting a tube change before leaving the room in the morning. That delay was okay with me; as predicted, the weather had changed, and rain poured from the morning sky. An hour later, clad in our rain gear from head to toe, we rolled our bikes once again through the Biltmore's fancy lobby.

"Good morning" the two doormen again said in unison as they held open the outer door. Did they always do that?

A photo with us in front of the Biltmore gave evidence to our brief encounter with high class. Minutes later we were on the Brown University campus for another brief encounter with high class, or at least the smart class. We cycled by a lot of smarties, pedaling through the Ivy League university, across the river and into East Providence.

That was where Terry and I expected to end the day before. We remembered the man's warning about not going through East Providence in the dark. We discovered it was bad enough in the light, with streets full of potholes, construction, debris, and traffic that flashed by too fast and too close. Since entering New York, our hopes to dash through towns were often stymied by lengthy delays at stop lights, and Providence was no exception. No wonder it took people so long to do their commutes in the east– they were stuck at traffic lights for half their commute.

The internet's recommendation for a bike route took us over the choppy streets of East Providence before burping us out onto Highway 44, giving us a straight shot to Plymouth and the Atlantic Ocean. Once there, we would hang a Roscoe, veer south to Cape Cod, and ride the scorpion tail all the way north to Provincetown. Our goal for the night was Sandwich, a tiny town facing Cape Cod Bay.

Barely out of Providence, it was *dejá vù* all over again:

Hello, Massachusetts.

CHAPTER 21

Eyes on the Atlantic— Massachusetts Two

Since it was our second time in Massachusetts, the state got straight down to business with road signs pointing towards towns, not bothering to waste reflective lettering on something as frivolous as a welcome.

A man walked by while I shed rain clothes.

"Gud muh-nin. How ah yah?"

Ah, the Boston accent. A friend describes it as the law of conservation of Rs. Lose the R in *park your car* (pahk yoah cah) and add them to the end of other words, like *idear*.

A nearby sign read *Entering Rhehoboth, Established in 1643.* Wow, what a long time ago. What was life like in 1643? I pondered as I pedaled. The modern New England population seemed to live on doughnuts and pizza. Whatever did the residents of Rhehoboth eat before doughnuts and pizzerias ruled the roads?

I stopped at a busy produce market along the highway and

waited for Terry. A trip through the checkout counter netted more Boston-speak.

"That'll be five dolluhs."

"He-uh at the sto-uh..." (Here at the store).

"He-uh you ah, de-uh." (Here you are, dear.)

"Shoo-uh." (Sure.)

The large market lacked a front wall. I sat at a picnic table just inside, close to my bike. With my helmet on the table and my safety vest on my body, it wasn't hard for people to connect me to the loaded bike outside. Soon, I was answering questions about our trip. Unlike many states earlier, when I told people that my husband and I were headed to the Atlantic, not a single person told me that we were crazy.

Chirp, chirp. My walkie talkie called.

"I'm at the bike shop buying another tire tube," Terry's voice came over the walkie-talkie. "They've got bike mirrors. Want to come take a look?"

I paused.

"No, not really. I don't feel like turning around. We've only got two days of cycling left, so I'll just make do with the mirror I've got." My toy mirror wasn't great, but it was workable. I went back to eating my pumpkin bread, and Terry showed up ten minutes later.

"Are you sure you don't want to go to the bike store? It's only 100 yards behind us."

We went to the bike store.

The bike shop employee grinned hearing about our journey to the Atlantic. Terry filled him in a half hour earlier while buying his tube, but he was eager to learn more. We told him we planned to end the trip at Cape Cod.

"Are you planning to stop in Plymouth?"

Terry and I hadn't talked about Plymouth, other than that it was our turning point to go south.

"You should definitely see Plymouth Rock – it's cool. There's a beach there, plus Plymouth has a fantastic ice cream shop."

On the road again, I mulled over his words. Plymouth. Hmm. I never considered ending our trip at Plymouth. It's on Cape Cod Bay, and not on the shore of the wide-open ocean. I always envisioned our tire dip on a sandy beach, with unobstructed waves. I couldn't envision Plymouth having that.

Although Terry and I would reach the Atlantic in just a few hours, we would need to keep riding two additional days to end at the northern point of Cape Cod.

Plymouth is where the Pilgrims landed. Cape Cod Bay is still the Atlantic Ocean, and we were told it had a beach. If it was good enough for the Pilgrims to land there, why shouldn't it be good enough for me?

I decided it was. Now I just hoped it was good enough for Terry.

"Hey, I've got an idea. Let's pull over and talk."

We pulled over.

"How about if we end our trip at Plymouth? That's where the Pilgrims landed – if it was good enough for them, I think it's good enough for us."

"That's an interesting idea."

"We can end our own pilgrimage at Plymouth Rock. I think that sounds perfect."

Terry smiled and extended his right hand. We shook on it. Now we would be ending our cross- country bike trip in just a few hours, not a couple of days. How crazy was that?

Resuming our cycling, I felt light and unfettered. We were going to end at Plymouth, a fitting destination, and one that was coming up unbelievably soon. How weird that suddenly we were going to be done with our trip. Excitement over our new destination gave the heave-ho to any lingering melancholy.

I had never been to Plymouth, nor had I seen pictures of Plymouth Rock. I envisioned Terry and me sitting up on a giant rock eating ice cream cones, with our bikes parked below us near the Atlantic. It was a gray and windy Tuesday in November – not the kind of day likely to have crowds hanging around. Without Clifton and his family, Terry and I weren't going to have anyone with whom to celebrate our arrival. The ending of our trip was likely to be quietly acknowledged with a handshake and a kiss, with nobody present but Terry and me.

My imagined ending of our trip was interrupted at a stop light when a man rolled down his passenger window.

"Wheh-uh ah yah going?"

"Atlantic Ocean."

"Wheh-uh'd yah stoht?"

"Pacific Ocean."

"Wheh-uh at?"

"Mouth of the Columbia River, between Oregon and Washington."

"How-uh long have yah been gone?"

"Today's the end of our 12th week of cycling."

"How-uh many miles?"

"Over forty-four hundred."

He gave me a thumbs up. "That's supah." The light changed and he drove off.

I felt supah.

It rained again. Layered in rain gear, I thought about the Pilgrims. They landed in December, and I knew that half of them died within the first six months. At the end of a cold, wet day, they couldn't just go to a motel and warm up for the night, nor could they casually show up at a Dunkin' Donuts or a pizzeria for dinner. Despite the challenges we had been through, our bike trip was trifling in comparison with the hardships that the Pilgrims experienced.

Highway 44 took on the look of a freeway and felt like an increasingly crummy place for Terry and me to be. Other people apparently thought so, too, honking as they went by.

I stopped for Terry at the crest of a hill. While cars zoomed past, I looked back expectantly.

No Terry. Neither my phone nor the walkie-talkie produced an answer. I stood in the rain for twenty minutes, and was just about to turn around when a car with red and blue flashing lights zoomed up.

"Is that your husband back there?" a police officer asked.

Oh no, not again. Something's happened to Terry, I thought. "Yes."

"It's illegal for cyclists to be on this road. I just ordered him to get off. You need to get off too."

I breathed a sigh of relief. I thought he was going to tell me Terry had been hit.

"I gave your husband directions on where to go. I told him to wait for you at a hot dog stand that's at an exit behind you."

The policeman gave me directions to find the hot dog stand. Get off at the next exit, turn here, turn there, turn here, turn there, and *voilà*, I'd be at the hot dog stand.

"We've gotten a lot of phone calls from drivers on this road who reported you two. This is a dangerous road." He looked at me sternly.

"Yes, it is dangerous, and I will be happy to get off." That was the truth.

If it was illegal for cyclists to be on that road, why hadn't there been signs indicating that? Or maybe there were, and neither Terry nor I saw them. It explained the many honks we'd been getting, and they weren't the short, friendly beep beep kind, either.

I rode to the exit ramp ahead, feeling guilty as I pedaled now knowing I was illegal. Happy to be leaving Highway 44, I wasn't happy to reverse my direction and go backwards. With this turn of events, and now needing to take side roads to Plymouth, perhaps we'd get there after dark. That would be an anticlimactic ending.

I turned here, I turned there, I turned here again, and cycled for fifteen minutes. Terry and I still hadn't been able to connect with our phones or walkie-talkies. Maybe we'd just waste the rest of the day trying to find each other. So close, and yet so far.

Finally I came to the highway, turned right, and pedaled to an outdoor hot dog stand. Why the policeman sent Terry to an outdoor hot dog stand when it was raining and cold was beyond me, unless the policeman just wanted to get his jollies and punish an illegal cyclist. Across the road from the stand were several businesses where Terry could have waited inside instead.

Terry sat at a picnic table underneath an awning, the solitary customer in the rain. Bundled against the weather, he sipped his customary hot chocolate. We grinned at each other. We were so close to the end of our trip, only to be kicked off the road and sent backwards. Do not pass Go, do not collect $200.

We recounted our stories.

"I had three different police officers stop and talk with me before I was able to get to the exit and get off the highway. The third one was pretty agitated," Terry said.

I only had one police officer talk with me, who was Terry's third guy. He hadn't struck me as agitated, only stern.

The rain wasn't inviting, but we wanted to reach Plymouth before dark, so Terry swigged the rest of his drink and we embarked on what we hoped was our final leg. This time we were legal, aiming for Plymouth on a side road.

The new route was heavenly. What a relief to be on a quiet road after the speed and congestion of Highway 44. At what point did we become illegal? We didn't know, but we did know that getting kicked off the road was probably a good thing.

Set back from the quiet, two-lane road, the stately New England homes transported me back two centuries. What was life like in the 1800's in rural New England? Horse-drawn wagons must have rolled along this road. I looked down at the fresh puddles on the asphalt and imagined horses sloshing, pulling heavy wagons on a muddy road.

My musing about life two hundred years ago was cut short by the approach of a modern yellow school bus in the oncoming lane, whose blinking yellow lights warned me to stop. I stopped so that my dangerous bike would not run over school children. I felt important, stopping my bike for a school bus.

And then modern time flung me back four centuries with another road sign:

Entering Plymouth, Inc. 1620.

1620. Good grief, that was really a long time ago.

And Plymouth. We were so close.

Our pleasant rural side route gradually became a busy, populated road, with other streets intersecting and spitting out yet more vehicles. Soon, it was just another fast and dangerous four-lane road, like so many of our end-of-the-day roads that swept us into the hearts of towns before dark.

With no shoulders, there often wasn't enough space for a car to safely pass us. Sometimes Terry and I just declared the entire right lane as ours and let the cars behind us deal with it. It was 3:30, rainy, chilly and gray, with increasingly congested traffic. What a shame it would be if we were killed during the last two miles of our cross-country trip.

The road pulled us downhill towards the coast. Vehicles aggressively zipped by, but as the bulk of the traffic curved left, Terry and I continued straight.

There we were, at the edge of the Atlantic.

Less than a hundred feet from us, sail boats graced the little harbor, whose gray water matched the color of the clouds above. The wet street shimmered in the headlights of a few cars but was otherwise deserted – no more frenzy, no more confusion, no more horn honking or close calls with traffic. Matching the tranquility of the street, Terry and I cycled in quiet rhythm along the harbor's edge to Pilgrim Memorial State Park, a small patch of trees and grass that hugged the water's edge. Between the tiny park and the street, a plain black and white sign above the sidewalk proclaimed: *Plymouth Rock, Landing Place of the Pilgrims, 1620.*
We'd made it.

I straddled my bike in the drizzle, looking up at the sign. We'd actually done it. Terry and I were at Plymouth Rock with our bikes, at the edge of the Atlantic Ocean, an entire continent away from where we started at the Pacific Ocean forty-five hundred miles earlier. A subdued excitement enveloped me, but even more, a sense of gratitude. We arrived, despite weather, traffic, and conditions that challenged us from one coast to the other. Even the last hour of our trip had been a knuckle biter with wet roads and increasingly menacing traffic.

We were at the Atlantic – it seemed surreal.

In typical Rudd fashion, Terry and I shook hands, kissed, and hugged. It wasn't our routine hug, though. It was a long, silent hug, where we squashed the whole North American continent between us and tightly squeezed. I felt a profound sense of gratitude for this phenomenal journey of ours.

Terry tilted his head as we broke apart.

"There are some people who could take our picture."

He pointed to three people standing fifty feet away under an open-sided, stone pillared gazebo. I walked to the gazebo where the trio peered down over an iron rail. A few feet below, a gray rock about the size of a sofa lay on a bed of wet sand. The year 1620 was engraved in large numbers on one half of it, and a big crack ran from top to bottom on the other half, making it look as though the rock had broken into two pieces and had been shoved back together.

At first, I looked at it uncomprehendingly, and then I understood. This was Plymouth Rock. It looked so small and insignificant. How could the Mayflower have landed there? I expected Plymouth Rock to be huge as a fortress. This rock wasn't at all what I envisioned. But I wasn't there for the rock. I turned to the tourists.

"Would one of you be willing to take a picture of my husband and me by that sign?" I pointed to where Terry stood in the drizzle. "We just finished a cross-country bike trip ten minutes ago. We started at the Pacific Ocean and are ending it right here."

The three looked from me to Terry and our loaded bicycles.

"Wow, that's amazing! Of course, we'd be happy to take your picture."

"When did you start?" another asked.

"We started on May 10th, but at seven weeks when we were in northern Minnesota, a car hit my husband and broke his arm. We had to wait for three months while his arm healed, and then we flew back to Minnesota five weeks ago and started up again at the same place we'd left off. So, it's been a total of twelve weeks of cycling. And 4500 miles."

"Wow."

"I'm from Minneapolis," a woman said. "Where were you in northern Minnesota?"

"Bemidji."

"I know Bemidji. Itasca State Park is one of my favorite places."

The three enthusiastically asked questions about our trip--two middle aged women and a younger man. In just a few minutes, they learned about our general route, our summer camping, our autumn motels and some of the random hospitality, and bicycling in snow, rain, and wind. I easily could have talked with them longer, but Terry stood in the lightly-falling rain, waiting for a photo. The trio and I walked to the sign.

"This is pretty exciting for us to be with you at the end of your trip," one woman said.

"This is even better than Plymouth Rock," noted the other.

I handed my camera to the man and my iPhone to a woman.

"You may not believe this, but this is Ray Charles' daughter," said the man, nodding his head and smiling towards the woman with my phone. "She's giving a concert tonight."

"Could I get a photo of you and me?" I asked after she'd handed back my phone.

She had a name, of course, but did I ask it before I requested to have a photo with her? No. I felt ashamed. There I was, getting caught up in her celebrity, reacting only to the surface and not to her substance. I wanted an immediate redo, to go back 15 seconds, introduce ourselves, and acknowledge her for her kindness in taking our picture.

I'd just seen a side of myself about which I wasn't happy. None of the three showed disdain for my lack of manners, however. Maybe they were used to it. Our conversation continued and we introduced. Sheila Raye Charles and her manager Pat were going to be guests at Seth's church, where Sheila Raye would be giving a concert in three hours.

"You should come!" they said.

The Vineyard Church was only three miles away, with a motel and restaurant across the street. Terry and I didn't hesitate. Celebrating the end of our bike trip with them was so much better than what I'd imagined.

"We're also involved in a church, a Methodist church, back in Portland," Terry told them.

"I joined the Methodist church a couple of years ago," Sheila Raye told us. "It's a good place."

"I like being part of a church community," I reflected. "It's been a powerful part of my life."

We briefly talked about the importance of church communities in our lives and in the lives of others. After a few minutes of church talk, the topic turned back to the bike journey.

"I'm just amazed at the two of you and your bike trip," Sheila Raye said. "I am so glad that we met you here, and I'm so glad that you'll be coming tonight. You two are inspiring."

What an unexpected turn of events.

"This is such a terrific way to end our trip," I told them emotionally. "I figured Terry and I would be all alone with nobody to celebrate with us. Meeting you three here has already made our ending wonderful, and the invitation to your church concert makes everything even more fantastic. You know how to make a great ending for a cross-country bike trip."

"Give me a ring if you run into any problems," Pat told us as she gave us her phone number. Warmth and congeniality radiated from those three.

"See you soon!" we called to each other.

Despite rain and darkness, Terry and I pedaled off with renewed energy, arriving to a motel with not only a large room, but also a pool and a hot tub--a fitting way to celebrate our trip's end after the concert. In no time, we trashed the room in our customary end-of-a-wet-day manner.

Feeling cozy from a hot shower and clean, dry clothes, we settled in at a nearby Mexican restaurant.

"How ah yah doin' tonight?" our young waitress asked.

"We're doing great. We're celebrating the end of a cross-country bike trip that we just completed this afternoon."

"Oh, that's cool," she casually replied, and then went about taking our orders.

I don't think she thought it was as cool as Terry and I did.

The waitress left, and we looked at each other across the table.

"We rode our bikes across the country."

We'd been so lucky. We hadn't been stopped by snowfall on the second leg of the trip, and we had a warm place to sleep every night. For our entire coast-to-coast trip, our spirits were boosted by people along the way. When we began, I knew that friends and family would be an important part of our route, but I had no idea how much the kindness of strangers would impact us.

And what a surreal ending to our journey. Terry and I decided to end our trip only hours before we did. We were kicked off the highway after getting separated from each other, we met Sheila Raye, Pat, and Seth at Plymouth Rock, and were now about to attend Sheila Raye's concert. When our morning started in Rhode Island, we had no idea this was in our future.

Leaving the restaurant, we saw a flyer about Sheila Raye Charles and her upcoming program. The flyer noted that Sheila Raye's turbulent life included serving time in federal prison as a crack addict. Tonight, she'd give her testimony and sing. Her appearance at Vineyard Church was sponsored by Celebrate Recovery and the church.

Terry and I walked across the highway to Vineyard Church, where people filled the lobby. Through the crowd, we spied Pat.

"Ah! It's so great to have you here tonight! Sheila Raye's inside the sanctuary doing a sound check."

Pat introduced us to two people from the church, who then introduced us to more people. By the time the concert began, we'd shared our story a dozen times.

Terry and I settled in a pew near the front, where Sheila Raye saw us and came over.

"I am so excited that you are here." She smiled broadly as she hugged us. "For me to have been there at the completion of your bike trip was so special. What an incredible trip, and what wonderful timing."

About seventy-five people filled the pews, a mix from Celebrate Recovery and the church. Maybe some were both. A man opened with prayer, and then introduced Sheila Raye Charles. She radiated energy and enthusiasm as she told her story.

Sexually abused as a child, she became addicted to crack, was in federal prison three times, and had five kids with four fathers. Three of her children were crack addicts at birth, and all five of her children were taken into foster homes. Sheila told her sobering story by alternately booming her voice and then dropping to a whisper, mixing humor and tragedy.

In prison, she decided to turn her life around. She made peace with God, and began living a transformed life, resolving to have her life ministry be working with "people in prisons, recovering addicts, and people in the dumps."

"God's love is powerful, forgiveness is powerful, and God provides the power to change," she passionately told us. The sanctuary was quiet, absorbing her message. As she talked about her reconciliation with one of her children, many people cried –including me.

Then she donned dark glasses and began impersonating her father, Ray Charles. She bobbed her head and belted out some of his famous songs. She invited the audience to sing along and we sang to her new words.

Hit the road, crack, and don't you come back no more, no more, no more, no more, hit the road, crack, and don't you come back no more.

The audience roared with laughter at her brilliant impersonation. A great talent with a beautiful voice, Sheila Raye alternately subdued, entertained, and moved us.

Towards the end of her program, Sheila Raye looked at Terry and me, and asked us to stand.

"This is Terry and Mari, who I met a few hours ago at Plymouth Rock. This afternoon, they just finished doing a 4500-mile cross-country bicycle trip. They started their trip at the Pacific Ocean in May and made it to Minnesota by the end of June, when Terry was hit by a car. His arm was broken, and then they waited three months before starting again. They started again in Minnesota five weeks ago, and just ended their trip this afternoon at Plymouth Rock, when Seth, my manager Pat, and I were there. Terry and Mari are an inspiration, too." People clapped.

In the lobby afterwards, Terry and I waited to say good bye. People congratulated us on our ride, asking questions and leading into a discussion of my favorite topic.

"Could you please take a picture of the five of us?" I asked someone.

Suddenly, a dozen cameras were pointed at Sheila Raye, Pat, Seth, Terry, and me.

"Look over here!"

"One, two, three!"

I felt like a celebrity, and then remembered that I was *with* a celebrity.

Terry, Sheila Raye Charles, Seth, Pat, and me

"What a wonderful and powerful evening," I told Sheila Raye, Pat, and Seth. "Thank you so much for inviting us and being so welcoming. This was an amazing ending to our trip, to meet you three and be here tonight. The work that you're doing impacts so many lives. It's clear you impacted many tonight, and you've certainly had a good impact on us."

I paused and eyeballed each of them. "Thank you for being who you are." They nodded silently.

"Sheila Raye's coming to Portland in the spring and will be looking for venues. If you know of any good places, let me know," Pat told us.

"Well, sure, we know of a great place – our church. It hosts a program for recovering women alcoholics. I'm sure that our church would be thrilled to have Sheila Raye come and give her testimony. I'll start the inquiries."

"I'm so glad that we all met today," Sheila Raye declared again with another round of hugs. "Blessings to you in your lives."

"Thank you! Good bye!"

What an amazing evening we had, and how privileged we were.

Back in the motel preparing for bed, it felt like any other day of cycling. I was tired from having biked all day in the rain. Our wet clothing and gear covered our bikes and the room. The physical ending of the day seemed pretty standard—a good fatigue and a messy motel room.

The psychological part hadn't set in yet. The day progressed so unexpectedly and there hadn't been time yet to process the completion of our trip. We hadn't planned that today would be the end, and it didn't seem real that our bike trip was actually over.

I did, however, feel an overwhelming sense of gratitude for our safe arrival, and for the privilege of experiencing our extraordinary adventure together.

I awoke in the morning with that immediate and familiar flash of anticipation.

Oh wait. We were done.

I mused over a favorite quote. *The afternoon knows what the morning never expected.*

We certainly hadn't expected this.

There was no hurry to get on the bikes. There was no hurry to get anywhere. As Terry slept beside me, I reflected. We were lucky to have made it to the east coast. The second part of our trip was a gamble no matter how you sliced it. Heavy snow could have ended it at any time. No cars plowed into us on the rainy days, no ice derailed us, and neither Superstorm Sandy nor any nor'easters blew us into trouble.

We found indoor lodging every night. Our tent would have been useless in the brutal winds and rain of the three converging storms in southern Ontario.

Terry and I weathered not only the physical storms, but we weathered relationship storms as well. I thought we knew each other well before the trip; I discovered there were still important things to learn about each other, even after 32 years. Adaptability is paramount in life, relationships being no exception. If you can learn to bend, but not break, you can mold yourself to the contours of new conditions, and not break relationships. As our bike trip progressed, I learned to bend better.

For our entire trip, we saw a narrow swath of the country, but we followed it for 4500 miles. We watched as the country transformed from one terrain to another: farmland into mountains, forests into prairies, rivers into oceans. We saw nature up close and in slow motion, experiencing the wonders of Yellowstone, the Badlands, the headwaters of the Missouri and the Mississippi Rivers, the rain, the wind, the snow, the sun.

We persisted and made it, despite Terry's broken arm.

As much as our goal was to reach the Atlantic Ocean, it was clear that it was the journey along the way, and not the destination, that gave meaning to our trip. Most importantly, it was the people who defined our journey. Terry and I received so much kindness and hospitality along our 4500 miles. Planned reunions with family and friends were anticipated highlights of our route. What we hadn't anticipated were all the people, unknown to us when we began our trip, who were now so important to us, too.

We felt the kindness of strangers in their hospitality, supportive words, and simple gifts like root beer and oranges. We felt their friendly car honks, waving arms, and encouragement from passing cars. What may have seemed insignificant to the giver often became a remembered kindness for the rest of the trip, and beyond.

I realized how energized I felt when people engaged me with their curiosity and enthusiasm.

Hospitality and kindness—I vowed to become a more frequent giver of both.

I reflected on the impact of words. Facebook, e-mail, and phone calls connected me with so many people during the trip. Written and spoken words energized, inspired, and supported me, both during the easy, good times of the trip and also during times of disappointment and discouragement. Supportive words fueled me daily.

And I still basked in the glow from last evening. What an emotional ending to our trip. Just to hear Sheila Raye's powerful message of hope would have been enough, but her welcoming inclusion of Terry and me into her program touched us deeply. We marked the completion of our trip not in isolation, but in a gathering of people who celebrated with us. How lucky we were.

I gave thanks.

The Pilgrims are associated with Thanksgiving, and in a strange twist of timing, Terry and I arrived at Plymouth Rock the week before Thanksgiving. We anticipated being home in time for Thanksgiving dinner with our family in Oregon. I was thankful for a lot: Terry, Erik, family, old and new friends, health, a safe journey – my list was long.

Only one thing remained to complete: dip our tires at Plymouth Rock.

Terry and I loaded our gear and set out. So much for being

done with our bike trip—that was only a theoretical concept. We still had bikes as our only means of transportation, and we looked as bike-trippy as ever. Unlike the rainy day before, the sun peeked out from the clouds.

Sunshine near Plymouth Rock, a day after our rainy arrival

With Plymouth Rock's gazebo in the background, we removed panniers, tent, sleeping bags, and Thermarests. A colorful pile of rubble decorated the sidewalk, generating interest from passersby.

"Could you please take a photo of us dipping our bike tires in the water?" I asked two of the onlookers. "We just finished a cross-country bike trip, from the Pacific to the Atlantic. We dipped our rear tires in the Pacific, and now we're going to do the front dip in the Atlantic."

"Sure, we'd be glad to." I handed over two cameras as the men looked at our pile of junk.

"How long you been doing this?" one asked.

"We did twelve weeks of cycling, but we actually started in May. A car hit my husband in Minnesota after seven weeks of cycling and broke his arm, and we had to take a three-month break. We just started up again back in Minnesota five weeks ago. It's been a 4500-mile trip."

"That's fantastic."

Terry and I lifted our bikes and gingerly picked our way down through the boulders at the water's edge.

Two busloads of school children watched from the gazebo, and they knew something was up. Several boys ditched historic Plymouth Rock and ran over to our pile of gear.

"What are they doing?" I heard one boy ask another.

Terry and I braced our feet firmly on the rocks, held our bikes by their seats and frames, and dipped the front tires – in the water of the Atlantic Ocean, in Cape Cod Bay by Plymouth Rock. We smiled for our cameras. The joy was compounded by the growing crowd up on the sidewalk, watching us and recording our big event on their cameras, too. I wished I could have taken a picture of all of them from my vantage point at the water.

Front tire dip in Cape Cod Bay, Atlantic Ocean, with Plymouth Rock in the background, November 14, 2012

After a minute of dips and photos, Terry and I carried our bikes back up the bank, parking them on the sidewalk. Some of the boys already ran back to their bus, but a stalwart group of six remained. They stared at Terry's long recumbent bike.

"Did you really ride your bike across the United States?" one of them asked Terry.

"Yes, I did," Terry replied.

"Maybe someday you'll ride your bikes across the United States, too," I told the boys. "It's a great adventure."

"I want to do that."

"That's a cool bike."

They stared at Terry's recumbent.

"May I get a photo with you all in it, with him and his bike?" I nodded towards Terry.

Someone shouted and three of the boys ran off towards the buses. The remaining three hesitated, then stood with Terry by the bike. I snapped a picture, and they ran off, too.

The allure of people with their bikes.

For thirty-two years, I felt the pull of a bike and of this cross-country trip.

The school buses pulled away.

I replayed the scene of energetic, curious boys running over towards us from Plymouth Rock, forsaking a monument depicting four hundred years of history, gravitating instead to us and our bikes, as had so many people along our trip.

"What are they doing?" a boy had asked.

And as usual, I was happy to tell.

EPILOGUE

Nine months after completing our cross-country bike trip, Terry had a sudden cardiac arrest, followed by triple heart bypass surgery. Looking back at his undiagnosed heart issues during our bike trip, his fatigue and slow speed make a lot more sense.

He's had two more sudden cardiac arrests since then, but some prompt CPR, zaps from an automatic external defibrillator, and medical intervention have put him back on his bike-- an electric bike.

Now it's Terry who waits for me at the top of a hill.

The End.

REFLECTION QUESTIONS

Chapter 1: **Anticipation**
What have you eagerly anticipated in your life? Did it happen? How did you prepare for it? What have you anticipated with dread? Did it happen? How did you prepare for it? What are some effects of anticipation in your life?

Chapter 2: Farewell to the Pacific—Oregon. **Community**
To what communities do you belong? How has community shaped and influenced you? What are positive/negative aspects of belonging to a community? How can you be a good influence on your community?

Chapter 3: River Travels—Washington. **Momentum**
What barriers have prevented you from starting big goals? How does momentum assist in reaching a goal, and what happens when momentum stops? What do you want to do, but have never started, or have stopped before it was complete? What can you do to start, or continue?

Chapter 4: Water—Idaho. **Kindness**
What acts of kindness have had the most impact on you, and what was that impact? What kindness have you given, and how has that affected you as the giver? What can be done to create a ripple effect of kindness? What are new ways you can show kindness to people?

Chapter 5: Snow and Pain—Montana. **Trust**
Would you have been as trusting as Mari and Terry in their circumstances? How has trust, or the lack of trust, affected your life? When have you trusted and there was a good outcome? When have you trusted and there was not a good outcome? When have you wanted someone to trust you and they were skeptical?

Chapter 6: Bison and Geysers and Bears, Oh My—Wyoming. **Anxiety**
How has anxiety affected your life? Has anxiety kept you from doing what you wished to do? How has anxiety protected you from negative circumstances? How do you manage your anxiety?

Chapter 7: Endurance—South Dakota. **Endurance**
What situations in your life have required significant endurance? What has kept you going? What aspects about endurance have been the most challenging? How did you manage to endure? What have you learned over the years about your ability to endure?

Chapter 8: Tailwinds—North Dakota. **Tailwinds**
How do easy times influence your life? What have been some of the easiest times in your life, and what factors made it easy? What lessons are there to be learned from easy times?

Chapter 9: The Uninvited—Minnesota. **Surprises**
How do you plan for life's surprises? What surprises have happened to you and how did you deal with them? How have you managed grief when the surprises brought disappointment?

Chapter 10: Processing—Skogfjorden. **Processing**
How do you process change? Over the years, what have you learned about how you process? When have you processed well, and what was the outcome? When have you processed poorly, and what was the outcome? Who or what supports you as you process? How can you improve how you process change?

Chapter 11: Resilience—Van Life. **Resilience**
How has being resilient shaped the person who you are, or how has the lack of resilience shaped you? What has shaped your ability to be resilient? How do you increase your ability to be resilient? Who are role models for you regarding resilience, and what can you learn from them?

Chapter 12: Waiting. **Control**
How do you deal with lacking control over situations? When have you had no control of an outcome and have had to manage the consequences of it? When have you been in the Waiting Zone, and what was your experience with it? What helped, or made things worse, while you waited? What do you do to increase your sense of control?

Chapter 13: Back in the Saddle—Minnesota Resumed. **Persistence**
In what situations have you shown persistence and how was it manifested? What factors go into a decision to persist or to give up on a plan or person? When have you decided to stop persisting, and let something go? What regrets did you have about letting go? What were the positive aspects of letting go?

Chapter 14: Rails to Trails—Wisconsin. **Standing on the Shoulders**
In what situations have you stood on the shoulders of those who have gone before you? Who has gone before you, and what work did they do? Will people be standing on your shoulders and thankful for the foundation you have provided? If so, what are the circumstances?

Chapter 15: Electrifying—Michigan. **Norms**
How did the norms of Terry and Mari clash with the norms of Mike and Ardie? How did the differing norms meet in the middle? What are your norms that are significantly different from those of others you've encountered? In what situations have you needed to adapt to other peoples' norms, and what have been the challenges

— — — —

in doing so? What factors caused you to view peoples' opinions and situations in a more favorable light?

Chapter 16: Stormy—Ontario. **The Bigger Picture**
When have you been focused on a smaller picture, and neglected to see the bigger picture? What were the consequences? Who in your life is noted for seeing the bigger picture, and how does that skill affect a situation? What circumstances make it less likely that you will see the bigger picture of some situations? How can you increase your ability to see the bigger picture on a routine basis?

Chapter 17: Winter—New York. **Navigating Disappointment**
What were some of the disappointments Terry and Mari encountered, and how did they each navigate those disappointments? What disappointments have you encountered, and how have you managed them? How do you choose your battles? What second chances have you experienced, and for what second chances do you still hope?

Chapter 18: Winding Down—Massachusetts One. **Reaching Goals**
What is the purpose of a goal? What are your goals? What is your experience with reaching goals, or not reaching them? When you've reached a goal, has it produced the satisfaction you expected? How so, or if not, how so?

Chapter 19: Eat Your Broccoli—Connecticut. **People**
What experiences have you had with diversity of people, and how have those experiences been positive or negative? What effect do you think you have on other people? What effect do you want to have on them? What are some simple ways in which you can have a positive effect on people?

Chapter 20: The Island That's Not an Island—Rhode Island. **Assumptions**
When have you assumed what others told you to be true, and then discovered it wasn't? How did that affect you, and others? What

is the consequence of believing others without pursuing to learn more about a situation? What assumptions are made by individuals or society when we don't look deeper? How can we look deeper?

Chapter 21: Eyes on the Atlantic—Massachusetts Two. **Adaptability** What were the consequences of not being adaptable during Mari and Terry's bike ride? How has adaptability, or the lack of it, affected your life? How does one discern whether to adapt to a situation, or stand firm against it? What are some situations in which you are struggling to adapt? What biases do you bring to situations that hinder your adaptability?

ACKNOWLEDGEMENTS

Thank you to early readers Charlie Adams, Joyce Auxier, Mike Cochran, Neelima Courtney, Frank Holman, Tanya Jacobsmuhlen, Jamie James, Jane Lewis, Debbie Laughlin Mathews, Teri Meyer, Joan McNamara, Terry Rudd, Becky Steed, Mary Ellen Warren, Ruthe Williams.

Thank you to Tom Hallman for writing classes.

Thank you to Jen Harold for graphic artwork.

Thank you to Michael Staudinger for initial abridging and editing, and for your mentoring.

Thank you to all who have supported me throughout the bicycling and writing process.